D1268775

CHRISTIAN-MUSLIM DIALOGUE IN THE TWENTIETH CENTURY

Christian-Muslim Dialogue in the Twentieth Century

Ataullah Siddiqui
Research Fellow
The Islamic Foundation
Leicester

First published in Great Britain 1997 by
MACMILLAN PRESS LTD
Houndmills, Basingstoke, Hampshire RG21 6XS and London
Companies and representatives throughout the world

A catalogue record for this book is available from the British Library.

ISBN 0–333–67358–1

First published in the United States of America 1997 by
ST. MARTIN'S PRESS, INC.,
Scholarly and Reference Division,
175 Fifth Avenue, New York, N.Y. 10010

ISBN 0–312–16510–2

Library of Congress Cataloging-in-Publication Data
Siddiqui, Ataullah.
Christian-Muslim dialogue in the twentieth century / Ataullah
Siddiqui.
p.   cm.
Includes bibliographical references and index.
ISBN 0–312–16510–2
1. Islam—Relations—Christianity.   2. Christianity and other
religions—Islam.   I. Title.
BP172.S53   1997
297'.1972—dc20   96–17954
                                                                        CIP

This book is printed on paper suitable for recycling and made from fully managed and
sustained forest sources.

Printed and bound in Great Britain by
Antony Rowe Ltd, Chippenham, Wiltshire

10   9   8   7   6   5   4   3
05   04   03   02   01   00   99   98

To the memory of my mother

Contents

Glossary

'Abdullāh	Servant of God
Da'i	One who invites
Ahkam [Hukm (sing.)]	Commands, legal rulings
Ahl al-Kitāb	People of the Book
Ahl al-Zahir	People of outward forms, the literalists
al-Arabiyyah	The language of the ancient Arabs
al-Dajjāl	Anti-Christ
Amanah	Trust
Amir	Leader
Anbiyā [Nabi (sing.)]	Prophets
'Ashura'	The tenth day of *Muharram* (special day in Shi'a calendar). Iman Husayn, the grandson of the Prophet Muhammad, was killed on this date
Ayah	Sing/a verse of the Holy Qur'an
Bazaar (Urdu)	Market
Chador (Farsi)	A woman's veil
Dahri	Atheist/materialist
Da'i	One who invites
Dar al-Ahd	House of agreement/or fellowship
Dar al-Harb	The house of war
Dar al-Isalm	The house of Islam/Peace
Dargah	Shrine
Da'wah	Invitation
Dawah ilā Allah	Invitation towards God
Dhikr	The reminder
Dhimmī	One who is protected/protected by the State
Falsafah	Philosophy
Fard	Obligatory
Fatwa	Religious edict
Fiqh	Jurisprudence
Fuqaha'	Jurists
Hadīth (Ahadith pl.)	Narrative relating deeds and utterances of the Prophet Muhammad and his Companions
Hajj	Pilgrimage
Hanif	One who is inclined to One God
Haqiqah	Reality/truth

Harām	Prohibited
Hidāyah	Guidance
Hijāb	Veil
Hijra	Migration, associated with Prophet Muhammad's migration from Makka to Madina and beginning of the Islamic Calendar
Hizb al-Watan	Party of Fatherland, Social Movement of the *Muhammadiyah* movement
Hizb Allah	Party of God
Ihsān	Moral excellence
Ijtihād	Exertion. A major source of Islamic jurisprudence
Islami Jami'at-e-Talabah	Students Islamic organization in Pakistan, associated with *Jama'at-e-Islami*
Jama'at-e-Islami	Islamic organization, a religious-*cum*-political organization in Pakistan
Jami'at-Ulama'-i-Hind	Organization of scholars in India, a religious organization in India
Jihād	An effort or strife
Jizyah	Poll tax
Khalifa (Khulfa pl.)	Successor, Caliph
Khatmiyyah	A Sufi order in the Sudan
Khilāfah	Caliphate
Khutbat (Urdu) (*Khutbah, Khutab* pl. Arabic)	Sermons, orations
Madrasah (Madaris pl.)	Religious school/seminary
Maghrib	West (direction)
Mahdiyah	A movement headed by Muhammad Ahmad (1849–99) of the Sudan belonging to *Sammaniyah Sufi* order
Mahjubiyyah	A Sufi order in the Sudan
Majlis al-Shura [*Majlis-i-Shura* (Urdu)]	The consultative Assembly
Makhluq	Creature
Makruh	Disliked, blameworthy
Malik al-Mulk	The Lord of the Kingdom
Maqasid	Objectives
Maqasid al-Shari'ah	Objectives of the Shari'ah
Ma'rūf	Well-known, universally accepted
Mashi'at Allah	Whatever God wishes/will of God
Mubah	Permissible
Muhammadiyah	A religious organization founded by Haji

	Ahmad Dahlan in 1912 in Indonesia
Muharram	The first month of the Islamic calendar
Munkar	Not recognized, detestable
Mursalin	Messengers
Mushrikin	Associationist
Mustahab	Preferred/advised, praiseworthy
Nadwat al-'Ulamā	Council of 'Ulamā, a well-known seminary in Lucknow (India)
Na'ib Amir	Deputy leader
Nawab (Urdu)	A ruler of a territory
Nechari (Urdu)	Naturalist
Pir (Urdu)	Saint, venerated by the people
Qanun	Law (canon)
Qiblah	The direction in which all Muslims turn to pray, i.e. the *Ka'bah* in Makka
Raja (Hindi)	King
Sāhib	Companion
Sammaniyyah	A *Sufi* order in the Sudan
Sarekat Islam	A religious organization founded by Haji Tjokroaminoto in Indonesia in 1912
Sha'b	People
Shakhsiyah	Personality
Shari'ah	Path/Way
Sirah	Biography, the biography of the Prophet Muhammad
Sirat (Urdu) as in *Sirah*	
Subhān (Tasbih)	Glory, glorification
Sufi	A mystic in Islam
Sunnah	Traditions and practices of Prophet Muhammad
Tafhīmat	Explications
Tafsir	Exegesis, A commentary of The Holy Quran
Tahrīf	Alteration
Tanqihat	Evaluations
Taqarrub	Intimacy/nearness, drawing near
Tawhid	Oneness of God
'Ulamā'	Religious scholars
Ummah	Universal Muslim community
'Urūbah	Arabism
Wahdat al-Adyān	The unity of religious
Walī	Guardian/protector
Zakah/Zakat	Poor due

Introduction

This is a study of Muslim perceptions and sensitivities in the context of current Christian–Muslim relations. It examines the concern that Muslims express, individually as well as institutionally, in their dialogue with organized, ecclesiastical Christianity.

Historically, the origin of the present dialogue can be traced to the inner problematic of the Christian mission, to the realization that the challenge of religious pluralism required a new initiative on the part of the Churches. The serious debate that emerged within Western Christianity immediately before and after the 1914–18 war was thus instrumental in forcing the Western Churches to shift their emphasis from mission to dialogue. However, despite the recognition of the new context within which the indigenous Churches of Asia and Africa were playing an ever more important role, the centrality of Western Christianity was never renounced in dialogue discourse. This study provides a brief account of the theological developments which eventually led to the establishment of a Secretariat within the Roman Catholic Church and a Dialogue Unit within the World Council of Churches to deal with other religions. The Evangelical Churches, in contrast, viewed organized dialogue as a betrayal of the universality of Christ and as a denial of the relevance of the Christian mission. Thus, they hold major international conferences with the express goal of opposing the 'creeping syncretism' of the major Churches.

This study also traces Muslims' encounter with the Western forces of imperialism and colonialism. It takes special notice of the assault of modernity and the social, psychological, economic, political and theological upheavals that followed in its wake. It was in this context, the context of modernity and imperialism, that Islam entered into a new encounter with Christianity. It was an encounter that initially puzzled Muslims. For whilst they were prohibited, by the dictates of their faith, from speaking against the central figures of Christianity – Jesus and Mary – and whilst they were bound to accept Christians as adherents of a genuinely revealed religion – *Ahl al-Kitāb* – they found no corresponding restraint or recognition on the part of the Christians who came to preach the Gospel among them. Christians, on the other hand, found that Islamic belief about Jesus in particular and Christianity in general does not correspond with their belief, and therefore perceived the Islamic faith to be flawed and in need of correction.

Even greater, however, was the Muslims' dilemma concerning Qur'anic injunctions in an age, informed by the intellectual climate of modernity, which denied the legitimacy of all religious values and world-views. Muslims were faced with the inevitable choice between resorting to a new *Ijtihād* and, adopting the world-view of modernity, reinterpreting their religion, or ignoring the issue of *Ijtihād* altogether and keeping their religion 'unaltered'. This study seeks to provide an understanding of the Muslims' concerns and to demonstrate that the question of religious pluralism and mission, so central to the heart of ecclesiastical Christianity, constituted the least important item on the Muslims' agenda. Instead, Christianity was perceived by Muslims as one, albeit less lethal, arm in the arsenal of Western modernity. It was seen as part of the problem and not a cure. For, despite the political independence of the Muslim countries today, Muslims are fully aware of their economic, technological, and indeed even their psychological, dependence on the Western Powers. And so their theological attempts to debate the question of the Shari'ah and to achieve a pragmatic solution to the problem of religious pluralism get entangled with, and become an intrinsic part of, their struggle with the more secular forces of the West.

From the perspective of Christian–Muslim relations, then, the contemporary situation raises new hopes as well as new fears. Though the dialogue has become institutionalized and Muslim participation is now an unquestionable fact, Muslims nonetheless remain cautious and reluctant. It must also be recalled that whilst Muslim participation started with the formation of a united front against atheism and socialism in Bhamdoun (Lebanon) in 1954, gradually, and since 1970 in particular, the focus of the dialogue has shifted to the sociological and theological questions affecting the two communities.

Chapter 3 takes account of the Christian criticism of Muslim issues, viz. the demand for the Shari'ah and its implementation *vis-à-vis* Christian minorities in Muslim states, and the question of mission within the Muslim community, both in Muslim countries and elsewhere. Muslim opinion, though moving towards an accommodating and pluralistic understanding of society in accordance with the 'catholic' temper of the Muslim tradition, is still suspicious and fearful of the Christian position. Muslims seem to be both unable and unwilling to adopt a dual approach to the problem of modernity: one for dealing with the hard-headed secular power structures and the other for accommodating the idealistic Christian conscience. Muslims would prefer to deal with the more utopian 'problems of conscience' only after they have dealt with the real 'problems of power'.

Thus, as the situation has developed, there is much genuine fear on both sides, which is compounded by the political feuds in the Balkans, the Sudan, Nigeria and elsewhere. However, the new situation also signals new opportunities. Perhaps, dialogue may ultimately cross-fertilize the moral conscience of the two traditions: Muslims will become sensitive to the individual dimensions of the ethics of human rights, whilst Christians will accept the political rationale of a just World Order morality.

Part I is an account of the historical and contemporary dimensions of Christian–Muslim relationships. Part II provides specific information on six individuals who have participated in various dialogues initiated by the World Council of Churches and other Christian and Muslim organizations. Their approaches to dialogue with Christians, and their concern with Christian–Muslim relations, may thus be viewed as representative of wider Muslim thinking.

The most striking feature of the Christian–Muslim debate is the absence of a Muslim institution that can legitimately represent Muslims in this encounter. Classical Muslim thought revolves around the institution of *Khilāfah*, but ever since the abolition of the Ottoman *Khilāfah*, Muslims have had to live without even this fig-leaf of juridical theory. There are some Muslim organizations that are trying to fulfil some of the 'ummatic' functions of the caliphate, and these include: the *Mu'tamar al-'Alam al-Islami* (World Muslim Congress), *Rabitat al-'Alam al-Islami* (World Muslim League), *Jam'iyat al-Da'wah al-Islamiyah al 'Alamiyah* (The World Islamic Call Society) and the Organization of Islamic Conference (OIC). However, it soon became clear that the freedom and wider vision needed for such institutions to flourish was constrained by the location of their headquarters, financial uncertainty and dependency on one or two states, all of which limited their much-needed projects. Furthermore, their priorities, perhaps quite rightly, were directed towards the social needs of Muslim communities, and these came under increasing pressure as their resources were directed to the increasing numbers of Muslim refugees escaping famine and war all over the world. The overwhelming priority seemed to be to deal with the social and cultural upheavals created by the aftermath of colonialism. At the regional and institutional level, one finds some progress has been made on participation in dialogue with Christians. Presently this is still at the nascent stage, and more time is needed before this can be an influential contribution to society. But the growing number of 'dialogue units' in various Muslim centres cannot match the human resources available to the Churches.

It is rare in these units to find people with knowledge of Hebrew, Latin or Greek and some European languages on the one hand, and Arabic and other languages spoken by Muslims on the other. This human resource still is a long way off. Nor do Muslim institutions express the same enthusiasm that the Churches and their units and councils show on the question of dialogue. In a sense, Muslim institutions respond as institutions as far as dialogue is concerned, but are not initiators of dialogue with other religions and beliefs.

The year 1970 marks a turning point in the history of Christian–Muslim dialogue. The World Council of Churches, after years of debate, began a dialogue with other religions in 1970 and established its Dialogue with People of Living Faiths (and Ideologies) unit a year later. The unit merged, in 1990, with the Secretariat of the WCC, and is now called the Office on Inter-religious Relations. This step marked an official recognition, on the part of the Protestant and Orthodox Churches, of the importance of forging a new relationship with Muslims and other faiths.

The Second Vatican Council (1962–5), whose initial concern was pastoral, accepted *Nostra Aetate* as part of the official teaching of the Roman Catholic Church. It established a Secretariat for Non-Christians (now called the Pontifical Council for Inter-religious Dialogue), whose efforts concentrated on preparing Church members for dialogue with other faiths through training and publications. It produced its first guidelines in 1969. The first higher level delegation of Muslims from Cairo was received by the Secretariat (Council) in Rome in 1970. This was the first official Christian–Muslim encounter following the declaration of *Nostra Aetate*.

The Evangelical Churches viewed the growing dialogue with Muslims and other religions as a compromise. They criticized the World Council of Churches for involving itself enthusiastically in favour of dialogue and saw in the WCC's statements a denial of the uniqueness of Christ and, by extension, of the mission to save the souls of unbelievers. Thus in 1970, the Evangelical Churches met in Germany and produced a forceful declaration known as the Frankfurt Declaration. This Declaration and the subsequent pronouncements of the Evangelical Churches have exerted a tremendous pressure on both the WCC and the Roman Catholic Church to return to the missionary understanding of the concept dialogue. All these factors are taken into consideration in this study.

The most obvious limitation of this study is that it is restricted to English language sources. It does not drawn on the French, Arabic and Urdu constituencies, unless this is absolutely necessary.

This study is also limited in its historical background. It begins with the mid-nineteenth century, but is mostly concerned with the twentieth century. Therefore, the debates regarding Christians and Christianity in the Qur'an and *Hadīth* literature and the subsequent development of Christian–Muslim relations in the medieval period, e.g. in Spain, are not considered. Many works, available in various languages including English, cover these aspects adequately, and at appropriate places, some of these are referred to in the notes. Nor does this study examine the question of *Jihād* (or Just War), although it recognizes the importance of the subject. A fresh and thorough study is needed to elaborate the concept in today's international atmosphere and interdependent world. It would be challenging to study the motivation for *Jihād* in Afghanistan and the religious factor in the Gulf War and the Balkans.

This study is based on a combination of library research, interviews, questionnaires and correspondence.

The first two chapters are based exclusively on published sources. The following chapters draw on interviews, questionnaires and personal correspondence. Twenty-four interviews were conducted, including five with Christians. Twenty-two responses, from 134 questionnaires sent to various Muslims – both male and female – have been accommodated, especially in Chapter 3. The six prominent Muslims who are studied in Part II are from both the Shi'i and Sunni denominations of Islam. They come from different geographical regions and their mother tongues – Arabic, Urdu and Farsi – also differ. In extensive interviews with four of them some of their opinions on various aspects of relations between the two communities were put on record for the first time. An attempt has been made to allow them to express themselves freely. The international organizations discussed in Part III are mainly Sunni institutions. I corresponded with them, and their relevant responses are recounted here. It was difficult to find parallel institutions in the Shi'i community, which have participated in organized dialogues. However, Shi'i Imams have pioneered Christian–Muslim dialogue, e.g. Imam Musa al-Sadr of Lebanon. A study of Shi'i institutional initiatives in this direction would be worthwhile.

In this study 'Muslim' refers to both Sunni and Shi'i Muslims, and the use of the word 'concern' is understood in the sense of apprehensions as well as priorities in dialogue – cultural, religious and theological concerns related to Christianity in the West. 'Dialogue' is used in a wide sense, to cover all aspects of the term as understood and defined in Chapter 3.

The study starts from the assumption that institutional and organized dialogue with Muslims is a Western Christian initiative born out of the necessity of defining mission in the new context in which the Churches find themselves.

The first objective of this study is to examine, very briefly, the social and theological developments between Muslims and Christians up to the beginning of the organized dialogues. The second objective is to identify the reasons for Muslims' participation, their expectations as well as apprehensions. We shall also assess how far Muslims are prepared to consider various sensitive issues raised by Christians in relation to Muslims and to explore whether a wider debate between the two traditions is possible. It is hoped that this study will provide a fresh insight into Muslims' concern about contemporary Christian–Muslim relations.

In the preparation of this monograph, I am obliged to the Islamic Foundation, Leicester for sponsorship and secretarial assistance. I wish to express my gratitude to so many people that it is not possible to mention them all here. Their willingness to talk to me on various critical issues of the subject, and others who found time to reply to my queries, were the main sources of this research. I am grateful too to various institutions, including MISSIO (Aachen, Germany), the *Nostra Aetate* Foundation (The Vatican), The World Assembly of Muslim Youth (WAMY) (Riyadh, Saudi Arabia), The International Institute of Islamic Thought (London office), Al-Karim Bursary Trust (Birmingham) and The Spalding Trust (Oxford) for their help at various critical moments in my research. I also wish to acknowledge my appreciation to Dr Christian Troll and Professor Jørgen Nielsen for their critical comments and constant support, and to Dr Parvez Manzoor, whose suggestions have been a great help. Finally, I express my gratitude to my family who endured the brunt of this work.

I
Dialogue –
Background and Beginning

1 The Challenge of Modernity

Modernity began with the emphasis on reason. René Descartes' famous dictum, 'I think therefore I am', brought reason to the centre-stage of human conduct to such a degree that it became the sole arbiter of all human actions. Metaphysical realities began to be tested by the criterion of reason alone. Kant's *Religion Within the Limits of Reason Alone*[1] is representative of the mode of the time. The followers of modernity began to question even 'unquestionable' beliefs – God, Revelation, Judgement, Hell and Heaven. Anything beyond the reach of reason in time was declared irrelevant. A new epistemology widely and confidently took root in Europe.

Technological innovation in the West drastically changed the means of production and unleashed unprecedented social and political upheaval. It demanded heavy capital investment and large-scale production. Products had to be sold and therefore expanding markets were required. The attempt to secure these markets and maintain an uninterrupted supply of raw materials resulted in the occupation and colonization of countries in Africa and Asia. At the social level, it was responsible for creating large cities and nuclear families; these families became increasingly dependent on the state and gradually the security of large, extended families was lost. In the social, political and economical fields, the guiding philosophy remained the self, with self's reasons at the centre. Secularism – the separation of State and Church – became the state philosophy and utilitarianism its economic and social justification.

The dominant modernist trend in Europe and America continued to exist side by side with the 'traditional' view, or the metaphysical world-view. Christianity began to respond to the impact of modernity. The question was, how to bring Christianity into conformity with the demands of modernity. Any supernatural beliefs had to be explained 'within reason'. The German theologians Heinrich E.G. Paulus (1761–1851) and David F. Strauss (1808–74) explained the supernatural events of the Gospel narratives 'scientifically' and 'objectively', in an attempt to 'desupernaturalize' the Gospel narratives. Two other German theologians, Christian F. Baur (1792–1860) and his student, Albrecht Ritschl

3

(1822–89), stressed the 'community', in contrast to the 'individual', to which, they argued, the Gospels were committed. They, therefore, implied that Christianity is more concerned with society's 'salvation' than with individuals' atonement. Generally, dialectical principles were employed to explain the New Testament. An attempt was made to differentiate between the religion *of* Jesus – simple, ethical and practical – and the religion *about* Jesus, which was regarded as metaphysical, miraculous, supernatural. Ludwig A. Feuerbach's (1804–72) *The Essence of Christianity* (English translation 1854) had a wide influence in establishing the former view. Later, Adolf Harnack (1851–1930) regarded the metaphysical aspect of Christian theology 'as an alien intrusion from Greek sources (Hellenization)'.

The theologians' obsession with trying to make theology conform to modernity was challenged by Søren A. Kierkegaard (1813–55). He attacked Hegelian philosophy, on which a number of Christian theologians based their liberal interpretations, and launched a vigorous attack on Western Christendom. He denounced the established Church in Denmark, where he was born, for its obsession with objectivity and 'proving the truth' of Christianity. His writings later influenced Karl Barth (1886–1968), who revolted against liberal theology. Barth insisted on the supremacy of the Word of God – the Word itself, the Word of Scripture and the Word of Proclamation. His language was deeply influenced by the Bible and emphasized the transcendence of God. But the main attack on liberalism came from the Fundamentalists. A series of twelve booklets, published in the United States of America, entitled *The Fundamentals* (1909) asserted that liberal Christian theologians were trying to reinterpret the Bible, so that those beliefs should not look odd to a 'modern' audience. They asserted and affirmed the 'inerrant verbal inspiration of the Bible, virgin birth, miracles of Christ, physical resurrection, total depravity of the human being, substitutionary atonement, premillennial second coming'.[2] Fundamentalism grew as a movement as a counterpoise to the liberal views of Christianity.

Muslim experience was almost the same as Christianity's – but with an added dimension. For most Muslim countries were under the direct (in some cases indirect) control of the colonial Western Powers.[3] Muslims faced the challenge of epistemology and the reinterpretation of Islamic theology on the one hand, and the political and economic control of the Western Powers, who had drastically changed the social fabric of their societies, on the other. Furthermore, during the period of organized Christian mission in the eighteenth and nineteenth centuries, Protestant missionaries were active in the same territories as the colonial powers. Although the Roman Catholics had been present in various parts of the world since the fourteenth century, increasing Protestant missionary activities created an urgency amongst Catholics, too, to compete with them. Western missionaries' attitude to Muslims created unprecedented tension between the two communities. The West's sense of superiority, both political and economic, gave Western man little chance to see the spiritual treasure within his own tradition and to relate to others, nor to respect the 'otherness of the others'. Their desire was to invade and conquer, and literature was provided to prepare the missionaries towards this end. Samuel Zwemer, for example, wrote in the Preface to his book *The Moslem World* (1908):

> At a time when the missionary societies are awakening to the needs of the unevangelized Mohammedan world, everyone should know what Mohammedanism is, how it arose, what are the elements of its strength and its weakness, and what Christian nations have done and can do for Moslems. . . . In a general view of the Moslem world, the social and moral evils of Islam, together with the power of this system on the lives of its votaries, are exhibited. The story of missions to Moslems is briefly sketched, and shows by typical examples what can be done and should be done to meet the present problem and peril in this day of opportunity. May the study of this theme lead many to pray for the millions still under the yoke of the false prophet, and arouse the spirit of Christian chivalry in the hearts of young people who read these chapters, so that they may devote their lives to carrying the gospel to every Moslem land.[4]

Muslims thus faced a multiple crisis: How to relate and interpret Islam in this new situation; and how to counter the Western political forces who were occupying their lands and were in control of all their important institutions – financial, educational and civil and military. In many cases, the *Ulamā* encouraged the Muslim community to wage armed struggle against the Western colonial powers. But there was another crisis to be faced – the Christian missionaries. In the pre-colonial period, with few exceptions, Muslim–Christian relations had been largely cordial. In south India, for example, the situation was such that the shrines of Christian saints were venerated by the Muslim population as well. But the situation soon changed when aggressive Western missionaries arrived in Muslim countries, and the *Ulamā as* well as the Western-educated Muslim elite began to respond, through participation in public debates and publications. It was the Western-educated Muslims who, in some cases, supplied the *Ulamā* with material published in the West by liberal Christians against the fundamentalist position. Here we shall discuss some of the major events and approaches made by Muslims, as they play an important part in contemporary Christian-Muslim relations.

MUSLIM LEADERSHIP *VIS-À-VIS* COLONIALISM, MISSION AND MODERNITY

In the second half of the nineteenth century and the early twentieth century, Muslim leadership remained with the *Ulamā*. They became the vanguard in preserving Islamic identity, especially when political leadership was almost non-existent. They were able to inspire a considerable amount of respect for the Muslim cause. We shall take first the situation in India. It is important to note that as far as the opposition to Christian mission was concerned, the Indian *Ulamā* supplied a great deal of ammunition to co-religionists in other parts of the world. The alternative leadership consisted of those who were educated in the colonial education system in their respective countries or in Europe, and were heavily influenced by modern ideas. They wanted to reform the Muslim community in the light of dominant Western ideas. However, it seems there was little disagreement between the two groups as far as the opposition to Christian polemics was concerned. At times, it was the modern-educated people living in the West who supplied the necessary materials to the *Ulamā*, in their public debates with Christian missionaries. For example, Rahmatullah Kairanawi (see below) was helped in his debate with Karl Pfander by Wazir Khan, a practising physician in London, who collected historical criticism of the Bible and sent it to Kairanawi.

In **India**, the British first entered the country as traders through the East India Company. After the fall of the Mughal Empire in 1707, with the country virtually run by *nawabs* and *rajas*, the British increased their sphere of influence through a mixture of alliances and battles. By 1800, British influence in India had generated fear amongst the *Ulamā*, and several *Fatawa* were issued, indicating that India under the British were no longer a *Dar-al-Islam* but a *Dar-al-harb*. However, even during such periods of tension, the *Ulamā* were not opposed to sending Muslim children to British-run schools. The 'missionary activity' until then, as Powell remarks:

was not identified as a separate and peculiarly dangerous aspect of British influence until the escalation of preaching and publication in the late 1830s caused some of the '*Ulamā*' to recognise the urgent necessity for a radical rethinking about the position of the Muslims *vis-à-vis* Christianity.[5]

Missionary activity at this stage was not considered a contentious issue, and was in any event mainly targeted at the Hindus. Gradually, however, the missionaries moved into the predominantly Muslim areas. There they published pamphlets in Urdu and addressed people in the bazaar and on street corners. It was not so much what, but the way they preached to the Muslims which alarmed the *Ulamā*. The content and nature of the pamphlets derived their material from the Muslim scriptures in order to prove the 'authenticity' of the Bible and Jesus – and therefore the 'falsity' of Islam. In this respect one name stands out, that of Karl Göttlieb Pfander (1803–65). The British missionaries were not well acquainted with the languages spoken by the Muslim community (Farsi, Urdu, Arabic) or with Islamic theology; study of these subjects was not part of their training. But the German missionaries' curriculum, especially at the Basil Mission Centre where Pfander received his training, included Islam and Arabic. After completing his training, Pfander was sent to Central Asia where he worked for ten years. But when the Czar ordered the closure of the Basil Mission Centre, Pfander was sent, by the Mission, to India in 1839 where he transferred to the Church Missionary Society (CMS). The CMS posted him to Agra in 1841 where he began his preaching career.[6] His book, *Mizan-al-haqq* (The Balance of Truth), which adopted the style mentioned earlier, created a sensation amongst Muslims. For them, the question was: is British policy in religious matters neutral? Rahmat Allah Kairanawi (1818–1890), who held a public debate with Pfander in Agra (1854), believed it was not. Powell remarks:

[Kairanawi] had no complaint about the first phase of British rule and even tendered moderate praise to the good organization and sense of security which the British presence had at first guaranteed. But the touchstone of this security had been the fact that there was no religious proselytism. He identified the beginning of the second phase of British rule with the abandonment of this religious neutrality in favour of support to missionary activity.[7]

The British authorities issued a warrant for Kairanawi's arrest after

his involvement in the 1857 revolt against the British, and he went
into hiding. Subsequently, the authorities confiscated his property in
Kairana, which compelled him to leave India. But the legacy of the
bitter debate with Pfander and the political tension of the time left a
lasting impact upon the *Ulamā* and the intellectuals of the Deoband
seminary (established 1867).

The spiral of antagonism generated in India witnessed a renewed
phase between Hindus and Muslims. Maulana Sanaullah Amritsari (1868–
1948) was one Muslim champion, who debated against the Hindus. He
also used his 'polemical talent' against the Christians, and used the Christian Scriptures in his exegesis of the Qur'an, known as *Tafsir Sanai*. The
Old and New Testaments were also used as sources to prove the 'authenticity' of Islam. He cited various events of his time in support of his
argument that the British government was prepared to go to any lengths
to support Christian missionaries. In explanation of one of the verses of
the Qur'an on *Jihād*, he referred to the British Prime Minister, Lord
Salisbury's speech of 15 August 1895 in which he expressed his concern about missionaries in China and threatened that if a satisfactory
solution was not found which would allow the missionaries to work
there, then the British would take action against China.[8] This was enough
to make *Ulamā* like Amritsari distrust the religious intentions of Britain. This played an important role when the *Ulamā* involved themselves in Indian nationalism against the British, viz. *Jamiat-Ulama-e-Hind.*

The Deoband Seminary was, and is today, a symbol of the ortho-
doxy of the Hanafi school of thought. Deoband put up overwhelming
resistance to the pressure for change. *Ijtihad* in relation to the new
circumstances became irrelevant. They discouraged Muslims from ac-
quiring the new education introduced by the British, believing that
Muslims would thereby lose their religious and cultural identity. The
opposite view was presented by Sayyid Ahmad Khan (1817–98). He
saw the rigidity and inflexibility of the *Ulamā* as indicative of their
fear of facing new challenges. In 1877, he founded the Oriental College, which later became the Aligarh Muslim University. In this intellectual and social turmoil, he, as Christian Troll puts it:

> concentrated on laying the foundations of a 'this worldly' progress
> of the Muslim community. He viewed education [including the learning
> of English and the acquisition of Western knowledge and acceptable
> Western values] as the basic means for improvement. All his other
> activities were rooted in his one basic desire – to restore Islam in
> India to its pristine dignity and prestige.[9]

Sayyid Ahmad Khan's approach was conciliatory. To this end he cultivated socialization with the British in India. He attended their dinner parties and invited them to his home. For many Indian Muslims this was enough to question his integrity as a Muslim. But his views on the Bible further strengthened the hands of the critics. When Muslim *Ulamā*, like Rahmatullah Kairanawi and others, were busy pointing out how the very authenticity of the Bible was in doubt, Sayyid Ahmad wrote *The Mohamedan Commentary on the Holy Bible*. He argued that in so far as the Bible contains original text, one could, perhaps, rely on its authenticity, and accept it as a Revealed Book.

The aspirations of Sayyid Ahmad and the founders of the Deoband seminary for their community were hardly in dispute. What was in dispute was their methodology. The *Ulamā* wanted to wait and let history pass by and then, when the time was right, participate again. Sayyid Ahmad wanted to travel along with and be part of the forces of history, and disembark only if it became necessary to do so.

Altaf Hussain Hali (1837–1914) recognized Sayyid Ahmad Khan's approach and his concern as 'that of the revitalizer of the Muslim community';[10] he urged the Muslim community to avoid any confrontation with the British authorities. This suggestion was in contrast to the prescription of the Deoband seminary *Ulamā*. Nevertheless, Hali was in agreement with the introduction of *madaris*, like Deoband, throughout the country. He wanted to create a network of *Ulamā* who could establish educational institutions and seminaries amongst the Muslims. The *Ulamā*, he argued, could promote an awareness of the religious heritage of the Muslim community through seminaries and sermons. Hali's non-confrontational approach also avoided any confrontation with Christianity.

The debate between the 'old' and the 'new', between the 'modernism' of Aligarh and 'preservationist' approach of Deoband, created a conciliatory approach in Shibli Numani's (1857–1914) writings and in the *Nadwah* school. Shibli pointed out the importance of both and enhanced those aspects of 'modernism' which had a close affinity to the classics. For him, heroes could be found in the past who could give renewed confidence in the present. He wrote *Al-Farooq*, *Al-Mamoon* and *Al-Ghazali*, in order to highlight how Muslims could face the challenges of their time. The *Nadwat-al-Ulamā* was founded in 1893. The spirit behind the movement was to bring about reconciliation between the Aligarh and Deoband approach and produce a new breed of *Ulamā* who would be schooled in both modern and classical knowledge of Islam and provide a new direction to Muslims. Both Shibli and *Nadwah* gave new confidence to the new generation of thinkers and writers. Shibli alluded to the debate of *Fiqh* and *Falsafah* and pointed out that if the Muslim community could make the Qur'an the central point of their progress, rather than the history of the *Ummah*, then the *Ummah* would be able to face the challenge of modernity successfully. Shibli and the *Nadwah* school provided much-needed flexibility in the interpretation of Islamic jurisprudence and theology. Subsequent Muslim thinkers increasingly advocated a middle way between the classical and modern approaches. Christianity figured less prominently in Shibli's writing. He concentrated more on answering the interpretation of Islam by the Orientalists. His famous biography of the Prophet Muhammad – *Sirat-un-Nabi*[11] – was one such step in this direction.

Muhammad Iqbal (1873[5]–1938), the philosopher-poet, approached the Muslims' condition critically. He pointed out that in Muslims who have adopted a lifestyle that compromises with the demands of the modern trend, lies their conscious adoption of a value system which is contrary to the Islamic spirit. He argued that in the past Muslims had adopted Greek philosophy and mysticism without judging them by Islamic criteria; now Muslims were repeating the same mistake by adopting modern Western values. His poetry, especially his later poems, indicates that he was concerned with the materialist outlook, nationalism and irreligiosity in general of the Muslim society which came as the direct result of the acceptance of values contrary to Islam. However, he suggested reconciliation between the 'traditionalist' and 'modern' view, and not confrontation. He saw a new role for the *Ummah* in the situation – a confident Qur'anic approach and vision.

Iqbal appreciated the spirituality of Christian individuals. He wrote:

> The great point in Christianity is the search for an independent context for spiritual life, which according to the insight of its founder, could be elevated not by forces of the world external to the soul of man, but by the revelation of a new world within his soul.[12]

He welcomed the newfound way between 'modernity' and 'rigidity' – what he called the new 'liberal movement in Islam' – and compared this 'to that of the Protestant Reformation in Europe'. He warned Christians of the danger of 'a gradual displacement of the universal ethics of Christianity by systems of national ethics'. On the other hand, he appealed to Muslims, particularly their leaders, to 'understand the real meaning of what has happened in Europe' and not be dismissive, and asked them to move forward with 'self-control', and 'clear insight'[13] in the new situation of the world in which Muslims found themselves.

Others, like Abul Kalam Azad (1888–1958) and Abul A'la Mawdudi (1903–79), were fiercely critical of Christianity in general and the West in particular. Azad saw the West as an anti-Islamic force, a silent conspiracy against the Muslim world. The Western domination of the Muslim world he associated with 'Christian forces', and identified colonial imperialism as a '*Jihad* of the Cross'.[14] However, his belief in *Wahdat al-Adyān* (the Unity of Religions) was perhaps the basis on which he co-operated with other non-Muslims against British colonial power. This motivation remained with Azad until his death. Mawdudi began his career as a journalist. He received instruction in traditional Islamic learning but accused the *Ulamā* of not giving a clear lead to the Muslim community. He was astounded when the *Ulamā* joined ranks with the Congress Party in India.[15] He criticized the Aligarh School for propagating secular and liberal views of Islam. He identified the need of the *Ummah* as awareness of Islamic roots and a holistic view of Islam. Like Azad, he was extremely critical of the West and saw Christianity in the same light as did Azad. He argued that Western civilization had encountered Islam at a time when it was at its lowest ebb; the West had encountered a 'shadow of the real Islam': 'true spirit of Islam is neither in their mosques nor schools, neither in their private lives nor in the public affairs. Their practical life has lost all its association with Islam. The law of Islam does not now govern their private or collective conduct.'[6]

The holistic approach of Islam and the implementation of Shari'ah became Mawdudi's vocation. Christianity, he remarked, had lost its way, especially after the Council of Nicaea in 325 and Ephesus in 431 CE (Common Era); he saw Christianity in juxtaposition to Western colonial rules. He drew on *The Gospel of Barnabas* extensively in his interpretation of the verses of Surah al-Saf (The Ranks) of the Qur'an.[17] He responded to Pope Paul VI's letter to observe 1 January 1968 as 'Peace Day'. He asked the Pope to 'use your good offices and the immense influence that you command in the Christian world as the highest religious leader of the Catholic Church to remove the causes which are poisoning the relations of the two world communities . . .'. 'I request you also to likewise frankly and unreservedly point out those deeds and acts of commission or omission of the Muslims anywhere in the world which have been a source of annoyance to the Christian brethren and to assure you that I shall use all the influence I may be able to exert to remove those sources of annoyance to the Christian world.' He pointed out four areas of Muslim grievance: the attack on the Prophet Muhammad and the Qur'an by the Christian scholars; the methods of Christian mission amongst Muslims; the creation of Israel and the occupied lands; and finally, the question of Jerusalem.[18]

An emphasis on the Qur'an with the exclusion of *Sunnah/Ahādith* and the reinterpretation of the Qur'an in the new climate which the *Ummah* was facing, is found in the writings of Enayatullah Khan Mashriqi (1888– 1960) and Chaudhury Ghulam Ahmad Pervez (1903–88). *Sunnah/ Ahādith*, in their opinion, should be seen as a historical development, a narration of events, but should not be one of the basic tenets of Islam. Their views were in contradiction to the generally accepted principles that *Sunnah* is the source of Islamic jurisprudence. Both had a small following and had little impact on the wider Muslim society.[19]

In **Indonesia**, Dutch colonization created similar tensions to those in India and Egypt. It created two groups: the traditionalists, *Kaum Tua* (Old Group) and the modernists, *Kaum Muda* (Young Group). The Muslim religious leadership was to the fore in opposing colonial rule: 'Islam was then synonymous with nationalism'.[20] The Dutch saw Islam as a threat; and Muslims saw in the Dutch presence 'an attack on Islam'.[21] In order to resolve this tension the Dutch adopted two strategies.

On the one hand, the Dutch wanted to foster a feeling of contentment with Dutch rule among the Indonesians. Therefore, they attempted to disseminate Western culture among the population in such a way that the Indonesians would adopt it as their culture 'without necessarily neglecting their own'. This was known as 'association'.

And on the other, they set out to convert the 'Indonesians, Muslims as well as pagans, to Christianity'. This was not necessarily for spiritual reasons; rather, the aim was related to the first, that is to strengthen Dutch rule in Indonesia. 'The missionaries themselves were of the opinion that if the aim of the first view was fulfilled, they "will be able to make themselves more acceptable to those natives who had been culturally assimilated"'.[22]

The growing reaction of the nationalist movement against the Dutch forced the colonial powers to introduce the Ethical Policy. This policy strengthened the hands of the Christian missionaries and, under their pressure, the authorities banned Sunday markets and trading. In order to curb Islamic influence, teaching Islam without obtaining a special licence from the Dutch authorities was made illegal. These measures created a further rift between the Dutch rulers and the Muslims. Conversion to Christianity was seen by Muslims as a betrayal of the Muslim community, and converts were lumped together as 'Dutch Europeans' or the 'white man'.

The two figures who stand out in this phase of Indonesia's social and political crisis are Hadji Ahmad Dahlan (1869–1954), the founder of the *Muhammadiyah* Movement (founded 18 November 1912 in Surabaya) and Hadji Oemar Said Tjokroaminoto (1882–1934), who became the leader of *Sarekat Islam* in May 1912.

Hadji Dahlan is generally considered 'the great reformer of Islam in Indonesia'. Although he was greatly influenced by the intellectual trends in Egypt, he began his reform movement at the grass-roots level. He emphasized the importance of hygiene, and the proper *Qiblah* of mosques (many Muslims were unconcerned about the direction of the *Ka'bah*, while they pray, a condition of prayer in Islam). Education for children and special training were arranged for those working in the civil service. Education became the cornerstone of the *Muhammadiyah* Movement. Within a year of its formation, it had branches in a number of places in the country and had established a women's wing. Dahlan adopted and modified several methods of Christian missionary activity and incorporated them in *Muhammadiyah*. He adopted the Scout Movement programmes and, in 1918, created *Hizbul Wathan* (Party of the Fatherland). The high profile of the Christian mission was, perhaps, responsible for the success of Dahlan's movement. He met Rahmat Allah Kairanawi in Makkah and encouraged him to publish his debates with Pfander in book form. He also established good relations with Hendrik Kraemer.

Sarekat Islam was founded in 1911 and became an influential political movement in Indonesia. Here, we are concerned with Tjokroaminoto's participation (in 1912) in the *Sarekat*, and the organization as a whole. Tjokroaminoto's participation gave the *Sarekat* a sense of direction. In 1916, it formulated a Declaration of Principles and Action Programmes which was further endorsed at its Second Congress in 1917. The Congress noted 'the exclusion of Christian missionaries from Muslim areas' and felt it their duty to 'keep intact and to hold in honour our religion, Islam, by every means'. *Sarekat*, though it opposed Christian mission, organized its educational and religious teachers' training on the missionary model. In 1921, *Sarekat* came into direct conflict with the Dutch, who arrested Tjokroaminoto for his activities and opposition to the Dutch Ethical Policy. *Sarekat* propagated that: 'It was Europe . . . that had transformed "almost all the people in Indonesia into labourers" including intellectuals who were "only of value as tools of the capitalists".'[23] After Independence in 1945, a new era was ushered in, in which, the military played an important role. Muslims and Christians were locked in multifaceted problems. The perception of Christians amongst Muslims and vice-versa changed little with Independence. The Muslims believe that Christian mission and the Churches influence the governing of Indonesia. The conversion of aborigines on the various islands of Indonesia (some 13,000 islands) remains a source of mistrust and suspicion.[24]

In **Egypt**, the long occupation of the Western colonial forces began with the invasion of the Napoleonic army in 1798. By 1801, the French had retreated and the British, with the collaboration of the Turks, entered Egypt. But soon the Mamluk governor was deposed and replaced by Mehmet Ali (ruled 1805–49), who carried out a massive Europeanization of the administration. He implemented changes despite opposition from the *Ulamā*, whose power was in decline and whose unity was shaken. The seat of Islamic learning in Egypt, al-Azhar, though respected, became increasingly peripheral. After Mehmet Ali, his son Said (ruled 1854–63) and grandson Isma'il (ruled 1863–79) modernized the education system and technological development and pursued a programme of active reform. From 1882, for all practical purposes, the ruler of Egypt was Lord Cromer, the British Consul General in Cairo until 1907. His economic and administrative changes had a far-reaching effect on the Egyptian people.

An immediate reaction to this situation was to see whether the dominant European ideas could be understood in a new Islamic framework. Rifa'a al-Tahtawi (1801–73) qualified in traditional and European education, and forcefully propagated a policy of merging the traditional and European education systems. He argued that within the universal Islamic community there is room for a special national community like Egypt. Egypt's ancient civilization, he argued, had an important place in history. This emphasis on Egypt's unique place in history was a contributing factor in subsequent Egyptian nationalism.

The idea of coexistence and convergence – of classical and modern – in the socio-political sphere was not acceptable to Jamal al-Din al-Afghani (1839–97). Afghani, who taught in Egypt for eight years and influenced a group of students including Muhammad Abduh, led a restless life. He travelled in India, Persia, Syria and Europe, and died in Constantinople. During his visit to India, Afghani saw the development of Sayyid Ahmad Khan's approach to Muslim education. He disagreed strongly with him. Afghani had various articles published in India, in which he called Sayyid Ahmad Khan a naturalist (*nechari*) and materialist (*dharī*). The new approach was unacceptable to Afghani. He argued that where the West generally associated itself with the emancipation of a new world, for him, this was the very point where the West started to engulf itself in general decadence and dissolution.[25] For Afghani, Christian beliefs like the 'Incarnation', the 'suffering of God' and others were 'odd beliefs'.[26] He saw Christianity in the context of Western imperialism.

Muhammad Abduh (1849–1905), a student of Afghani, was considerably influenced by him. But the turning point of Abduh's life came when he was arrested after the unsuccessful 'Urabi rebellion'. He was prosecuted for his part in the rebellion, but the court freed him. Soon he approached Cromer and offered his services in the field of education. Muslims saw in Abduh's actions a betrayal of the community, but he argued that it was practical politics.

In a period when the debate on science and religion, the traditional and modern, were high on the agenda, Abduh argued that religion should not be forced into 'scientific' interpretations. Nevertheless, a collection of his articles, under the title *Al-Islam wal-Nasraniyyah min-'ilm wal-madaniyyah* (Islam and Christianity and Their Attitudes to Science and Civilization), appeared, claiming that Christianity was essentially contrary to science and preached irrational dogmas. Here one has to keep in mind that writers like Abduh were confronting Christian polemics as well as trying to find a new framework where Islam could become relevant again. It is interesting to note that Abduh saw the progression of humanity in three stages:

Childhood, when man needed stern discipline as a child: the law of Moses. Adolescence, when man relied on feelings: the Age of Christianity. Maturity, when man relies on Reason and Science . . . the Age of Islam.[27]

He saw the Muslim ailment as their internal divisions and sectarian attitudes. He disagreed with the pan-Islamic efforts of the Muslims and feared that it might incur the 'wrath of Europe'. After the fall of *Khilāfah* in Turkey, Muslims all over the world began to look for an alternative and in 1926 formed *Mu'tamar al-'Alam al-Islami*, which we shall discuss in a later chapter.

Rashid Rida (1865–1935) was an ardent follower of Abduh and Afghani, his views being closer to Afghani than Abduh. While Abduh avoided the controversial area of politics, Rida involved himself in it. *Al-Man'aro* journal which Rida edited, had a tremendous influence on Abduh, who at times interfered in its policies. Rida remarked: 'We sometimes wished to indulge in it [politics] but *Al-Ustaz al-Imam* (Grand Imam) used to stop us. We did not get what we wanted until after

Allah had called him.'[28] The contemporary political situation and a strong desire to reform society moulded Rida's mind. This directed his views on Christianity too. His writings expressed a strongly combative attitude and a sense of urgency to expose Christianity's 'follies'. It was this motivation that in 1908 directed Rida to translate the *Gospel of Barnabas* into Arabic after it was published in English (Oxford University Press, 1907). He argued that the four Gospels of the New Testament were written at different periods of Christian history by different authors – therefore, the Gospels could not be accepted as revealed books. He assessed all the Scriptures against the Qur'an to prove them right or wrong and wrote *Shubuhat al-Nasara wa-Hujaj al-Islam*[29] (Objections of Christians and Proofs of Islam).

Muhammad Abu Zahra (1894–1973) was another Egyptian whose approach to Christianity was both hostile and critical. In his book, *Muhadarat fil nasraniyah* (Lectures on Christianity), he argued that Jesus' original message was simple monotheism, without intermediary beliefs. He claimed that there had been a number of external influences in Christianity which had changed the course of its history. He was critical of the early Christian Councils, which, he believed, were responsible for changes in Christian beliefs.

The focus on Christianity by Muslim authors gradually shifted from the Bible, Church History or Contemporary Christianity to the personality of Jesus. This provided new trends in Muslim scholarship because Jesus was revered in Islam. The perspective on Jesus remained broadly the framework provided by the Qur'an which disagreed fundamentally with the Christian understanding. But, at a time when Christians were widely seen as 'intruders' because of their colonialism, the new approach to the personality of Jesus appeared to be a breakthrough. The new generation of writers saw the very legacy of Islam as being under attack, especially the Prophet Muhammad. Some of them approached the life of Jesus, to avoid the colonial and missionary controversy and secure Jesus for both Muslims and Christians. Others introduced the biography of the Prophet in new circumstances and to a new audience of Muslims and non-Muslims alike. Abbas Mahmud al-Aqqad (1889–1964) wrote a biography of Jesus, *Abqariyat al-Masih*[30] (The Genius of Christ) and *Abqariyat Muhammad*. Writing on al-Aqqad, Dajani comments that:

> [he] fully realised . . . the great battle taking place in his time between the West, claiming to represent a Christian civilization, and the world of Islam, believed that in the missionary writings on Is-

lam, facts were at times presented out of context to convey impression of faults, and faults were magnified, and great achievement of the Prophet and other remarkable Islamic figures were under emphasised. To him all this is done under the name of 'science' and 'scientific' methodology.[31]

There were other attempts at reconciliation with the dominant Western civilization. Muhammad Hussayn Haykal (1888–1956) argued that Western civilization could even become a means of civilization for Egypt, but he opposed the missionary endeavour to convert Egypt to Christianity. He emphasized that:

Europeans are Christians, and we do not propose to make Christianity our religion, but we propose that European means of civilization should become Egyptian means of civilization, because we cannot live otherwise, nor progress, nor become masters.[32]

Whilst the traditional approach, which reflected Christian mission and the 'European means of civilization', was perhaps accepted by modernist Muslims as a fact of life, nevertheless they disapproved of the colonial and missionary endeavours in Egypt.

Sayyid Qutb (1906–66) had a Western education. He also spent two years (1949–51) in United States, where his suspicion that the West was basically anti-Islamic was confirmed. Like Azad and Mawdudi, he saw the West as an amalgam of Christian nations. His writings were deeply motivated by the establishment of an Islamic state. The progress towards this desired Islamic state, Qutb suggests, is hindered by two factors: the subjugation of Muslims by the West, and the ignorance of the Muslim community of Islam. Qutb puts the blame squarely on the Church for giving way to the modernist trend and not providing proper leadership:

the final blow that established the hideous schizophrenia that put to an end any working relationship between religion and practical life in Europe, finally separating the religious ideal from the social order. It is the greatest crime committed by the Western church against itself, the Christian religion and against all religions of the world up to this time.[33]

Today Qutb's influence is increasing especially amongst the younger generation in the Middle East and in the countries of North Africa.

The future of Christian–Muslim relations in these countries may take the route shown by Qutb, but most importantly, the future Western political role in these countries will be a deciding factor in severing or cementing the relations between the two communities in these regions.

The nature of Muslims' encounter with modernity and Christianity in **North Africa** was different from that in Asia. In Libya, Tunisia and Algeria, Islamic identity was emphasized through various Sufi orders. These orders had an influential role amongst Muslims and were able to maintain a continuous social and religious pressure upon the colonial forces. The French and Italian colonialists were less enthusiastic about converting Muslims to Christianity. But unlike the British in India, the French, especially in Algeria and Tunisia, were more settlers than colonizers. They were more concerned with re-education and the civilization of the indigenous population and there was a sense of urgency to inculcate the French language and culture amongst the indigenous population, at times even by force. The Muslim leadership in general resisted anything foreign and took up arms against forced enculturation.[34] There is little evidence that the modernist movements were fully successful in these countries. Since Christian mission amongst the indigenous population was banned, there was virtually no indigenous Christian population in these countries.

The country that was still open for the missionaries was the **Sudan**. Muhammad Ali, who introduced a wide-ranging modernization programme in Egypt, also introduced modernization in the Sudan when it was under Egyptian administration. These reforms provided an opportunity for various European Churches to begin missionary activities there. In 1857, the Mazya Institute in Verona organized a mission to the Sudan whose best known missionary was Daniel Comboni (1831–81). He was famous for his indigenous mission, preparing missionaries from native converts. Cardinal Lavigerie (1825–92), a Frenchman, founded the 'White Fathers' movement in 1868, which is now known as the 'Missionaries of Africa'.

In 1878, Charles Gordon (1833–85), the Governor General of the Sudan, at the request of Comboni, invited the Church Missionary Society (CMS) (headquarters in London) to evangelize the Sudan. But before the CMS could organize properly, the *Mahdiyah* movement erupted. Muhammad Ahmad al-Mahdi (1844–85) found little enthusiasm among the *Ulamā* to denounce the corruption of the Egyptian-Turkish rulers. The colonial experience of the Sudanese people came from two sources. The Egyptian-Turkish administration, which was thoroughly corrupt, was in partnership with the actual masters, the British.

The Funji Sultanate could not control the external forces. The modernization process, introduced by both the Egyptians and the British, had a far-reaching effect on the country. Sudan responded through the Sufi orders. For they could either accept the dominant Muslim 'government', supported and sustained by the British, or oppose the 'foreign' rulers and support the local religious teachers and educated group. They chose the latter (especially by *Sammamiyyah* and *Madjhubiyyah* and the former position was adopted by the *Khatmyyah* orders of the Sufis). Towards the end of the nineteenth century dissatisfaction with the Egyptians increased. Finally, a *Sammaniyyah* teacher, Muhammad Ahmad, began a movement to oppose the physical and spiritual exploitation by the ruling elite. His successor, Abdallahi (1848–99), maintained a Mahdist state until the British and Egyptian armies conquered Sudan in 1899. Despite the suppression of the Mahdist movement, the followers of the Mahdist order did not die.

Muslims associated this phase of their tribulation, especially colonial rule, with *al-Dajjāl* (Anti-Christ) and awaited the second coming of Jesus. Invasion of the Sudan by the colonialists was a reclaiming exercise. Reclaiming, that is, for Christianity as the land was taken away from them by the Muslims. Christianity 'must be planted here again. We are only reclaiming what once belonged to him and belongs to him still. Never must the Christian church rest until she has retaken her own possessions.'[35]

In the Sudan, as in other Muslim countries, the people could not distinguish between the Western colonial powers and Christianity, especially when the death of one representative of the imperial power – that of Governor General Charles Gordon – was commemorated by the Church Missionary Society, which opened the Gordon Memorial Mission and collected some £3000 in order to maintain missionary training in Sudan.

We have briefly discussed the emergence of modernity in some Muslim countries and their approach to it. We have identified two major modes – one that advocated the traditional and classical methodologies of preservation; the other, much more adventurous, which attempted to accommodate many modern trends and redefine Islamic tradition in the new circumstances. Arguably there was a third trend the revivalist approach, where Muslims did not reject the tradition of the earlier scholars as such, but looked at critically and derived their inspiration from the sources of Islam – the Qur'an and the *Sunnah* – to form a new framework in a new context. Although the three approaches disagreed amongst themselves, at times bitterly, there was a degree of unanimity at the level where they opposed colonialization and Western-

ization and Christian mission. Cantwell Smith remarks of Western
Christian missionaries amongst Muslims:

> To a considerable extent, modernization of Islam was, in form, re-
> action to the stimulus of Christian assault. Almost without excep-
> tion, the reformers wrote their expositions of the new Islam as
> apologetic answers to the criticism of the missionaries.[36]

Rosenthal rightly remarks of this encounter that it 'led the Muslims to
identify the West with Christianity'.[37]

POLITICAL CHANGE AND ITS RELEVANCE TO DIALOGUE

A large number of Muslims who graduated from secular institutions
gradually became influential in the creation of nation-states; they became the flagbearers of nationalism. Once a number of independent
states had emerged, the national leadership wanted to mould their countries on the European model. But there were internal struggles amongst
various factions. Some preferred a Western-style, secular government
and wanted to change, among other things, the law and education policies;
whilst others opted for a Marxist or socialist style of government with
a command economy. In both cases, Islamic law and policies in any
form would be marginalized. As pointed out earlier, a third, revivalist,
approach to modern problems seeks to redress the Muslim problem in
newly formed states by reverting to the Qur'an and the *Sunnah* and
sees Western-style government as a threat. They argue that it will bring
all the 'evils' of Western society, and 'moral decadence' will be trans-
planted into Muslim countries. They also oppose the Marxist-socialist
style of government in which they foresee the implementation of an
atheistic, Godless society. In such circumstances the call for dialogue
by the Christian Churches, especially from the West, was a very at-
tractive option. They saw the Churches as an ally in their fight against
materialism and socialism on one hand, and injustice of any kind on
the other. Furthermore, the newly-created Muslim states were independent as well as being on an equal footing with other nations in
international political fora, e.g. the United Nations. Therefore, dialogue
between the Churches and Muslims was a dialogue of 'common cause'
between 'equals'. Thus, at the first 'Muslim–Christian Convocation' in
Bhamdoun (Lebanon, 22–27 April) 1954 they participated in both its
preparatory meetings and in the Convocation.

Issue of materialism, especially the increasing influence of communism, dominated the Muslim-Christian Convocation. Western-educated Muslims, members of the Muslim Brotherhood and Shi'a *Ulamā* were enthusiastic participants. In the Convocation, Mostapha as-Siba'i, then dean of the College of Shari'ah Law in the Syrian capital, Damascus, and a leading figure in the Muslim Brotherhood, made an emotional speech in which he proclaimed.

> I am a man of faith, and I believe that my spiritual enjoyment is to live with believers. If I had the choice either to be in prison with people such as ... Mr. Hopkins, [chief organizer of the Convocation] I would prefer to stay with ... [him] in prison for six months rather than have a good trip to Hollywood with an atheist.[38]

The creation of new Muslim states also coincided with the creation of Israel in 1948. This resulted in the displacement of hundreds of thousands of Palestinians. A large number took refuge in neighbouring Muslim countries, Jordan and Syria. Muslims put the blame for the creation of Israel and the displacement of refugees squarely on the Western nations. Muslim participation in dialogue was motivated by the fact that the issue of Palestinian justice could be raised as well as support from the Western Churches, if not from the Western governments, if it is raised from a platform of dialogue. Furthermore, a large number of Palestinian refugees were Christians. This motivation was reflected when Muslims had the opportunity to participate in dialogue with Christians. In the Bhamdoun Convocation, Mostapha As-siba'i said:

> Is it not Zionism, with its political ambitions, a materialistic movement contradictory to all spiritually and moral values even of the Jewish doctrine itself? Can we ask our masses who are suffering Zionist atrocities and imperialist terrorism in their very land to believe that the Christian West is sincere in its materialism and its threat to religions and ethics, while they see how Western powers deride all the principles of truth and justice in their relations with them; while they cuddle the Zionist movement as a petted child whose parents are only too eager to answer his demands and aspirations.[39]

The issue of the West as Christian, as we have pointed out earlier, consciously or unconsciously permeates Muslim leaders' and writers' understanding. So too the issue of Zionism continuously reverberates through the subsequent consultations and organized dialogues. And it became an embarrassment to the Holy See when a statement on Zionism was included in the joint communiqué in the Tripoli dialogue in 1976.

We have discussed the impact of modernity within Christianity and the opinions of some theologians. However, the general Christian trend remained loyal to the fundamental tenets of Christianity. But, Western Christianity, perhaps for the first time, now confronted the important question: What is the mission of Christianity in a religiously and culturally pluralistic world? The next chapter will deal with this question.

2 The Churches' Move Towards Dialogue

DEVELOPMENT WITHIN THE PROTESTANT CHURCHES

Inter-religious dialogue owes a great deal to the nineteenth century's Christian missionaries. Their hopes and aspirations were for closer association between the various Christian denominations, especially between Protestants. They saw the whole world as an unexplored field, an opportunity to win for Christ. William Carey (1761–1834), a Baptist missionary, proposed in 1806 a meeting of all denominations of Christians at the Cape of Good Hope in about 1810. He further proposed a similar gathering for consultation amongst Christians to be held every ten years. Carey's wish was not realized in his lifetime, but, in 1846, an initiative which commenced in Germany made it possible to hold an international conference. Some 800 delegates, representing over 50 denominations, gathered in London and launched the Evangelical Alliance. This historic move paved the way for further international assemblies and ecumenical movements and brought renewed enthusiasm to the global Christian mission.

These gatherings were also motivated by another factor. Modernist thinking was responsible for the secular outlook of society. Charles Darwin (1809–1882) and Karl Marx (1818–1883) challenged fundamental beliefs about God and His creation. These new beliefs began to question the established Churches' tenets and dogmas. But Christians became alarmed when Christian theologians too began to question Christian beliefs in the same vein as the secular protagonists. For example, Ernst Troeltsch's (1865–1923) apparent denial of the *absoluteness* of Christian Revelation and his doubts about the reliability of the biblical accounts were projected as 'modern discoveries' into Christian thought, and were seen as trying to drive a Trojan horse into the camp of Christianity. As a result, many Christians began to emphasize the *fundamentals* of Christianity.

Islam came under scrutiny as well. The organizers of the conference were aware of the Muslims' discomfort at colonialism and their growing protests. John R. Mott, a moving force behind the conference, associated the nationalist movements against the colonial rule with 'pro-Moslem movements' and therefore distinctively against the Christians. The overall thrust of the conference, as far as Islam was concerned, was that their religion is 'buried under masses of error'. Muslims were seen as searching for 'the unknown God'. Christians, as elder brothers, should take Muslims by the hand and show them how God could be known. Muslims were seen as both stubborn about and strong in their faith. Some of the participants even thought of denouncing 'Islam as a "gentile Judaism" or [a] degraded form of Christianity'.[1]

A missionary conference at Edinburgh in 1910 took the initiative in reviewing the mission field world-wide. The conference, with 1200 participants representing 160 Christian bodies, set up eight commissions to deal with the following major areas of mission:

1. Carrying the Gospel to all the non-Christian world.
2. The Church in the mission field.
3. Education in relation to the Christianization of national life.
4. The missionary message in relation to non-Christian religions.
5. The preparation of missionaries.
6. Home-based missions.
7. Missions and governments.
8. Cooperation and the promotion of unity.[2]

The major theme of the Edinburgh conference was 'evangelization and unity' – 'evangelization' amongst non-Christians world-wide and 'unity' of 'all' Christians across the world. But 'unity' was understood in terms of the Eastern Church merging with Western Christianity. A minority view persistently challenged this view; for example, J.N. Farquhar's book in which he drew a distinction between Christ and religion. Christ is the central figure to which other religions yearn to arrive. To explain this Farquhar used Hindu symbolism and expressions.[3] Kraemer remarked about the conference:

> It was not only the age of faith, but also the eye of the Westerner, who subconsciously lived in the conviction that he could dispose of the world, because the absorption of the Eastern by the Western world appeared to come inevitably.[4]

By 1928, when the Jerusalem Conference took place, the missionary mood had changed. To borrow Kraemer's words, the conference moved from being 'strategical' to 'introspective'.

The First World War had a tremendous impact on the Christian attitude of the Western countries' imperialism and the emergence of communism. The conference emphasized that the Christian Gospel could provide answers for the troubled world. But the most significant thing to emerge from the conference was that it recognized and affirmed the 'values' in other religions. It appealed to 'all believers' to join forces with Christians in order to confront the growing secular culture.

The third missionary conference, at Tambaram in 1938, was arguably the turning point in Christian missionary approach amongst non-Christians. Hendrik Kraemer made a great impact at the conference. He emphasized the importance of the indigenous Churches being free from Western influence; as well as the importance of first-hand *contact* with the followers of other religions so that a missionary should have first-hand knowledge of his cultural milieu. He found the missionary ideal of 'conquest' or a 'crusading mission' out of date and out of place, and talked about the conversion of 'values' in the non-Christian religions. He articulated new ways for missionaries. 'Kraemer meant', Hallencreutz remarks:

> that the missionary, when witnessing to 'reality', had to express himself in such a way that he could be understood by the non-Christians in his religious situation, which was dominated by a radically different apprehension of that reality. He had to apply indigenous terminology, 'converting' its elements into a radically different framework.[5]

Kraemer's writings suggest that he was prepared to try to understand the culture and religion of non-Christians. However, his belief about other religions being the products of human endeavour and therefore unable to provide the right answers to mankind was unshaken.

One important element that helped to mould his view about other religions was, perhaps, Kraemer's long stay amongst the Muslims in Indonesia. He was a keen observer of the modernist movements – their initiatives to reform the Muslim society, and their reactions to Dutch colonialism. He

> regarded Islam as a religious and social unit, with legalistic connotations. He saw its social and political dimensions as being very important, particularly for its current development. For him, the Reformation within Islam did not mean a deepening of its spiritual life but 'political and social reform'.[6]

Kraemer was critical of the modernist trends in Islam. He built a close relationship with Dhalan and in the development of the *Muhamma- diyah* movement of Indonesia he saw a positive development within Islam. But, perhaps in this development he 'foresaw a strengthening of the Moslem consciousness of the movement . . . [which] would not favour the Christian dialogue with Islamic renaissance'.[7]

Kraemer noted with concern the indigenous Christians who looked to and depended on Western Christians for their needs and therefore became increasingly isolated from their own people. This perhaps made a lasting impact on Kraemer, and, in turn, an impact on Tambaram. Here we find that he increasingly emphasizes the importance of indigenous Christians entering into dialogue with Muslims.[8]

The Edinburgh Conference, whilst stimulating wider debate of mission in subsequent years, also gave birth to three organizations.

The International Missionary Council (IMC) was established in 1921 in New York. This united the Protestant National Missionary Councils and Council of Churches in Africa, Asia and Latin America. Although many non-Western Churches were involved in the creation of the IMC, 13 of the 17 founding members were Western missionary councils. Its objectives were:

• To stimulate thinking and investigation on missionary questions,
• To make the results available for all missionary societies and missions.
• To help coordinate the activities of the national missionary organ- izations of the different countries and of the societies they represent.
• To help unite Christian public opinion in support of freedom of conscience and religion and of missionary liberty.
• To help unite the Christian forces of the world in seeking justice in international and inter-racial relations.[9]

The IMC called five major world mission conferences: in Jerusalem (1928), Tambaram (1938) (both we have briefly discussed earlier), Whitby (1947), Willingen (1952) and Accra (1958). The IMC merged with the World Council of Churches in 1961.

The Faith and Order Movement, established in 1927 in Lausanne, by 400 participants, was also an outcome of the Edinburgh confer- ence. The Protestant Episcopal Church in the United States resolved that 'a joint commission be appointed to bring about a conference for the consideration of questions touching Faith and Order'.[10]

The Movement's aim was described as:

to proclaim the oneness of the Church of Jesus Christ and to call the Churches to the goal of visible unity in one faith and one eucharistic fellowship, expressed in worship and in common life in Christ, in order that the world may believe.[11]

The Faith and Order Movement staged world gatherings in Edinburgh (1937), Lund (1952), Montreal (1963) and Santiago (1993).

The Life and Work Movement, established in 1925 in Stockholm, was also one of the outcomes of the 1910 Edinburgh conference. The name states clearly the reason for its establishment – the implication of the Gospel for the daily life and work of men. The architect of this movement was Bishop Nathan Söderblom. The movement concentrated its efforts on social and international relationships. The unjust industrial relations of the time compelled the Churches to take the side of the workers, especially as their cause was taken up by the socialists, thereby obviously marginalizing the religious groups. Bishop Söderblom avoided doctrinal discussion, perhaps believing that doctrines divide but ministry unites the Churches. The Life and Work Movement held a world conference in Oxford in 1937. In 1938 a provisional committee, with members from 'Faith and Order' and 'Life and Work Movement', was set up for the formation of the World Council of Churches. The Second World War intervened but, in 1948 in Amsterdam, the two organizations merged to form the World Council of Churches. The IMC merged, as pointed out earlier, into the WCC in the New Delhi Assembly in 1961.

The World Council of Churches

The World Council of Churches (WCC) formally came into existence on 23 August 1948 and became the visible, symbolic expression of Christian ecumenical life in the twentieth century. The Council includes all the main denominations of the Eastern and Western worlds, with the exception of the Roman Catholic Church and the Uniates. The Vatican has sent representatives to the WCC Assemblies quite regularly and cooperates at various levels. In 1968, the WCC and the Vatican created a joint secretariat for social and international justice and peace.

The purpose of the WCC has been described by one of its organs, *One World*, as:

To facilitate the common witness of the Churches in each place and in all places.

To support the churches in their world-wide missionary and evangel-
istic task.

To express the common concern of the churches in the service of
human need, the breaking down of barriers between people and
the promotion of one human family in justice and peace.

To foster the renewal of the churches in unity, worship, mission and
service.[12]

The discussion and debate related to the formation of WCC and its
subsequent development, important as they are, are not within the or-
bit of the present study, although some of them will be referred to if
necessary, in relation to dialogue and Christian–Muslim relations.

WCC and Dialogue

As pointed out earlier, the World Missionary Conferences at Edinburgh, Jerusalem and Tambaram, with different emphasis, approached
the question of relations with other faiths. While the Tambaram conference raised several issues – for example, how Christians should
understand the revelatory character of other religions – other similar
issues were unresolved. After the formation of the WCC, the International Missionary Council once again turned its attention to relations
with other faiths. The WCC had established a Department on Evangelism, and this Department and the IMC were anxious to open the debate again. But the political and social climate had changed radically;
the approach, even the understanding of the relation with other faiths
compared to the pre-war period, had also changed.

Nationalism was on the move throughout Asia and Africa. A number
of new countries emerged on the world map. With their newly gained
confidence these new nations sought to create a separate identity distinct from Western influence. The Churches in these countries now
found themselves at odds with the rapidly changing social climate.
Many thinkers, especially from India, like P. Devanandan, D.T. Niles
and S. Kulendran, challenged the Churches to take seriously the experience of the younger Churches in the newly independent countries
where they worked together with peoples of different religious traditions in nation-building.

Christian thinkers and leaders were eager to participate in nation-
building as Christians in their countries. On the one hand, they did not
want to lose their respective cultural and social context, and on the
other, they wanted to maintain their wider relationship with the Church

outside the country. They were aware of the perception their co-citizens had of them. The relationship which existed during the colonial period between the local and the Western Churches had created suspicion amongst the non-Christians. They perceived a Christian church in their neighbourhood as a legacy of Western imperialism. For their part, the Christian Churches in the newly created states, anxious to change this image, became increasingly contextualized and gradually dissociated themselves from the Western Churches, although without totally severing their relations with them. For the Western Churches, the very 'understanding' of the others' 'self-understanding' was the beginning of dialogue within the wider ecumenical movement and with other religions.

In 1961 when the IMC merged into the WCC, the Departments of Evangelism of the WCC and IMC formed a Division, later to become the Commission on World Mission and Evangelism (CWME). Its first meeting, in Mexico City in 1963, had as its theme 'Witness in Six Continents'. Section 1 dealt with the 'Witness of Christians to men of other faiths'. Though consensus was not reached on the nature of dialogue as such, dialogue was understood in the framework of mission.

A consultation among Christians, mainly from the Muslim world, about relations with Muslims took place at Broumana (Lebanon), in June 1966. Thirty Christian scholars, from 17 countries, participated. Victor E.H. Hayward, a research secretary to CWME, points out the reason for the consultation in these words:

> . . . speaking in general terms, no religion, save Judaism, has showed itself so impervious to the Christian appeal as Islam, the third of the 'religions of the biblical God'. Islam presents a deliberate challenge to the Christian Church. But Christians, by and large, fail to take steps to make any real approach to Muslims . . .[13]

But the consultation was widely divided on such basic issues as: Do the Muslims worship the same God, or does God in some way work within other religions too?[14] However, the participants of the consultation agreed to meet with Muslims. In this respect the consultation has moved very little from the Edinburgh conference of 1910.

Another consultation took place in March 1967 in Kandy (Sri Lanka). The Second Vatican Council had already taken place (we shall discuss this later) and, as a result, three Roman Catholics nominated by the Vatican Secretariat for Non-Christian Religions (now Pontifical Council Inter-religious Dialogue) participated in the discussion.

Agreement was reached on a statement that highlighted that 'Salvation in Christ has often been too narrowly understood'.[15] Pointing out the nature of dialogue, that statement emphasized that:

> Dialogue implies a readiness to be changed as well as to influence others. Good dialogue develops when one partner speaks in such a way that others feel drawn to listen, and likewise when one listens so that the other is drawn to speak. The outcome of the dialogue is the work of the Spirit.[16]

The consultation recognized that Christians will not understand the place of other religions and their traditions, including Islam, unless they have a living experience with them.

In a study considering the subject of dialogue, it seems that there was some kind of realization among Christians 'to live down the suspicions and prejudices perpetuated by Christians against Muslims and to covert Muslims invitations for dialogue'. The study also urged Christians to 'take seriously also the Qur'anic doctrine of the primeval covenant of God with man'.[17]

The Kandy consultation resulted, a year later, in the appointment of Stanley J. Samartha to explore the implications of the programme on 'The Work of God and the Living Faith of Men'. Samartha's paper found two defects in the wider debate for dialogue:

> The whole discussion was moving almost exclusively in the sphere of Western philosophy and theology. The discussion about other faiths was almost totally unenlightened by any real dialogue with people who held these faiths.[18]

Dialogue between Muslims and Christians under the auspices of the WCC took place in Cartigny (Switzerland) on 2–6 March 1969. The 22 participants recognized that 'Christian–Muslim dialogue is occurring in many places' but this gathering 'represented an attempt to take up the conversation on an international level'. The participants agreed that followers of both religions are facing the 'questions of the modern world' and argued that dialogue must concern itself with what serves the true liberation of man.[19]

The Cartigny consultation affirmed the threefold aim of dialogue:

1. Dialogue should lead both religions to greater mutual respect and better understanding of each other.

2. Dialogue should raise the questions which can lead each of the religions to a deepening and a renewal of spirituality.
3. Dialogue should lead both Christians and Muslims in accepting and fulfilling common practical responsibilities.[20]

Muslim participants raised the issue of Palestine as a common responsibility. Hassan Saab from the Lebanon, in fact, made it a condition of dialogue.[21] A separate Appendix was prepared, but it was not intended for publication. The Appendix was submitted to the General Secretary of the WCC for transmission to the Executive Committee in order to have a much clearer view of the problem in the council about the issues in dialogue.

A multi-religious dialogue was organized in Ajaltoun (Lebanon) in 1970 – a turning point for the WCC. Dialogue concerned the experience of living together with other faiths, rather than a discussion about them and the nature of dialogue. Invitations were sent on a personal basis to 28 Christians, 3 Muslims, 3 Hindus and 4 Buddhists. For the participants what was important was 'not just dialogue but the special kind of community that the dialogue seemed to bring about'.[22] After Ajaltoun, Christians associated with the WCC held a number of meetings the same year on the issue of dialogue with people of other faiths. The following year, at the 24th meeting of the Central Committee of the WCC at Addis Ababa, the sub-unit on Dialogue with People of Living Faiths and Ideologies (DFI) was established.

WCC began its dialogue programme with enthusiasm, opening multilateral dialogues with Muslims, Hindus, Buddhists and others. However, the dialogue organized at the international level with Muslims did not seem to take the path the WCC wanted. At times these organized dialogues dissolved into heated debates, in which the participants seemed to want to pour out their grievances. In the absence of an international representative body of Muslims, the WCC was dependent upon individuals. Initially, the Muslims invited by the WCC's Dialogue Unit were, broadly speaking, those whose views were not widely endorsed within the Muslim community itself, e.g. Hassan Askari. Subsequently, the WCC's Unit looked for participants whose views were well known and understood, and 'widely accepted' by the Muslim community. But these people have proved to be very obdurate partners in dialogue, e.g. Ismail Faruqi.

The WCC, after the Colombo dialogue of 1982, eventually shifted its focus from the international to the regional level and, by the early 1990s, due to financial restraints, decided to close the Dialogue Unit and merge it with the Secretariat of the WCC. Above all, the WCC could not decide how relations should be established between 'mission to' non-Christians as well as 'dialogue with' them. The WCC were put under enormous pressure from the Evangelical Churches, which understood every step in the direction of dialogue differently from the decision-makers of the WCC. However, there was a lack of clarity in defining the relation between 'mission to' and 'dialogue with'. Stanley Samartha sums this up incisively:

> ... dialogue emerged out of the womb of mission and it has never been easy for mission to cut the umbilical cord and to recognise the independence of the growing child without denying the relationship.[23]

DEVELOPMENTS WITHIN THE ROMAN CATHOLIC CHURCH

The Second Vatican Council was held at the initiative of Pope John XXIII. He wanted to bring the Church up to date on its 'teaching, discipline and organization'. The overall consideration was unity of the Church and unity of Christians all over the world. The Council began in 11 October 1962, held four sessions at various intervals and ended on 8 December 1965. The Council also dealt with the Church's relation with people of other religions. The councillors' approach to other religions had been moulded by a number of Roman Catholic theologians who wrote extensively on the subject. Before discussing the Council's statements about other religions, especially Islam, we shall discuss very briefly three important theologians whose views had a great impact on the Council's attitude about other religions.

Jean Danielou (1905–74) during the 1950s and 1960s put forward a theology of other religions. He distinguished between 'religion' and 'revelation'. For him, religion was a human search for God, whereas revelation is God's search for human beings, where God breaks into human history. For him, Christianity alone was in a position to atone for 'Original Sin', simply because only in Christianity does God intervene in history, and men and women receive God's grace. However, he found aspects of truth in other religions; they are aware of the sacred dimension in reality. He argued that though Islam and Judaism know God, their knowledge is incomplete. Therefore he proposed that:

> Christians must try to see that this good is assumed, purified, and transformed by the gospel. Indeed, assumption, purification and trans-

formation sum up Danielou's position with respect to how Christianity is related to the values in the non-Christian religions.[24]

Danielou suggested that the revelation of God, which is the unique belief of Christianity, in fact, 'frees the values and truths in the non-Christian religions from their errors and corruption, or completes the partial revelation in them in the case of Judaism and Islam'.[25] Salvation outside the Church, for Danielou, was possible through the 'mysterious workings of God'.

Karl Rahner (1904–84), like Danielou, understood Christianity 'as the absolute religion, intended for all men'. To him other religions were instituted religions of man, which in his view were not valid. He argued: 'lawful religion for Christianity is rather God's action on men, God's free self-revelation by communicating himself to man.'[26]

Rahner's important thesis is: When does 'absolute religion' begin in a person's life? Does it begin at christening or only when one becomes aware of the 'absolute religion'? However, the question *when* one becomes aware of the 'absolute religion' remains unanswered. Since that *when* is not known, Christians do not confront others simply because they are non-Christians but because they are 'anonymous Christians'. Rahner argued:

It would be wrong to regard the pagan as someone who has not yet been touched in any way by God's grace and truth. If, however, he has experienced the grace of God – if, in certain circumstances, he has already accepted this grace as the ultimate, unfathomable intelechy of his existence by accepting the immeasurableness of his dying existence as opening out into infinity – then he has already been given revelation in a true sense even before he has been affected by missionary preaching from without.[27]

Christian mission and the Church's relation with other faiths has changed: a non-Christian is not seen as an object to 'win', but rather a person who is already approaching and needs to be shown the direction towards the path of Christianity.

The other person who influenced the reshaping of the attitude of the Church towards Islam was Louis Massignon (1883–1962). Massignon identified Muslims as 'the sons of Ishmael'. He emphasized that instead of 'looking at Islam from the outside and violently attacking it, one must place himself, by a kind of Copernican somersault, at the very centre of Islam, where this spark of truth lives from which all the rest is invisibly and mysteriously sustained'.[28] A disciple of Massignon, Father Giulio Basetti-Sani, developed his ideas further and appealed to the Church to adopt a positive approach to the revelation of the Qur'an and the Prophet Muhammad's authenticity. He argued that the 'convergence of Muslim and Christian thinking on the significance of an Abrahamic–Ishmaelian origin of Islam also has importance from a theological point of view and merits special attention in assessing the authenticity of Muhammad's message'.[29]

Texts that discuss inter-religious dialogue are *Lumen Gentium*, promulgated 21 November 1964; *Nostra Aetate*, 28 October 1965; *Dei Verbum, Gaudium et spes, Ad Gentes* and *Dignitatis Humanae*, all 7 December 1965. The important thing to note here is that none of these texts contains highly developed concepts of inter-religious dialogue. None refers explicitly to Islam. Furthermore, regarding relations between the Jews and Christians, two approaches have to be kept in mind:

> . . . the *ethnic* reality of Israel is identified and described *theologically* with a series of quotations from the New Testament . . . it affirms the ongoing reality of Israel as a people mysteriously chosen by God, and as such related to the Church. Or shall we put it the other way round: the Church related to Israel, Israel being what it is? Both perspectives are complementary. If *Lumen Gentium* has chosen the former, *Nostra Aetate* has chosen the latter.[30]

Again, although Rahner's view of 'anonymous Christians' had a profound impact on the Council, the Council was not yet prepared to accept Muslims as part of an 'inner circle', as the Jews were, and was not prepared to identify Muslims as 'the sons of Ishmael', as perhaps Massignon would like to have seen. However, a number of Catholic theologians are beginning to adopt a more conciliatory understanding of Islam in their writings.

Here we shall discuss a few texts, which are more explicit in their pronouncements on other religions. *Nostra Aetate* (In Our Times), as far as other religions are concerned, is a very significant document. It challenges Roman Catholics as well as the Protestant Churches to open up and rethink their attitude towards other religions. The statement, in its first section, exhorts that 'the Church examines with greater care the relation which she has to non-Christian religions' and emphasizes that all human beings are 'but one community'.[31]

Pope John XXIII, summing up the Second Vatican Council, perhaps did not foresee that it would be necessary to make a statement on

Muslims as well. He was concerned about the future relations and status within the Church of the Jewish people. The Pope asked Cardinal Bea, who was President of the Secretariat for Promoting Christian Unity, to prepare a statement regarding the Jews. However, the text was not ready until after the Pope's death. The text was introduced as the fourth chapter in *Unitatis Redintegratio* (The Decree on Ecumenism). It is significant that relations with the Jews and their status was introduced within the broader ecumenism of the Christian Church under the presidency of Cardinal Bea, who informed the Council that the late Pope John XXIII had approved the 'basic lines of the document'. However, the Cardinal's pronouncement raised two important objections. Some conciliar fathers strongly objected that any Jewish–Christian relationship should be addressed separately and outside the Catholic concerns for ecumenism.[32] The other objection was raised by bishops from Arab countries. They feared that accepting the document as it stood would be seen by Arab Muslims as the Council taking a pro-Jewish – and, by extension, a pro-Israeli – view, which eventually would damage the Church's image amongst Middle Eastern Muslims. The text presented by Cardinal Bea thus underwent further revision and was approved only in the final session of the Council. In relation to Muslims, the approved text addresses them as those who 'worship God, Who is One', they 'strive to submit themselves' as 'Abraham submitted himself'. Regarding Jesus, it says, 'they venerate Jesus as a prophet', and they also honour the 'Virgin Mother' and believe and await 'the Day of Judgement and reward of God'.[33] But the important section of the document continues:

> Over the centuries many quarrels and dissensions have arisen between Christians and Muslims. The Sacred Council now pleads with all to forget the past, and urges that a sincere effort be made to achieve mutual understanding for the benefit of all men, let them together preserve and promote peace, liberty, social justice and moral values.[34]

The statement on Muslim beliefs has thus moved from a position of condemnation to the acknowledgement that Muslim beliefs are a set of beliefs in their own right. However, the document ignores the question of Revelation (Qur'an), and the Prophethood of Muhammad. Although it compares Muslims' submission to the submissive act of Abraham, this does not mean it accepts the spiritual lineage of Muhammad (peace be upon him), through Ishmael to Abraham. It is also significant that the document, reconciliatory in tone, nonetheless emphasizes 'forgetting the past' in order to acclaim 'peace, justice and moral values'. How Muslims reacted to this statement we shall discuss in some detail later.

Lumen Gentium (Light of the Nations). The light referred to here is an affirmation that 'Christ is the light of humanity'. *Lumen Gentium* is basically a Christocentric document. For example, in paragraph 6 it emphasizes that reconciliation of Jews and Gentiles will be possible in Christ:

> The Church is a cultivated field. On the land this ancient olive tree grows. . . . That land, like a choice vineyard, has been planted by the heavenly cultivator (Mt. 21:33–43; cf. Is. 5:1f). Yet the true vine is Christ who gives life and fruitfulness to the branches, that is, to us, who through the Church remains one Christ without whom we can do nothing.[35]

The document also speaks about an 'invisible structure', implying the Catholic Church, through which Christ communicates truth and grace to all men. Section two of *Lumen Gentium* refers directly to Muslims. After some references to the Jewish people, 'who have not yet received the Gospel', the text continues:

> But the plan of salvation also includes those who acknowledge the Creator, in the first place amongst who are the Moslems: these profess to hold the faith of Abraham, and together with us they adore the one, merciful God, mankind's judge on the last day.[36]

Again referring to Jews and Muslims, and other non-Christians, the text reads:

> Those who, through no fault of their own, do not know the Gospel of Christ or his Church, but who nevertheless seek God with a sincere heart, and, moved by Grace, try in their actions to do His will as they know it through the dictates of their conscience – these too may achieve eternal salvation.[37]

These statements certainly express some marked improvements in respect of other faiths. It shows the urgent desire of the Church to reach non-Christians, and non-Catholics, who are the 'children of God', including Muslims, and all Children of God 'have been called to membership of this new people'. Commenting on this document, Hastings remarks that non-Christians, despite having some valuable qualities, 'still lack much' and, therefore, he says, to achieve the ultimate desired goal, 'missionary work is absolutely necessary'.[38]

Ad Gentes Divinitus (The Universal Sacrament of Salvation) commonly known as 'Decree on the Church's Missionary Activity'. As we have seen earlier, the plan of salvation includes those 'who acknowledge the Creator'. The *Ad Gentes Divinitus* emphasizes that knowing that they have been saved is equally important. Chapter 1, paragraph 3 reads:

> This universal plan of God for salvation of mankind is not carried out solely in a secret manner, as it were, in the minds of men . . . their efforts need to be enlightened and corrected . . . [so] they may lead one to the true God and be a preparation for the Gospel.[39]

Then it refers to the importance of God's salvific act in Jesus. Now it is the duty of the members of the Church 'to save and renew every creature, so that all things might be restored in Christ'.[40]

It states, 'the church on earth is by its very nature missionary . . . it has its origin in the mission of the Son and the Holy Spirit'.[41] It is clear, therefore, that missionary activity flows immediately from the very nature of the Church. Missionary activity extends the 'saving faith of the Church'. It asks Christians to unite for the task: 'All baptized people are called upon to come together in one flock that they might bear unanimous witness to Christ their Lord before the nations.'[42] Those that the Church has to reach 'are two billion people – and their number is increasing day by day . . .'[43]

Dei Verbum (On Divine Revelation). This document emphasizes the importance of the Revelation and its completion. It briefly mentions the history of the prophets, where Abraham and Moses and others and their followers were taught 'to look for the promised Saviour'. The chain of prophets is seen as the preparation for 'the way for the Gospel'.[44] Jesus has been mentioned as 'a man among men' who 'speaks the word of God' (John 3:34) and accomplishes the saving work which the Father gave him to do (cf. John 5:36; 17:4), who 'completed and perfected Revelation and confirmed it with divine guarantees'.[45]

Here no room is left for further 'Revelation' and therefore the Qur'anic Revelation and Prophet Muhammad's ministry have relevance in the Council's documents. As the Council further points out, the earlier prophets were taught 'to look for the promised Saviour'. The Qur'an also points out that Jesus asked his followers to look for a Prophet after him (Al-Saff 61:6), but this also has no significance in the Council's documents. But it shows the difficulties ahead in the theological area of dialogue with Muslims.

Gaudium et Spes (Joy and Hope). This document addresses 'the whole human family' and the day-to-day problems in the world, viz. the dignity of man, moral conscience, promotion of human concerns like politics and economics. It points out that:

> Man is growing conscious that the forces he has unleashed are in his own hands and that it is up to him to control them or be enslaved by them. Here lies . . . the modern dilemma.[46]

And emphasizes that the solution is only in Christ – 'an ultimate foundation', who is 'the same yesterday, and today, and forever'.[47]

Dignitatis Humanae (Dignity of the Human Person). This document contains practical advice on religious freedom and human rights. The increasing pressure from the secular forces perhaps compelled the Council Fathers to issue a separate text on the subject. This document first appeared as part of the decree on ecumenism. The document advocates 'religious freedom'. 'Freedom', as it explains:

> means that all men should be immune from coercion on the part of individuals, social groups and every human power so that, within the limits, nobody is forced to act against his convictions nor is anyone to be restrained from acting in accordance with his convictions in religious matters.[48]

Section 2 deals with 'religious freedom and the light of Revelation'. It distinguishes between those who believe and are baptized and those who do not: 'weeds had been sown through the wheat but ordered that both be allowed to grow until the harvest which will come at the end of the world.'[49] This statement shows that Rahner's theological position of anonymous Christians has not been accepted.

To sum up what we have said so far: three broad patterns emerge from the Second Vatican Council's view on other religions, especially on Islam, showing that the Roman Catholics appeared to have discovered spiritual wealth amongst Muslim beliefs. Nonetheless, the perspective on beliefs is selective. The Council accepts the Islamic belief of one God as merciful, all-powerful; but that the same God could reveal with the Abrahamic covenant a new 'revelation' clearly seems unacceptable. Although *Nostra Aetate* inspired the process of dialogue with Muslims and other religions and a secretariat was established to initiate dialogue, the tension between 'mission' and 'dialogue' remained unresolved for nearly two decades. The Council and its various documents point out, on the one hand, 'mission to', and on the other 'dialogue with'. But is the 'dialogue' part of 'mission', or will 'mission' be 'dialogical' in relation to other religions? That is the crucial question. From the very begining the Church was under immense pressure to abandon its reconciliatory attitude towards non-Christians, as one of the commentators on the Second Vatican Council notes:

> a large number of practising missionaries were disturbed about the all too favourable judgement on non-Christian religions and the possibility of salvation for non-Christians, especially in *Nostra Aetate* and *Lumen Gentium*, they asked for a clear statement on these problems and an official pronouncement on the necessity of the missions even after the Council.[50]

To clarify this 'tension' or 'confusion', the Church's dialogue office issued a document, *The Attitude of the Church towards the Followers of other Religions: Reflections on Orientations on Dialogue and Mission in 1984.* Pope John Paul II's encyclical *Redemptoris Missio* 1991 is an important indication of how the Church regards 'dialogue' with non-Christian, and the subsequent statement published in the same year, *Dialogue and Proclamation*, is a further indication of the Church's future direction. However, these statements indicate that the 'dialogue' is exclusively under the domain of 'mission' and not vice versa.

EVANGELICALS AND DIALOGUE

The Evangelicals' understanding of dialogue is that dialogue is a missionary activity. Evidence suggests that dialogue with Muslims has not been accepted in the form and in the spirit that the Church leaders in the international arena so frequently express. In 1978, an inter-Christian consultation organized by the Conference of European Churches in Salzburg on relations with Muslims in Europe revealed the difficulty. Bishop Fitzgerald, one of the participants, remarked:

> I was a member of the theological workshop. We were to produce a theological statement underpinning the understanding of and practice of Christian–Muslim relations. There were some in the group

for whom the only possible attitude towards Muslims was one of direct evangelism, the explicit preaching of Jesus Christ with an invitation to accept him as Lord and Saviour. For them a broader view of God's plan for salvation, in which there might be a place for Islam, was anathema. They would not even agree to disagree. And so the final report from the consultation, in the section 'theology' carried an eloquently blank page![51]

The central point remains how to relate the question of mission to other faiths. Thirteen years after the Salzburg Conference, the problem remains. The WCC's Seventh Assembly in Canberra report admits:

> Interfaith dialogue has proved difficult for some churches and Christians because of our continuing problems in understanding religious plurality and God's relationship to people of other religious tradition.[52]

The Evangelicals, who emphasize the centrality of Christ as Saviour, were put on the alert with the publication of statements like: 'We should take careful note of the fact that Christ did not send His disciples to convert the whole world to the Church but rather sent them out to teach or make disciples of all nations,'[53] implying that it is not necessary to become 'Christian' in order to be a 'disciple'. The Evangelicals' suspicion turned to distrust even before the publication of such statements. In 1968 the WCC published its assembly report 'Uppsala 68', in which the Evangelicals saw a clear betrayal of mission. Donald McGavran remarks:

> From beginning to end the document is studded with the word mission ... But while the word mission is repeatedly used, its meaning is nowhere that of communicating the good news of Jesus Christ to unbelieving men in order that they might believe and live.[54]

Developments, especially in the Protestant Churches since Edinburgh 1910, directed Christians towards an ecumenical movement on the one hand, e.g. Life and Work, Faith and Order, which eventually created the WCC, and towards a collaborative effort of mission on the other, represented by the International Missionary Council. The tension that existed between the two approaches within the WCC was enhanced after the merger of IMC with the WCC in 1961, and further deteriorated after the Uppsala Assembly in 1968. A later document states:

Something happened after Edinburgh 1910 . . . the authority of evangelism began to shift from Scriptures to the organised church . . . Emphasis turned to men 'in this world' rather than 'in the next world'.[55]

The social dimension, 'the materialistic salvation of the *community*', taken up by Churches, during the height of the socialists' resurgence, caused the Evangelicals to put great emphasis on the spiritual rather than the material salvation of the people. The so-called Third World countries, including Latin America, wanted to know how their material salvation would be procured without the loss of their spiritual salvation.

The first declaration by the Evangelicals was issued in 1970, and is known as the Frankfurt Declaration. It renewed commitment to mission and strongly opposed the World Council of Churches' position on dialogue. The document was the brain-child of a number of German confessional theologians. It speaks about 'a fundamental crisis' in the organized Churches. The teaching that 'Christ himself is anonymously so evident in world religions' was strongly opposed by the Declaration, which rejects:

the idea that 'Christian presence' among the adherents to the world religions and a give-and-take dialogue with them are substitutes for a proclamation of the gospel which aims at conversion.[56]

The Declaration quite clearly establishes dialogue as a means of 'missionary communication' and nothing more. The Evangelicals, two years later, published their response to the WCC's call for a world-wide conference on inter-Christian consultation, *Salvation Today* (Bangkok, 29 December 1972 to 21 January 1973). Soon after the conference the Evangelicals published their response, *The Evangelical Response to Bangkok*,[57] which criticized the fact that the WCC had tampered with the term 'salvation'. As one of the commentators put it, terms like 'salvation' have been 'devalued'. Their 'eternal significance is being minimised and their temporal meanings underlined'. It also criticized the WCC's approach to other key biblical terms, like 'mission', 'evangelism' and 'conversion'. The commentator pleads that the 'Evangelicals should work and pray that this deliberate debasing of Christian currency ceases and that the reformation of the social order . . . should not be substituted for salvation.'[58]

This tension was present even while the dialogue programme with other religions was in progress. The gap between the Evangelicals and

WCC, as well as with the Roman Catholic Church, persisted and widened. The Evangelicals called one of the most successful missionary conferences in history, in Lausanne, in 1974, at which some 2500 delegates from 150 countries participated. Apart from issues like mission, evangelism, salvation and conversion, 'dialogue' became a serious term to be understood and clarified. Unlike the Frankfurt Declaration, the Lausanne Congress accepted the importance of dialogue as a means of evangelism. G.W. Peters, at the Congress, said:

> *Purpose* is evangelism, the *procedure* is dialogue – the friendly exchange of views and convictions, the ultimate sharing of experiences, needs, aspirations, and frustrations, with a view of dissolving the difficulties, obstacles, and prejudices in the heart and mind of the unsaved person.[59]

The term dialogue thus became increasingly part of contemporary missionary thought and vocabulary, and Evangelicals gradually accepted it. David Gitari remarks that dialogue

> is said to be necessary because Christians everywhere are living in a pluralistic society. It is urgent because all men are under common pressure in search for justice and peace, and are faced with the challenge to live together as human beings. Dialogue is full of opportunity because Christians can now, as never before, discover the meaning of the Lordship of and the implication for the mission of the Church in a truly universal context of common living and common urgency.[60]

In his conclusion he points out the urgency of the task of evangelism, which, he argues, has 'no hard-and-fast rules'. At times, he stresses that the Christian 'proclamation will be dialogical'.

Since Lausanne, the Evangelicals have quite comfortably pursued this line of dialogue. Soon after Lausanne, in 1978, 'the North American Conference of Muslim Evangelization' also took up the question of dialogue with Muslims. The conference discussed in great detail the ways and means of Muslim evangelism, conversion, indigenization, training and research, as well as intensive area studies.[61] Daniel Brewster argues that the WCC has changed its position on the role of dialogue. At the New Delhi Assembly of the WCC in 1961, it points out, dialogue was seen as 'a useful means of evangelism', but by Uppsala 1968, dialogue had moved out of the sphere of mission and had become instead part of a more general sphere of 'continuing Christian obligation'.[62] The Evangelicals point out that though one cannot force conversion, nevertheless they feel that they can 'compel them to come in',[63] by which they mean into Christianity; whilst 'them' implies Muslims. The paper points out the three stages of the WCC's engagement in dialogue: first, ecumenical reflection amongst Christians; second, gathering for actual dialogue with Muslims, and third, ventures in relief and development. The first two approaches they rejected. The WCC's approach to the third stage is tentative. Brewster suggests that if some form of dialogue programmes with the Muslims are found to be 'profitable' towards the 'winning of Muslims', then the Evangelicals must 'plan how it should be done'.[64]

There has been a number of Evangelical Protestant statements since Lausanne 1974. They have all been quite successful in maintaining pressure on the Churches not to go too far, and compelling them to return from the 'original positions' on dialogue with other faiths, and especially with Muslims.[65] There is a need for an in-depth study on Evangelical pressure and Evangelicals' understanding of dialogue and their impact on both the Protestant and Roman Catholic Churches. The Evangelicals were perhaps the true inheritors of the Edinburgh 1910 Conference. Mission in the traditional sense is the alpha and omega of the Evangelicals. Dialogue, to them, came as a challenge and, as far as they are concerned, dialogue is no longer an issue. For them there is no debate between 'dialogue' and 'mission'; in their perception dialogue with other religions remains a tool of mission. Dialogue on social issues for them seems impractical.

Furthermore, Fundamentalist Christians in America have adopted a pro-Zionist and pro-Israeli position and effectively, through literature and anti-Islamic fervour, have created a distance between the Muslim community and Evangelical Fundamentalist Christians. Any contact worth mentioning is Ahmad Deedat's debates with them in South Africa and in a number of Western cities. These contacts were of a more polemical nature, a debate, which had more of entertainment value than dialogue.

Despite the controversies discussed earlier, the Churches took a serious decision to establish special offices in order to promote dialogue with other religions. The Roman Catholic Church established a Secretariat for Non-Christian Religions, known (since March 1989) as the Pontifical Council for Inter-religious Dialogue (PCID), and the World Council of Churches established a Unit on Dialogue with People of Living Faiths and Ideologies now under the Secretariat of WCC and known as the Office of Inter-religious Dialogue. The former was established on 19 May 1964 by Pope Paul VI, even before the Council Fathers voted in favour of *Nostra Aetate* (on 28 October 1965), and the latter in January 1971. We shall briefly discuss the formation of the two dialogue offices and outline their objectives.

THE PONTIFICAL COUNCIL FOR INTER-RELIGIOUS DIALOGUE

The Pontifical Council for Inter-religious Dialogue (hereafter referred to as the Council) was established on 19 May 1964. Cardinal Paolo Marella (1964–73) was its first head, followed by Cardinal Pignedoli (1973–80) and Archbishop Jadot (1980–84); currently, Cardinal Arinze is the head of the Council.

The *aims* and *methods* of the Council, as described by Mgr Rossano, are threefold:

1. We try to open friendly relations, communication and dialogue with followers of the religious traditions of the world: personal relations, official relations, community relations, grass-root-level relations, youth relations, academic relations . . . in a spirit of love, service, hospitality, in mutual sharing, social and cultural collaboration. Such is our activity outside the Church.

2. Inside the Church we try to arouse interest in and promote knowledge of the followers of the non-Christian faiths, to stimulate dialogue and communication with them, to help and to serve the Holy See and the local Churches in this field: in doing this we make it our rule and our commitment to respect the particular circumstances and the authority of the local Churches, and to offer and foster ecumenical collaboration whenever possible.

3. We consider it also our duty to be attentive and helpful in the ongoing process of enculturation which is a true form of continuing dialogue in the local Churches, especially in Asia and Africa, between the Christian message and the religious cultures of the particular place. In a word, we consider ourselves, within the Church, as the advocates and the defenders of others as such, namely of their rights, their spiritual values, their religious traditions and identity.[66]

Rossano informs us that in the early stages the Council faced uncertainty and a lack of proper direction regarding its work. Its aims were not made clear like other offices, which came out of the Second Vatican Council's discussions. The problem the Council faced, as late as 1991, was the *purpose* of dialogue. The document 'Dialogue and Proclamation' was published in order to resolve the confusion surrounding the terms 'mission' and 'dialogue'. Reflecting on the history, ideas and tension, Rossano notes:

> To have dialogue with non-Christians, but why? A new form of mission, or a lack of courage in the mission? If it is not mission in the true sense of the word, is it merely seeking to assist non-Christians in their social development? Or is its purpose to make them better Muslims, Buddhists or Hindus? On what foundation should dialogue be built?[67]

In a press conference soon after the establishment of the Council, its first head, Cardinal Marella, said that the Council's

> aim was not conversation or the bringing about of unity. Its first aim was to promote mutual understanding between men of different religions. An effort would be made to acquire an objective knowledge of different spiritualities and of the different ways the human mind expresses its approach to God.[68]

However, the confusion remained in the minds of many Christians and was expressed time and again. Some believed, as Rossano quotes, that there were some

> talking of the 'end of the missionary epoch' and saying 'it is now the era of dialogue'. A person of great prestige said to me at that time: 'the Church is the only power which still has a ministry for the colonies'. Others said: 'Now that the colonial age is over, missionary activities should also cease'.[69]

The Council, however, after a period of uncertainty, concentrated its efforts amongst Muslims, through its 'Commission for Islam'. This Commission pooled its resources: people in the Church who either had regular contacts with Muslims and were living amongst them, or who had undertaken some special study on Islam. They were called regularly to Rome for consultation. Consultations were mainly concentrated at two levels: first, to explain to Church members the importance of *Nostra Aetate* and the purpose of dialogue with other religions; and second, to explain the areas and meanings of dialogue in a way that is appropriate for Christians and Muslims and other religions. The first task has been initiated through the laity and local and regional churches. The other level was to establish guidelines for dialogue. In 1969, the Council produced *Guidelines for a Dialogue Between Muslims and Christians*,[70] written by Joseph Cuoq and Louis Gardet. In 1981, Father Bormans revised the *Guidelines* and published in French *Orientations pour un Dialogue entre Chrétiens et Musulmans*, which was translated into English by Marston Speight and published in 1990.[71] Both *Guidelines* and *Orientations* provide Church members with the basic tools to enter into dialogue with Muslims and understand their culture and beliefs.

The Council restricted its meetings as far as possible. Muslims visited Rome and visits were made to Muslim countries rather than holding dialogue meetings. Although the Council regularly participated in organized dialogues all over the world, the first Muslim delegation to visit Rome was of the High Council for Muslim Affairs in Cairo, headed by its Secretary General, Mohammad Tewfik Oweida, which was received by the Council from 16 to 20 December 1970. A reciprocal delegation visited the High Council in Cairo, headed by Cardinal Pignedoli, from 9 to 16 September 1974. Also in 1974, Pignedoli visited Saudi Arabia and met King Faisal. In recent years the Council has participated and at times jointly organized dialogue on various issues with Muslim organizations on a regular basis; these will be discussed later.

THE OFFICE ON INTER-RELIGIOUS RELATIONS

The WCC established a unit in 1971, within the Division of Mission and evangelism, which we discussed earlier. After it was established it soon realized the importance of guidelines for dialogue with Muslims as well as with other religions. The WCC meeting in 1971 in Addis Ababa produced what might be called intrinsic guidelines. It was also in this meeting that the Committee decided to add 'and ideologies'. George Khodar, in his paper 'Christianity in a Pluralistic World – the Work of the Holy Spirit', argued:

Christ is everywhere hidden in the mystery of his self-effacement. Any exploration of the religious is an exploration into Christ. When grace visits a Brahmin, a Buddhist or a Muslim reading his scripture, it is Christ alone who is received as light.[72]

Khodar believes that the Christian task 'is to follow the footsteps of Christ through the shadows of the religions'.[73] Stanley Samartha's paper, 'Dialogue as a Continuing Christian Concern', identified the reason for dialogue with Muslims as well as other religions, arguing that 'God in Jesus Christ has himself entered into relationship with men of all faiths',[74] meaning, therefore, that dialogue with people of other faiths is a continuation of God's work. Secondly, he emphasizes that the Gospels point out that the 'Church is a sign and a symbol' of the 'true community inherent in the Gospel'. This 'inevitably leads to dialogue' and cooperation with the people of other faiths should include a 'fight against all that destroys the community'. This for Samartha is sufficient reason that 'Christians must at all times be actively involved in building up a truly universal community of freedom and love'.[75] For Samartha – and this is the third point – Biblical understanding of truth is not 'propositional but relational, and is to be sought, not in the isolation of lonely meditation, but in the living, personal confrontation between God and man, and man and man'.[76]

George Khodar and Stanley Samartha's papers became the basis of the 'Interim Policy Statement and Guidelines' adopted by the Central Committee of the WCC at the Addis Ababa meeting. However, the WCC's report of this meeting suggests that most of the Orthodox and Asian Christians were in agreement with the view proposed by Khoder and Samartha; most of the objections came from the European Christians.[77]

Guidelines for Dialogue was finally produced at the Chiang Mai consultation in 1977. However, the WCC's General Assembly, reaction to 'dialogue' in Nairobi (1975) was seen by many as 'syncretism' and strongly criticized. This was reflected in later dialogue guidelines. The *Guidelines* had progressed from *Interim* to full *Guidelines* by 1977. Two years later, the Dialogue Unit issued *New Guidelines*, which were adopted in the WCC's Central Committee meeting in Kingston, Jamaica in January 1979. The 1977 *Guidelines* consist of three parts: 'On Community', 'On Dialogue' and 'Guidelines Recommended to the Churches for Study and Action'. The 1979 *New Guidelines* reflect developments after the Nairobi Assembly.

The *Guidelines* moved its thrust on 'dialogue' in 1971 to 'dialogue on community' in 1977 to 'Search for Community' in 1979. This shift emphasized the importance of the Christian community as a part of a wider community and not one in isolation. Furthermore, the new guidelines avoided the use of terms like 'mission', 'evangelism' and use the term 'dialogue' perhaps in the same sense as the term 'mission' or 'evangelism'.

In 1971 when the words 'and ideologies' were inserted, the WCC's committee was burdened with a legacy of ecumenical missionary concerns. Since the Russian Revolution in 1917 and the founding of the Soviet Union on secular principles and the role of these in society, the term 'ideology' was implicitly referred to by the Churches in a pejorative sense. But soon this distinction between faith and 'ideology' found itself in conflict. Many in the Church believed that if the mission of the Church is for the whole world, then the Church's responsibility is primarily to those who have never heard the Gospel. In 1984 the WCC decided to remove the words 'and Ideologies' and in 1990 the Dialogue Unit merged with WCC's Secretariat and became the Office on Inter-religious Dialogue. This is the background against which Christian-Muslim dialogue began. But before we turn to Muslims in Dialogue, it would not be out of place to point out the difference between the two initiatives. The WCC's initiative compared to the Vatican's could be called 'adventurous'. In the 1982 Colombo dialogue, Muslim participants recognized that even though it was the WCC's sponsored dialogue, Muslims were able to choose their own delegation and it was the first occasion when Muslims and Christians jointly planned the agenda. It was a courageous step on the part of the WCC to allow the planning and execution of the dialogue to pass out of their hands. Acting upon the initiative provided by the WCC, the Council began to organize dialogues on the basis of each community appointing their own delegates and jointly preparing the agendas. This approach was welcomed by Al Albait Foundation, the Call of Islam Society and various other Muslim bodies at the international and regional levels.

3 Muslims in Dialogue: Assessment and Priorities

Muslims' participation in dialogue needs to be seen first, in a theological perspective, and second, as an encounter with Christianity in the contemporary situation.

For Muslims Christianity and Judaism are integral parts of Islam, in so far as Islam accommodates earlier revelations as a part of its own theology. Islam's relation with these two religions is further cemented by the Prophet Muhammad's familial lineage through Ishmael, Isaac and Abraham. Abraham is an important figure whom the Qur'an frequently mentions as a model for all Muslims to follow. As a result of this historical and theological linkage, the position of Jews and Christians is clearly defined in the Qur'an and in the *Sunnah* of the Prophet; they are declared to be *Ahl-al-Kitab* – People of the Book.

Religions do not meet in a vacuum. It is their followers who encounter each other. Their perceptions and apprehensions are moulded by events, and events play an important role in understanding each other. We saw in the previous chapter how Muslims' understanding of Christianity is informed by their loyalty to Jesus and the Christian faith, as they understand them; but at the same time, they see Christians not as part of that tradition, but a part of a tradition which they have encountered during the last two centuries. Christians and the Churches are seen a 'legacy' of Western colonial tradition. And it is at this historical and psychological juncture that Muslims are asked to participate in dialogue with Christians. It is also important to note that the Churches, especially in the West, are now beginning to develop a theology of religious pluralism. They are trying to relate their faith to others', but not without challenge and opposition from within the Church. In the absence of a clearly defined pluralist understanding of other religions, any encounter between Christians and Muslims in the past, as Martin Kretzmann rightly remarks is an

illustration of the determination of the Christian to meet the Muslim within the framework of our [Christian] understanding of him rather than willingness to meet him at the point of his self-understanding. If we now try to make clear to ourselves what that self-understanding is, we are handicapped, not so much be our self-understanding as Christians as by the difficulty of ridding ourselves of those concepts which have accrued to us through a confusion of our faith with our religion, and our religion with our culture, concepts which by contrast make us understand the Muslims in categories which he does not recognise as a true and essential image of himself.[1]

Historical events mould these 'images' of each other and perceptions of each others' religion. In Islam, Jesus and Mary, his mother, are given special status, and Christianity has been seen, though critically, as a revealed religion. However, this has not stopped Muslims assessing Christians and forming opinions about them from a different outlook. Christians and Muslims judge each other's religion in the light of their own experiences, and formulate opinions about each other on this basis. Hassan Saab puts this point remarkably:

> Christians and Muslims tend to judge each others' religion through the prevailing Christian and Muslim conditions. Muslims would associate Christianity with the aggressiveness of those Christian rulers from whom they have suffered for a century and a half. Christians would associate Islam with Muslims' state of backwardness, with which they became familiar in their modern contact with Islam. The rejection of aggressiveness would then imply a rejection of Christianity. Disgust with backwardness would entail disgust with Islam. This would happen unless Christians and Muslims could set a demarcation line between religious ideal and human realities.[2]

In this chapter, our focus will be Muslims' apprehensions and hesitations in dialogue with Christians. We shall investigate the reasons behind such hesitations and attempt to see how Muslims define dialogue and establish what priorities they assign in dialogue, especially with Christians.

APPREHENSIONS

The term 'dialogue' was first used by the Christian Churches in a particular context, which we have discussed in previous chapters, and this suggests that Muslim attitude to dialogue is still bound by certain apprehensions. Their participation began to question the whole approach to dialogue. Is it a genuine effort at 'reconciliation' and 'bridge-building' – terms commonly used to describe the purpose of dialogue – or yet another method of missionary 'strategists' to serve the purpose of 'evangelization'? Others see it as an act of Christian desperation in the face of crass materialism and remorseless secularization.[3] Furthermore, in the eyes of some Muslims there is no need to engage in dialogue simply because the Qur'an says so, that the Jews and Christians cannot be 'friend and protectors' of Muslims.[4] They bring historical evidence in support of their claims by reference to colonialism in the past and more recently the Gulf War.[5] Others suggest that the Qur'anic injunction, 'to you your Way and to me mine',[6] should be the norm, and dialogue an exception.

There are other reasons why Muslims mistrust dialogue. Some view dialogue, which emerged in the West, as part of the secular heritage of the West. They argue that when Muslims deal with Christians in the West, they are in fact dealing with secularism. As Gai Eaton remarks:

> We are not really facing for the most part the problem of dealing with Christianity, we are facing the problem of dealing with Secularism in a particular guise – let us say with a good leverage of Christian faith, but nonetheless by our standards . . . essentially a secular outlook . . . the modern Christian often seems to be more the child of that tradition than the child of Christianity when Christianity was a solid all-embracing, all-powerful faith.[7]

It seems there is some truth in this view. The Church has a role in society as far as individuals and social life are concerned, e.g. marriage, birth and burial, and to some extent counselling for those who need it. But increasingly, the Church is becoming secular in its outlook, even in its religious beliefs and practices. Furthermore the Church is becoming a reactive institution and not pro-active in social and political affairs, dictated by secular social pressures to conform to 'the norm'. At times it seems that the Church is doing all the things right but not the right things. It is becoming increasingly 'a pressure group' within society, where it is seen as relinquishing its role as the leading moral force. Ziauddin Sardar puts it in these words:

> Christianity is, and ought to be, an antithesis to Secularism. Yet it became tied to a particular culture, a particular scholarly trend and the historic experience of a particular people. Instead of explaining the Bible and Jesus's ministry within changing circumstances,

cultural settings and different languages, scripture and Jesus were
made to serve the ends of European Secularism.[8]

Therefore Muslims may be right to question a seemingly religious dialogue which has all the ingredients of secular liberal values with an
edge of Christianity.

The second important mistrust is that of Muslim representation itself. In dialogue, at times it has been the case that in the absence of a
single representative body of Muslims, dialogue organizers approach
the 'official *Ulamā*' to represent Muslims. Once the *Ulamā* become
'representative', Muslims question whom they are representing. Muslim governments who have no mandate from the Muslim community
on the one hand, and the *Ulamā* who have been appointed by such
governments with limited freedom to speak in the mosques on the other,
are further limited in any attempts to 'represent' the Muslim community outside their own countries. They are cautious in dialogue rather
than vocal representatives of the Muslim community, and confine their
presentation as far as possible to quotations from the Qur'an and the
Ahādith. Muslims, and especially the *Ulamā,* have another difficulty,
namely, language. Most of the dialogue initiated by Western Christians uses English, French or other European languages, whereas the
Ulamā are well versed in Arabic or one of the 'Eastern languages',
viz. Turkish, Farsi or Urdu. When they meet in dialogue their language
is imbued with the religious and cultural milieu of their country. Therefore
dialogue becomes distorted, and at times unhealthy.

The third area of mistrust appears at the political and intellectual
level. The Christian world can afford to engage in dialogue simply
because it is intellectually equipped and politically and economically
powerful, and has nothing to lose. Muslims do not have 'anything,
economically [and], intellectually' comparable, emphasizes one Muslim.[9] Christians, he says, 'dominate too many discourses in the world
today and so dialogue is an extension of a whole Western Christian
domination'. 'Dialogue', another Muslim claims, 'is the child of
secularization of Western society and those who engage in it are beneficiaries of a recent phenomenon in world history'.[10] The Christian
West, or the Churches in the West, have compelled Muslims, who
lack the necessary intellectual tools to respond to a situation which is
not under their control and participate in a dialogue whose agenda
they have not set, and have rarely contributed to. When Muslims send
their children to the West to acquire 'Western intellectual tools', it has
been noticed that most of them either become 'Westerners' in their

approach and attitude or decide not to return to their country of origin. Either way, Muslims believe they are losing them.[11]

The Muslim view of dialogue is that it is increasingly becoming a discipline like any other social science discipline. It is become part of university culture, a culture where a subject is taught, but little participated in, little lived, useful mostly in intellectual circles, but nonetheless valuable. This value Muslims question – who is it for, the Church, State, or others? As one Muslim puts it, dialogue is 'an extension of a dominant Western Christian Judaic intellectual scenario' and therefore they will be the beneficiaries of dialogue.'[12]

The fourth aspect of mistrust emerges out of history. In relation to dialogue, Muslims identify six elements of 'historical equation of colonialism and Christianity'. These are: 'crusade, curiosity, commerce, conversion, conquest and colonization'.[13] In India, historians suggest, the Christian Church existed from the very first century of the Christian calendar. The arrival of Muslims in the country did not upset relations between the two communities. Rather, relations seem to have been very close, until the arrival of the Western colonial powers. One such example is the burial place of St Thomas. Historians, on the basis of Marco Polo's account, believe that the saint's shrine 'seems already to have been a *Dargah* or *Pir* cult'.[14] Muslims used to visit the shrine, believing that a prayer there could heal 'blindness'. The account suggests there were 'Muslim officiates at the shrine' to receive Muslim visitors. However, when the Portuguese took over the site in 1523, they built St Thomas' Cathedral on the site and by the 1540s or 1550s the Portuguese had begun to impose strict Roman Catholic-centred church discipline on the surrounding, even on the Syrian Churches, who trace their origin to St Thomas.

Perhaps it would not be out of place to point out another reason for Muslims' distrust. The British entered into a trade treaty with the Mughal Emperor Jahangir in India, and subsequently obtained a considerable number of trade concessions under Shah Jahan, which opened the floodgates of trade with India. The greatest beneficiary of this was the East India Company. The company, which not only supplied arms and textiles, but also carried missionaries, gradually shifted from commerce and curiosity to conversion of the local people, and this eventually paved the way, arguably, for the colonization of India. This is an example from one country; many other countries in the Far East, Middle East and Africa faced similar problems. These historical factors play an important part in Muslim psychology and their reasons for distrust of dialogue.

The fifth aspect of Muslims' apprehension is related to the history and tradition of 'Orientalism'. Orientalism is understood as an effort to bring the knowledge of the Orient, by translations, editing and fresh writings on the Orient, to European languages. But the purpose went beyond this noble intention. The 'knowledge' was 'at the service of the empire' of the Western colonial nations, for commercial, diplomatic and missionary purposes. This process continued for centuries, and the Western view of the Orient was colonized with the deep animosity of the Orient, and vice-versa. The Muslim perception of the West and Christianity in general is that the West is determined to 'disintegrate' Islam, and that Muslim countries will never be allowed to exist independently of the West. The religious conflict with the Muslim world is also blamed on the Western powers and the Western Orientalist traditions.[15]

This Muslim apprehension about the Orientalist tradition is not imaginary. One of France's influential colonial journals, the fortnightly *Questions diplomatiques et coloniales* (QDC), conducted a survey in 1901 of Islam's prospects in the twentieth century, especially its prospects for revival. The journal asked 18 prominent Orientalists-*cum*-Islamists from various parts of the world to write on the subject. Without going into further detail, we would like to quote Baron Carra de Vaux of France. A specialist on Ibn Sina, he was a contributor to the *Encyclopaedia of Religion and Ethics*, especially on the life and work of Abd al-Qadir al-Jilani. He identified colonialization as a slow process of change in the Muslim world and the danger of 'native reaction'. In his view:

> The great and general danger menacing the Christian powers in their relations with the Muslim world was pan-Islam; a simultaneous uprising from the Maghrib to the Far East, although improbable, was still possible at any time and without any clear pretext.[16]

Note how he associates the colonial powers with 'the Christian powers'. His formula epitomizes both the Orientalist perception of the East and Muslims' fear of the West. With respect to Western Christianity in general, 'I believe', he wrote,

> that we should endeavour to split the Muslim world, to break its moral unity, using to this effect the ethnic and political divisions . . . Let us therefore accentuate these differences, in order to increase on the one hand national sentiment (*sentiment de nationalité*) and to decrease on the other that of religious community (*communauté*

religieuse) among the various Muslim races. Let us take advantage of the political condition. Egypt, for example, governed today by British power, must be a moral entity clearly distinct from French Sudan or from Egypt a barrier between African Islam and Asian Islam. In one word, let us segment Islam and make use, moreover, of Muslim heresies and the Sufi orders.[17]

His answer to the question of how to face the prospect of the revival Islam was 'to weaken Islam . . . to render it forever incapable of great awakening'.[18] These apprehensions form a psychological barrier in the Muslim mind. They prevent Muslims participating fully in dialogue with Christians.

The Roman Catholic Church's Second Vatican Council's document, *Nostra Aetate* (1965), highlights another important aspect of Muslims' apprehension. The Council appeals to Muslims:

over the centuries many quarrels and dissensions have arisen be-tween Christians and Muslims. The sacred council now pleads with all to forget the past, and urges that a sincere effort be made to achieve mutual understanding . . .[19]

Though many Muslims agree with the spirit behind the plea, 'forget-ting the past' is a painful task. When the Council was debating the issue, Muslims in France, Muhammad Hamidullah of Paris remem-bers, wrote to the Pope with a request 'to officially disavow and de-clare annulled the [Church's] past unjustifiable resolutions of former Councils, Synods and other writings of anti-Islamic character'.[20] The request seems reasonable. But whether the Church will do this remains to be seen. The process of dialogue and the excitement of looking to the future gives the impression that both the Roman Catholic and Prot-estant Churches would rather not to talk about the past; they show an urgency to move forward.

Muslims argue that there is another dimension to forgetting the past. One cannot and should not forget the past because it is memory and 'memory is a weapon. Forgetting the past is a way of getting us to disarm ourselves.'[21] Others associate this with Muslim identity. As one Muslim remarks: 'To ask Muslims to forget the past is tantamount to the denial of their own identity and the obliteration of their own his-tory.'[22] Others find 'forgetting the past' a contradiction of the Qur'anic spirit, simply because the Qur'an reminds us of the past 'in order to reconcile with the present and the future'.[23]

Muslims do however accept the spirit behind the document. And they also distinguish between the present and the past – a past which has gone and is concluded, e.g., in the political sphere, say in Spain or Sicily; no Muslim is saying let us go and reconquer them. And the other past, whose effect continues into the present, or in other words, has a consequence with which Muslims are living and which cannot be forgotten, namely Palestine (one may include the image of Islam in general in the West). Muslims read the document as an appeal to 'forget the hatred . . . prejudices and start afresh'.[24] They argue that if it means 'to forget the mentalities of the Crusades in all its ramifications,'[25] then it should be welcomed by all. Others point out yet another dimension. Perhaps the Conciliar Document does not want to forget the past, 'but to face and to try to put them aside and look at the practical considerations of the present day'.[26]

DEFINITIONS AND AREAS

Definitions of dialogue vary from person to person, depending upon the areas from where they come and the nature of the encounter they are facing. The dictionary defines dialogue as a 'conversation between two or more persons, especially of a formal or imaginary nature, an exchange of views in the hope of ultimately reaching agreement'.[27] Dialogue has also been referred to as 'consultation', 'conversation', 'meeting', 'exchange of views', 'encounter', etc. In other words, it is a means of communication which expects a reciprocal response. Today, the term 'dialogue' provides an 'umbrella' for all those meanings and understandings. The geopolitical situation also plays an important role in guiding dialogue. The following definitions prevail among Muslims. Dialogue is about communication:

The essence of dialogue is communicating one's stand in assembly . . . in a sympathetic way to the others . . . and also listening to the others . . . based on mutual respect [and] to operate in areas of packed social and other spheres whereby our common values can be exercised and can be utilized.[28]

Dialogue is about

communicating with other faiths, with another community . . . [in order] to create better understanding.[29]

Dialogue, others point out,

> represents the engagement between two individuals or two communities who wish to communicate their beliefs, their way of life to each other . . . but also to identify the areas of potential conflict and the areas in which they can co-operate.[30]

Dialogue is about reducing areas of conflict. It is the

> sharing of thoughts and exchange of views and an effort to understand each other, to try to reduce differences and conflicts and find out if there are some common grounds [this] may also lead to convergence in certain areas . . .[31]

Dialogue is about

> mutual understanding and therefore reducing the areas of conflict.[32]

and means

> establish[ing] a relationship with the other faith communities in order to understand their religious beliefs and their ways of life and how their faith affects their attitude towards mankind in general and particularly their understandings of other faiths.[33]

A comprehensive definition was provided by the editor of the *Muslim Minority Affairs Journal* in the WCC's regional colloquium in 1987. A dialogue is a

> process wherein people with diverse faith backgrounds come together and recognising each others' confessional identity and integrity, join hands in equality and respect to resolve a common and mutually perceived threat to all.[34]

In this respect Muslims are also guided by the Qur'an when it says:

> And dispute ye not with the People of the Book except with means better (than mere disputation) unless it be with those of them who inflict wrong and injury, but say 'We believe in the revelation which has come to us and in that which came down to you; Our God and your God is One; and it is to Him we bow (in Islam)'. (al-Ankabut 29: 46)

Another verse, which Muslims quote often, which was revealed when a Christian delegation arrived in Madinah from Najran, says:

> O People of the Book! Come to common terms as between us and you: that we worship none but God; that we associate no partners with Him; that we erect not, from among ourselves, lords and patrons other than God. If then they turn back, say ye: Bear witness that we (at least) are Muslims (bowing to God's Will). (Al-i-Imran 3:64)

These two verses have a common thread, and that is God; the centrality of God is the prime motivator in dialogue. Muslims have not forgotten this point, at least conceptually, as the basis of dialogue with Christians as well as with the Jews.

The centrality of God for Muslims brings two other important dimensions to dialogue. One, the way God communicates with people, i.e. the Revelation of the Qur'an, and the other the Vehicle of the communication, i.e. The Prophet Muhammad (peace be upon him). The Qur'an becomes the chief source of knowledge, which explains the Will of God and the Purpose of Creation. The Prophet becomes the first recipient and therefore the first person to act upon the Revelation. The act of the Prophet is known as the *Sunnah* of the Prophet. Revelation and *Sunnah* form Islam. Muslims point out that both are vital aspects of Islam and that both are the most important areas in dialogue with Christians.[35] Revelation has some common factors between the two religions. Though the Revelation is understood in entirely different ways, e.g. contrary to Islamic beliefs, incarnation of God in Jesus is at the heart of Christianity where God meets humanity. In Islam, it is the Qur'an through the Prophet. Muslims suggest that 'the need of human dependence on Divine Guidance and Revelation'[36] is a common area in dialogue and needs to be pursued.

There is another important aspect. The very concept that God guides humanity, reveals His Will and human beings need that Guidance in all spheres of life, brings a sharp distinction between Islam and modernity or the West. The beliefs and value system of modernity are based overwhelmingly upon secular principles where Divine Guidance is a private affair. The study of the two systems brings to our notice that Muslims tend to compare the perceived defeat as having emerged out of different sets of values as pointed out earlier, with the ideals of Islam on the one hand, and the tendency to strive and aspire to some Western values, especially technological achievements, on the other. This paradox, or 'love-hate' relationship, is confusing, not only intellectually but also in practice. The reason for pointing out this aspect is that it is an increasingly dominant factor, as we have seen earlier in Christian–Muslim dialogue, and highlights the observation that a deep debate within and between the two value systems is increasingly called for.

As far as the Prophet Muhammad is concerned, Muslims generally consider that his image has been vilified by Christians in the past and strengthened by the Orientalist traditions in the West.[37] Modernity may have 'rejected' Christianity and the role of religion in the society, but the 'image' of the Prophet has been carried forward from the past. In many respect that 'image' is still salient in Western society. A number of Christian theologians in the last two decades have moved considerably from the position held by earlier Christians regarding the Prophet, as 'immoral' and an 'impostor' to that of a 'respectable' and 'reasonable' 'religious leader' (e.g. George Khodar, Cantwell Smith). This position, although appreciated by many Muslims, nonetheless has been questioned by some, e.g. in a question raised by Ahmad von Denffer who points out:

> The real nature of the Prophet Muhammad (may God's mercy and blessing be upon him) is perhaps the central issue of Christian–Muslim dialogue, for if Muhammad is a true Prophet who delivered his message faithfully, what is there to prevent a sincere man to accept his call to Islam.[38]

This prompted David Kerr to prepare a paper on this issue and point out a very important area, which the Christian theologians are struggling with, i.e., to have a positive appreciation of the Qur'an and Muhammad without actually becoming Muslim in the fully confessional sense of the word.[39] Other areas of dialogue may arguably be called 'extra-theological', simply because they go beyond immediate theological concerns and focus on the existence of human beings on earth. As Zainal Abedin points out:

> humanity is threatened with extinction, the planet earth has become or is likely to become the area of perpetual strife. Those who subscribe to the belief in a higher life and have faith in the transcendent potential to human nature owe it to themselves to join hands and stem this drift toward extinction.[40]

They argue that the problems faced by all humanity, bearing on social life, should be the central point of Christian–Muslim dialogue.

Muslims, like others, prefer to emphasize the fundamental questions. If God has given us freedom and dignity and both religions believe in these, then

> why, is there so much poverty, hunger and oppression? If religion is the freeing of human beings, why is there so much violation of human rights? . . . If religion is for honesty and righteousness, why is corruption so rampant?

argues Chandra Muzaffar, and suggests that shared values:

> through dialogue and social action, through committed programmes, will in the end lead to a change in our perception of who God is, what God means to us.[41]

Revelation and the *Sunnah* of the Prophet take the discussion of dialogue to another area and that is Shari'ah.

THE ISSUE OF SHARI'AH

The Seventh Assembly of the World Council of Churches takes the question of Shari'ah seriously, and says:

> Many Christians, especially in Africa and Asia, feel threatened by Islamization and the introduction of the Shari'ah law. The WCC must take this very seriously in its dialogue with people of other faiths.[42]

The continents, the Assembly points out, are Africa and Asia, individual countries are not specified, but recent events suggest they are Nigeria and the Sudan in Africa, and Pakistan in Asia. The 'threat' that is mentioned could have arisen out of the fear of how the Christians could live as a minority in a Muslim country where the Islamicization process is either in progress or where there is a persistent demand by the Muslims for implementation of Shari'ah. The specific areas could be of Shari'ah and religious pluralism, human rights, the right to propagate one's faith and religion in general. Here we shall bring out, in brief, the Christian apprehensions or 'threats' and Muslims' response, and their debate on the issue of Shari'ah in the contemporary situation.

First, Christians say that 'Muslim scholars' have not given an answer as to what 'Shari'ah . . . contains';[43] 'which aspects of Islamic law are applicable to all citizens in an Islamic state, and which regulations refer only to Muslims'.[44]

Secondly:

> when a minority community feels that their legitimate rights and privileges granted it by Islamic teaching have been violated, are there structures and means for them to challenge and appeal the alleged violations?[45]

Or, in another situation:

> If you have a Christian and a Muslim who have a law case, one against the other, where is the court going to try this case? If the sentence of the court is not acceptable where would you appeal, if the sentence is of a Shari'ah Court, will the appeal court again be another appeal court?[46]

Thirdly, if the Shari'ah is applied only to Muslims, others who are exempted become a 'marginal group'. In some cases 'applying the Shari'ah lowers their status and makes them citizens of a second class in their own country'.[47]

Fourthly, Christians, especially in Nigeria, point out that it is 'discriminatory in a secular and multi-religious state to have a vital organ of government based solely on the religious laws of a particular religion'. Under such circumstances 'it is morally and politically wrong ... to have a Shari'ah Court based on Islamic laws established and maintained by state funds'.[48]

Fifthly, Christians have voiced their fear that in an Islamic society (state) Christians will not be allowed to preach what they believe is right. The question has been raised, does

> Islamic teaching consider it a right of non-Muslim minorities to propagate their religious beliefs in Islamic society? What distinguishes a proper invitation to another to share one's faith from exploitative or subtly coercive techniques of proselytism.[49]

Sixthly, will the Islamic society (state) allow the central act of worship, 'the sacramental life of the community', where a bishop or a priest is required to preside over the worship in Orthodox and Roman Catholic Christianity? And will they allow a 'foreign or visiting clergy in an Islamic country where [there are] a large number of foreign workers and technical advisors'?[50]

Finally, Pakistan has its own context and evolution of Shari'ah, what is known as the Shariat Bill. Christians argue that the Shariat Bill was moved by the Senate, where there is no Christian representation, and has a supra-constitutional character and therefore will jeopardize the 'fundamental rights of minorities, and by restricting the interpretative power of the Shari'ah exclusively to the *Ulamā*, these rights will be totally eroded'.[51]

How do Muslims define Shari'ah? Our purpose is not to answer these questions, but to see in what direction Muslim thinking on these issues is moving.

Literally, Shari'ah means 'the path' or 'the way'. It is difficult to find a precise definition of Shari'ah. It covers almost all aspects of Muslim life and society. Therefore, for Muslims it is the identity of faith (*Din*). It is not only law, but also prayer, *Zakāt*, fasting, *Hajj*; all the acts of worship are part of Shari'ah. Thus to equate Shari'ah simply with 'law' – as perceived in a secular society – is wrong. Although it is difficult to define Shari'ah, its objectives (*Maqasid al-Shari'ah*) are clear in the eyes of Muslim jurists and theologians. Al-Ghazali says:

> The very objective of the *Shari'ah* is to promote the welfare of the people, which lies in safeguarding their faith, their life, their intellect, their posterity and their wealth. Whatever ensures the safeguarding of these five serves public interest and is desirable.[52]

Al-Ghazali puts faith at the head of his list of *Maqasid* (objectives) because Islam regards faith as the most important aspect of human life. Wealth comes at the bottom of his list because it is not an end in itself. The welfare of the people is the very area of Shari'ah. Ibn al-Qayyim stresses that:

> the basis of Shari'ah is wisdom and welfare of the people in this world as well as the Hereafter. This welfare lies in complete justice, mercy, well-being and wisdom. Anything that departs from justice to oppression, from mercy to harshness, from welfare to misery and from wisdom to folly, has nothing to do with the Shari'ah.[53]

In brief, the compassionate society is the objective of Shari'ah. Today, due to a number of historical factors, Shari'ah is debated on a par with secular laws. The demands for Shari'ah immediately elicit apprehension and at times hostile reaction. The recent incidents in implementation of Shari'ah in some Muslim countries including the Sudan and

Pakistan have created justifiable fear among non-Muslims. Society was not prepared, and their immediate needs were not addressed, but was shown the worst kind of so-called Shari'ah by military generals, and the creation of a compassionate society was not the prime motivator of such laws. In various areas, this study will highlight that a number of Muslims are prepared to discuss various aspects of Shari'ah especially in relation to Christians.

Some Muslims argue that the 'Shari'ah is one legal system which is perhaps the most defined, elaborate . . . developed over a very long period of time' in the history of Islam. It has developed over the years 'different schools of law'. Therefore, it is difficult to believe 'that Shari'ah is not defined'.[54] Christians have raised this question of not defining Shari'ah. A participant in the Colombo dialogue of 1982 argues: 'Shari'ah is not invented today' and Christians would know from their Muslim neighbours what it means to them. If 'there are genuine apprehensions', he suggests, 'one should try to talk and to clear it because Shari'ah is about the welfare of humanity'.[55] Giving examples in Nigeria, Noibi remarks that Christians in Nigeria are aware of the contents of the Shari'ah. It has been in the country 'long before the colonialist . . . came and they stopped the application of the Shari'ah' partially, but not all. The colonialists, he stresses, in many parts of the country retained a number of Shari'ah laws and applied these to non-Muslims too. After independence, Shari'ah, in one form or another, continued, despite the changes in the name of the courts, viz. Alkali (Al-Qadi) courts to Area Courts, which is indicative of the recent regime's concern that Christians do not feel any apprehension about the existence of these courts.[56]

There is no disagreement amongst Muslims that the foundation of Shari'ah is the Qur'an and the *Sunnah*. The interpretation of these, known as *Fiqh* (jurisprudence), varies. Zaki Badawi finds that these can be traced back to the second Caliph Umar.[57] Muslims contend that interpretation might sound 'as if one is changing' the law altogether. It is the 'contextual interpretation' which matters; where the 'basic principles remain and the details keep changing to meet' the contemporary needs. We do not want to ignore, as one puts it, 'the previous interpretation'; rather we would like to 'build upon them'.[58] This approach to Shari'ah seems widely accepted among Muslims and is in the spirit of the objective or *Maqasid al-Shari'ah*. Badawi puts the point incisively, that those who think that the Shari'ah is a frozen entity 'and that we have got to freeze society into that mood . . . they don't understand that nature of Islam nor the nature of the society'.[59]

Clarification of this point comes from Fazlur Rahman. He suggests that the most basic principle to be observed in application of Shari'ah:

> is the concept of *Ma'rūf* which the Qur'an repeats all the time which it talks about inter-human relations. *Ma'rūf* means that which sound human nature regards to be good; it is the opposite of *Munkar* which means those actions which sound human nature rejects as evil. In fact, the reason why the Qur'an has given so few laws is because of these two concepts which are basic to the Qur'anic ethical teachings and which the Qur'an intends to be the source of actual legislation.[60]

The question of *Dhimmī* and citizenship is a widely debated issue amongst Muslim scholars today. Our study shows that a majority view is inclined to state that the concept of *Dhimmī* is a later development in Islamic history. 'The word *Dhimmī* does not occur in the Qur'an or the *Hadīth*', points out Fazlur Rahman, 'but it grew out of the early political military practice of Muslims'.[61] The application of *Dhimmī*, others argue, in history has created 'hostilities towards others' and especially 'towards the *Dhimmī* [was] ... highest when they are in difficulties, not when [they] are comfortable'.[62] Perhaps one can compare this situation with the hostilities against immigrant or guest-workers in Western countries, when they are perceived as a threat to jobs and housing in the society. Muslims suggest the *Dhimmī* status needs to be replaced by equal citizenship and equality before the law[63] and therefore 'all should be subject to the same order of taxation'.[64] Some argue that the question of '*Dhimmī*' cannot be resolved simply because 'Islam has chosen identity of religion as the basis of its nationality, while others think in terms of colour, language, birth place and the like'.[65] Others point out that in a situation where Shari'ah is fully implemented 'the distinction remains on the basis of collection of *Zakāt*' from Muslims.[66] But such opinions are contested. They suggest that although the

> Muslim jurists in the early centuries of Islam conceived of *Jizya* as a tax imposed upon the Peoples of the Book in lieu of military service because these communities could not be expected to join Muslims in *Jihād*. The case is recorded by historians where some tribes in Syria during the caliphate of Umar ibn al-Khattab decline to pay *Jizya* which they contend meant humiliation for them. Umar Ibn al-Khattab then asked them to pay *Zakāt* instead of *Jizya*.[67]

This implies that a uniform tax system can be adopted.

One further point in this respect. Muslims stress that the other terminologies, viz. *Dar-al-Islam* and *Dar al-Harb*, 'House of Peace' and the 'House of War' are 'much later thought among Islamic scholars' and need to be 'rethought',[68] especially in the present circumstances. First, because a large number of Muslims are now living as equal citizens in many non-Muslim countries and therefore one cannot say that they are living in a *Dar al-Harb*, though some argue that some of these countries' policies are to subjugate the Muslim, and are responsible for many hostilities. But another important point is that a large number of Muslims are fleeing from 'Muslim' countries to 'non-Muslim' countries as religious conscientious objectors. They enjoy far more freedom to practise their religion and express their religious views openly in these countries. Therefore the distinction between *Dar al-Islam* and *Dar al-Harb* is becoming increasingly irrelevant.[69] There are large numbers of Muslims in Europe and North America and they accept the countries in which they are living as *Dar al-Ahd* (the house of agreement or fellowship). They agree to follow the laws of the country and in return enjoy the rights and freedom provided by the state equally with other citizens.

There is growing recognition amongst Muslims that the minorities in Muslim countries need to be involved in the Shari'ah debate and especially in the law-making process and its implementation. There is general approval amongst Shari'ah scholars that where there are a substantial number of minorities in a country they will not be expected to conform to Shari'ah. As one Muslim points out, in the Sudan, 'the South has been exempted from the Shari'ah law', and negotiation is going on that the 'capital Khartoum [should also be] exempted from the implementation of the Shari'ah'.[70]

Regarding the debate of Shari'ah in Nigeria, Muslims argue that there are few assumptions. These assumptions, perhaps, as one puts it, are 'misleading'. First, that the 'Nigerian people have agreed to live together' and 'the whole government is being run on that assumption'. Who has decided? Where has it been agreed? asks Usman Bugaje, Secretary General, of the Islam in Africa Organization. He suggests that it is important 'to get representatives from the different people that constitute Nigeria, to sit round the table and agree as to whether they would want to continue with Nigeria as it is today or they would want some other arrangements'.[71] If they agree to live together, say in today's boundary, then the system of government could also be discussed. The second assumption is that Nigeria has 'agreed that this country should be secular'. He finds that the insistence on these is at the root of the problem.

Muslims perceive the secular laws in general as 'Christian',[72] which favour aspects of Christian daily life. A rejoinder in a Nigerian newspaper on the Shari'ah debate, reflects this point that in the name of secularism the 'public holiday in the North was changed to Sundays because it was recognized that for Christians, this work-free Sunday was religiously important. The concession was therefore given by the majority to the minority . . .' But the rejoinder contends that this religious consideration went against the 'Muslim workers and students . . . being refused permission to attend Friday prayers'.[73]

The demand for Shari'ah generated a strong sense of resentment on both sides. Muslims felt that their legitimate demands had been ignored and vilified by the Christians. The Christians, on the other hand, saw this development as an erosion of their rights and subjugation under new-found Islamic resurgence, which imposes its will through Shari'ah. A series of tit-for-tat demands made the situation worse; opposition to Nigeria's membership of the Organization of Islamic Conference (OIC) by the Christians was compared by the Muslims of Nigeria to its relations with the Vatican. Other points raised are the official calendar used by the government, New Year's day and salutation and ceremonies in the armed forces, etc. Although *Ulamā* and Muslims in general pressured the government to remain in the OIC, the government decided to 'withdraw'. The situation became more tense when the long-standing demand of the Christian Association of Nigeria (CAN) to establish diplomatic relations with Israel was successful early 1992.[74]

To bring out the situation of the 1989 constitution of Nigeria will not be out of place here. The 1979 constitution emphasized that the 'Shari'ah Court of Appeal' of a state will be

> where all the parties to the proceedings [whether or not they are Muslims] have requested the court that hears the case in the first instance to determine that case in accordance with Islamic personal law. (Section 242 (e))

The 1989 constitution limits this to Muslims only. It says that

> the Shari'ah Court of Appeal of a state shall, in addition to such other jurisdiction as may be conferred upon it by the law of the state, exercise, such appellate and supervisory jurisdiction in civil

proceedings involving questions of Islamic law where all the parties are Muslims. (Section 261)

Effectively, non-Muslims are no longer under the jurisdiction of Shari'ah, so if a case is between a Muslim and a non-Muslim, Muslims cannot resort in future to the Shari'ah Court of Appeal.

Another question is, should Christian preaching in an Islamic society be allowed? (We shall discuss this under the heading of *Da'wah/* mission.) Will it be acceptable or permissible to erect churches and perform the sacrament – an important act of worship amongst Christians – and, if it is acceptable, will a foreign priest be allowed to perform this act, if there is nobody else to do this, when and where it is necessary? Building churches has not been a big issue. Evidence suggests that new churches have been built and permission has been given in a number of Muslim countries (Saudi Arabia is an exception). The Qur'an also regards churches and synagogues as places of worship where God's name is mentioned. On this account alone there is no reason why Christians should not be able to erect their religious buildings.[75] Regarding worship, the Qur'an asks Muslims 'not to abuse the idol, the idol-worshippers used to worship let alone the rites of worship of Jews and Christians'.[76] The Qur'an recognizes, even praises, many monks and priests for their humility and lack of pride. Some Muslims have no objection if there is a need to bring in priests to perform religious services. However, they fear, with some justification, that priests may use their office for other than religious purposes.[77]

The demand for implementation of Shari'ah in Pakistan has a constitutional history. The Objective Resolution moved by Prime Minister Liaqat Ali Khan in the Constituent Assembly of Pakistan on 7 March 1949, was the beginning of the first phase. This Resolution set the tone of subsequent demands for implementation of Shari'ah. In Pakistan's three consecutive Constitutions, the Objective Resolutions of Liaqat Ali Khan remained as the Preamble, with minor changes. The changes indicate the profoundly different outlook of the rulers of Pakistan. Up to 1971 the rulers were least concerned about Islam and Islamization, except for ceremonial purposes. Their outlook could be said to be 'secular'. The major signature campaigns and agitations were organized in this period. From 1971 to 1977, the rule of Zulfiqar Ali Bhutto was of a socialist outlook. This period provided alignments and realignments amongst religious parties, who were at the forefront of the demand for Islamicization. They later formed the Pakistan National Alliance (PNA). The third phase began with the imposition of martial law on 5 July

1977 and the subsequent programmes of Islamicization. The Islamicization process in the constitution really began when two senators – Qazi Abul Latif and Mawlana Sami-ul-Haque of *Jam'iat 'Ulamā-e-Islam* Darkhawasti group – introduced the Shariat Bill on 13 July 1985. Section 1(4) of the Bill clearly states that nothing contained in the Bill shall affect the personal laws of non-Muslims. But this did not satisfy the Christian minorities who wrote a joint letter to the prime minister. Muslims argue that the situation in Pakistan has allowed Christian minorities, especially through the 'separate electorate',[78] an opportunity to participate fully in the National Assembly. By February 1985, the new electoral system allowed Christians to elect a member of their own community to represent them in Parliament. Four Christians were elected to the National Assembly (NA) and several to Provincial Assemblies (PA). One of the elected members of NA, Lt.-Col. (Retired) W. Heshant, then President of the Pakistan Christian Movement, was asked by General Zia-ul-Haq to represent the Christian community in the *Majlis al-Shura*. He also represented Pakistan in 1982 in the United Nations General Assembly. This system, Muslims suggest, is much fairer, where a minority representative can participate in the debates of Parliament, and the 'opinion [could] be considered within the Parliament . . . [and] Select Committees'.[79] They also compare this to the situation in Nigeria and the Sudan. A Muslim academic argues that Muslims are not allowed to implement Shari'ah because of objections from Christians; they do not want the Shari'ah implemented at all. He suggests that the model adopted in Pakistan could be adopted in European countries to safeguard minority rights.[80] The Shariat Bill was approved by both Houses and became part of Pakistan's law. But what turn the situation will take in future remains to be seen.

The Shari'ah issue in independent Sudan has a long history. In its early phase the protagonists of Shari'ah were also enthusiasts for North–South unity, especially Ali Taib-Allah, the first leader of the Sudanese Muslim Brotherhood. But for Southerners, 'national unity' meant imposition of an 'Arab Islamic' culture. The 'South' emerged as a political concept in terms of opposition to the 'Muslim and Arab' North.[81] Muslims argue that opposition to the North emerged out of the British 'Southern policy', adopted by the colonial rulers between 1930 and 1945, 'aimed not at creating a non-Islamic culture, but an anti-Islamic one'.[82] But the situation which brought the Shari'ah issue to the fore was Nimeiri's division of the South into three regions in June 1983, and the implementation of Islamic law in September of the same year in the country including the South, aggravated the situation. The demand for Shari'ah on the one hand, and opposition to it on the other, should be seen in these historical perspectives.

Christian Churches in mid-1984 published their concerns regarding the enforcement of Islamic laws. They declared that the declaration of the Sudan as an Islamic state was unacceptable 'when over a third of its citizens were non-Muslims'. They called it a 'discriminating law'. They raised objections to the 'Oath of Loyalty on the Qur'an' and stated that enforcement of Shari'ah laws 'reduces them to second-class citizens without rights and without freedom'. They also objected to the Shari'ah, which they saw as a tool 'to force non-Muslims to become Muslims'.[83]

Representatives of the World Council of Churches also met Nimeiri, who assured them that he would set up a 'committee of Muslims and Christians on the [issue of] Shari'ah'. However, before he could do so his government fell. The Churches (especially the Catholic Church) now demanded that the new military junta 'set up a Department of Christian Affairs' in order to handle religious affairs in the country. They suggested that the ruling military council did not have a national outlook because it did not have a Christian representation, and Muslims are unaware of 'the structure, terminology or even the nature and function of the Christian church'.[84] The SPLA (Sudanese People's Liberation Army), headed by General Garang, emerged as a powerful force in the South since Nimeiri's enforcement of Shari'ah, demanded a 'Sudanese identity', a term which has never been defined. If it means excluding Islam, then it is bound to be irrelevant in the Sudanese context.[85]

However, general Muslim reaction so far is to see the Christian 'demands' in the light of a new kind of crusade by the secular forces, a crusade that compelled Sadiq al-Mahdi's government to drop the idea of implementation of Shari'ah in the Sudan. The new regime of General Bashir has involved Christians in the process of Shari'ah implementation. Negotiations on various areas are in progress, but success will depend upon what role external forces will play in the Sudan and how much the country can bear.

To conclude this section, one could say that Muslims' understanding of Islam, that is of submission, is in fact understood through Shari'ah. This is the problem-solving methodology and an effective tool of decision-making in Islam. It seems that Muslims are prepared to see Shari'ah as a dynamic and future-looking tool, a view that comes from the depth of the Islamic consciousness of Revelation. Perhaps through dialogue Muslims will be able to understand how others feel about it and will be able to explain the importance of Shari'ah to others.

DIALOGUE, MISSION/*DA'WAH*

In Christianity, as in Islam, mission and *Da'wah* form the corner-stone of the religion. In Christianity, mission is based on the Biblical command:

> Go ye therefore and teach all nations, baptizing them in the name of the Father, and of the Son, and of the Holy Ghost:
>   Teaching them to observe all things whatsoever I have commanded you: and lo, I am with you always, even unto the end of the World. (Matthew 28:19–20)

'Mission', therefore, is an activity of God. The 'living God of the Bible is a sending God, which is what 'mission' means'.[86] Further-more, this command becomes an example in the life of Jesus, who commands his followers to go into the world and make disciples:

> As thou hast sent me into the world, even so have I also sent them into the world. (John 17:18)

In brief, mission is the very *raison d'être* of the existence of the Christian community.

The Qur'an commands Muslims to:

> Invite [all] to the Way of thy Lord with wisdom and beautiful preach-ing. And argue with them in ways that are best and more gracious. For thy Lord knoweth best, who have strayed from his path. (al-Nahl 16:125)

Therefore, *Da'wah* becomes the central part of the existence of the Muslim '*Ummah*'. '*Da'wah* is integral to Islam. To be Muslim means to continually strive to become Muslim, that means to do *Da'wah*.'[87]

The common theme between the two religions is the urgency to reach others in order to offer something precious which the others need to have. The purpose here is to find out whether both communities see mission and *Da'wah* as part of dialogue. What are the Muslims' ob-jections to mission? What areas of mission do Muslims now believe need reconsidering? But first, a brief assessment of the recent devel-opments of mission in relation to dialogue.

The Roman Catholic Church's understanding of dialogue and mission can be found in *Nostra Aetate*. As we pointed out earlier, this document deals exclusively with non-Christian religions. It praises their devotion to God and the richness of their understanding and love of God. The Church does not reject 'what is true and holy in these religions'. Nonetheless, it is 'duty bound' to preach the 'supremacy of Christ' to others. By implication it finds inadequacies in other religions and, therefore, there is a need to bring them to Christ so that they can 'find the fullness of their religious life'. The document further encourages its members 'to enter with prudence and charity into discussion and collaboration with members of other religions'. Anyone involved in the process is 'witnessing to their own faith and way of life' and appreciating and acknowledging the 'moral truths found among non-Christians'.[88] Involvement in dialogue 'demands respect for others as he is; above all, respect for his faith and his religious convictions'. But this conviction of respect for the 'otherness of the other' does not diminish the duty of mission. 'In virtue of her divine mission and her very nature', the document in relation to Jews emphasizes, 'the Church must preach Jesus Christ to the world . . . they must take care to live and spread their Christian faith while maintaining the strictest respect for religious liberty'.[89]

It is important to remember that the development of Vatican Council II has been seen by the Churches around the world as a step forward in the direction of renewal of mission. Though some thought *Nostra Aetate* too lenient towards other religions,[90] the subsequent development after Vatican Council II provides more clarification on the question of 'dialogue' and 'mission'. The three documents published by the Vatican in these respects are important: *The Attitude of the Church towards the Followers of Other Religions* (1984), *Redemptoris Missio*, the encyclical of Pope John Paul II (1991) and *Dialogue and Proclamation* (1991).

These documents need to be seen against the background of the late 1960s and 1970s when the Vatican was viewed by many as an enthusiastic protagonist of human concerns. And dialogue with the people of other religious traditions was manifestly a dialogue of human concern or rather 'involvement in the world'. Some Church members even stated openly:

> Non-Christians do not need membership in the visible Church in order to be saved; they do not need the Church to arrive at a deeper awareness of the saving mystery by which they are continually embraced.[91]

Questions were raised within and outside the Church about the perceived 'importance' of dialogue at the cost of mission. The Frankfurt Declaration of 1970 and the Lausanne Covenant 1974's presence and their impact was felt at grass-roots level. Most probably this was the reason why Pope Paul VI called the Synod of Bishops in 1975 and put three questions to them:

1. What has happened to that hidden energy of the good news which can have such a powerful effect on a person's conscience?
2. To what extent and in what way is that evangelical force capable of really transforming the people of this century?
3. What methods should be followed in order that the power of the gospel may have its effects?[92]

Although the questions were widely discussed, the Synod did not answer all three questions as perhaps the Pope would have liked. However, the Pope issued an encyclical, known as *Evangelii Nuntiandi* (Evangelism of the Modern World) in 1976. But the question about the relation between 'mission' and 'dialogue' continued unabated. Cardinal Pignedoli, then President of the Pontifical Council of Interreligious Dialogue, wrote a letter to all Bishops of the Roman Catholic Church emphasizing that dialogue with other faiths is to know the 'riches which God has given to the peoples (*Ad Gentes* No. 11) in order to bring them back to the Lord illumined by the light of the Gospel'.[93]

In the 1980s and after, there was more emphasis on 'mission' than on dialogue. Dialogue is increasingly understood as one important component of mission. The Vatican's PCID issued a statement in 1984. This was published in support of Vatican II's *Nostra Aetate*. It declared emphatically that 'dialogue is the . . . norm and necessary manner of every form of Christian mission, as well as every aspect of it . . .'. It emphasized further that 'dialogue . . . finds its place in the great dynamism of the Church's mission.'[94]

In 1990, the Roman Catholic Church, along with the Protestant and Orthodox Churches, joined in declaring the decade the 'Decade of Evangelization'. The Pope issued an important encyclical, *Redemptoris Missio*, in January 1991. It further clarified its position on inter-religious dialogue as:

a part of the Church's evangelizing mission. Understood as a method and means of mutual knowledge and enrichment, dialogue is not in opposition to the mission *Ad Gentis*; indeed, it has special links with that mission and is one of its expressions ... the Church sees no conflict between proclaiming Christ and enjoying inter-religious dialogue. Instead she feels the need to link the two in the context of her mission *Ad Gentes.*[95]

After the publication of *Redemptoris Missio*, for further clarification the Church asked its two important divisions, PCID and the Congregation for the Evangelization of Peoples, to declare jointly their position on 'mission' and 'dialogue'. Hence the document *Dialogue and Proclamation*. This document states clearly that the Church's purpose, in dialogue, could be of human concerns, but that is not its primary duty. Its interest in inter-religious dialogue 'is not merely anthropological but primarily theological'.[96] On the question of dialogue and its relation with proclamation the document states:

Inter-religious dialogue and proclamation, though not on the same level, are both authentic elements of the Church's evangelizing mission. Both are legitimate and necessary. They are intimately related, but not interchangeable: true interreligious dialogue on the part of the Christian supposes the desire to make Jesus Christ better known, recognised and loved; proclaiming Jesus Christ is to be carried out in the Gospel spirit of dialogue. The two activities remain distinct but, as experience shows, one and the same local Church, one and the same person, can be diversely engaged in both.[97]

It is here that a Muslim finds difficulty in reconciling a priest of 'mission' and a priest of 'reconciliation' in dialogue, in one and the same person. A priest of 'mission' a Muslim relates to the past memory of Christian mission and finds difficulty in seeing how that same person can genuinely be interested in 'dialogue' with Muslims.

Dialogue with people of other religions, amongst the Protestant and Orthodox Churches, began with their concern over mission. The dialogue debate, in August 1969, after the WCC's executive committee meeting at Canterbury, included a new study on missionary participation in human institutions and a programme of dialogue with the followers of other religions as well as secular ideologies; the WCC adopted the resolution that:

dialogue with another implies neither a denial of the uniqueness of Christ, nor any loss of his own commitment to Christ, but rather that a genuinely Christian approach to others must be human, personal, relevant and humble.[98]

Muslims were invited to dialogue by the WCC in Cartigny, Switzerland, in March 1969, prior to the Canterbury meeting, the participants agreeing that 'dialogue between Muslims and Christians is necessary' and identifying the necessity which arises as the result of four factors:

a. the specific historical roots which the two religions have in common;
b. the attitudes of self-criticism which is inherent in each religion;
c. the increased mobility and mixing of populations which has made meetings of Christians and Muslims much more common, and has increased the responsibility of the two religions to find ways of living together in the same society;
d. the special present situation, especially the common responsibility of both religions with regard to the political problems in the Near East.[99]

Like the Roman Catholic Church, the WCC also felt pressure from within the affiliated Churches as well as from the Evangelical Churches, who were actively pursuing a programme of 'mission' and 'evangelization' internationally. The internal disquiet about the relation between 'mission' and 'dialogue' came to the surface forcefully in the WCC's Fifth Assembly in Nairobi in 1975. Its approach to dialogue with other religions was seen as an act of 'syncretism'. In Section III of the WCC Report, Emilio Castro wrote that in November, 'a heated discussion took place on the report . . . Several delegates expressed their fears that dialogue with people of other faiths could lead us to religious syncretism'. Castro remarks: 'the preamble to the report safeguards it against this possible misinterpretation – Nairobi did not want to betray the uniqueness of Jesus Christ'.[100]

By 1991, the WCC had openly acknowledged the difficulty of accepting dialogue in the form in which it was generally accepted, i.e. human concern. The Seventh Assembly report points out the reason for the difficulty:

Inter-faith dialogue has proved difficult for some churches and Christians because of our continuing problems in understanding religious plurality and God's relationship to people of other religious traditions. It is important to continue to explore this issue in ways that open up our churches to the challenge of living in a world of many faiths.[101]

The approach of the Lausanne Covenant 1974 among the Evangelicals has been consistent. Dialogue has been accepted as a *means* to reach the other religion. Their motto was clear: To live 'dialogically is to live dangerously'. In 1989, when the Evangelicals gathered for the Second Lausanne Congress on Evangelism in Manila, they maintained pressure on the question of dialogue with other religions. Their final declaration, known as *The Manila Manifesto*, stated that they profoundly disagree with even an inter-religious dialogue with the Roman Catholic and Orthodox Churches, and they generally did not see 'any form of dialogue or co-operation with them', and therefore the question of dialogue with other faiths does not arise. This Manifesto urges the need 'to adopt a consistent biblical understanding of evangelism',[102] a poignant reminder of the WCC's involvement with other religions, which Evangelicals, as pointed out earlier, sees as 'betrayal of mission'.

Muslims generally argue that dialogue comes under the broad spectrum of *Da'wah*.[103] They point out that dialogue should not become a platform to demonstrate 'the beauty of Islam', simply because it would not be necessary, because the best form of *Da'wah* is 'to live Islam and set a good example for others to follow'. However, in dialogue, 'it may be possible . . . to pass on the message of Islam whilst in dialogue'.[104] Yet others point out in the clearest terms that dialogue:

is a part of the *Da'wah* as it generates better understanding between the groups. In dialogue the context especially the position of the other party has got to be studied and understood. *Da'wah* may not take the context into consideration though to be effective *Da'wah* must always do that. In any case, in today's context, both dialogue and *Da'wah* are closely related activities.[105]

Abdur Rahman Doi points out yet another principle of dialogue, that is:

the enforcement of righteousness and prohibition of evil (3:104, 119) . . . stopping (and indeed eradication) of evil in society is a common concern for all those who say they believe in God and hereafter . . . principles of which shape the methodology of da'wah might also apply to inter-faith dialogue.[106]

In a similar vein, pointing to the *Ma'rūf* and *Munkar*, others suggest that if 'dialogue or reconcil[iation] is to seek a common goal, then *Da'wah* is of great relevance'.[107] *Ma'rūf* and *Munkar* are a duty that must be performed by a group of people in the community. This group Abedin describes as 'conscious Christians and conscious Muslims', who 'step out of the confinements of their respective community to share a common duty and there', he argues, 'lies the importance of dialogue'.[108] And in this dialogue one becomes a *Da'i*, and *Da'wah* becomes the most important vehicle, calling towards God. As another Muslim puts it, 'we need to concentrate on the call to Allah rather than the call towards the Muslim community'.[109] But the question arises whether a Muslim will be content to see a Christian becoming a better Christian, simply because that is how a Christian understands the 'call of God'? Opinions differ. *Da'wah*, others point out, is 'an invitation to Islam'.[110]

Dialogue, some others suggest, is not possible unless a partner has a genuine point of view and something to offer. 'In fact there would not be any discourse at all if one of the partners did not have any point of view to contribute.'[111] '*Da'wah*' and 'mission' should not only be recognized as a duty of the two communities, but also be allowed to approach the other in dignity. Khurram Murad argues that 'there is no point in entering into dialogue unless it is *Da'wah*'. In dialogue, he says, *Da'wah* should be taken as it stands for 'extending the invitation'. He emphasizes that *Da'wah* should not be taken to mean 'one is out to convert'. He is prepared to give the same discretion to Christians as to Muslims. 'Christians', he points out, 'may also have the same purpose and so long as we are not out to impose our views and to go beyond invitation or use any means which would fall under the category of exploiting human beings . . . *Da'wah* is and should be a part of dialogue. This is true for both the parties.'[112] On this point, some other Muslims are also in agreement that dialogue 'of course implicitly is *Da'wah* . . . and if this is the case with me, it is only fair . . . to expect it from the Christians'. He further emphasizes that in dialogue, conversion 'does not have to be the main objective of getting together . . . not everybody is interested to convert in a formal way'.[113]

What he suggest here is that a person may convert from their previous position or stand within his/her own traditions. Their outlook will change as a result of participation in dialogue, and 'conversion' to a new and better outlook is itself an achievement. If this is the acceptable norm of behaviour in dialogue, then what do Muslims object to? There are two important areas of interest – proselytization and the historical political situation. The Muslims' 'fear' of 'mission' is not about 'mission' as such but about the 'ethics of mission'. This point has been put clearly by Khurram Murad:

> I think my objection personally to Christian missionary activities as such is not an objection that the missionary activity in itself is wrong, because everybody who holds something to be right and true has a right to witness . . . what we do *object* to is that the Christian missionaries not only go to that extent but they also use . . . genuine human needs for the purpose of conversion [and] use their political influence and they have tried to obstruct Muslims from living by their own faith and by Shari'ah.[114]

Others point out in the same vein that Muslims 'feel resentment and suspicion of the Christians because they suspect them of trying to proselytize and dominate the Muslims. This has much to do with the colonial experience . . . and is also borne out by the general myopia of most Christians towards Islam.'[115]

It is difficult for a non-Christian to point out where mission begins and where it ends, where it develops into proselytizing. But for Shabbir Akhtar, 'the difference in practical terms is very simple'. Giving an example, he elucidates:

> It is the difference between switching on your TV and seeing a live Christian worship programme and the Jehovah's Witnesses (who are not mainstream Christians), knocking your door when you have told them that you don't want to see them any more . . . but they don't listen and that is when it is getting towards proselytization, when it is getting a bit ugly.[116]

An important aspect of *Da'wah* and mission lies in the future. What Muslims have to accept, despite the centuries of generated mistrust, through encounters, at times very unpleasant, is that the world has changed drastically, especially in the fields of technology and science. In the past perhaps it was possible 'not to allow' mission and missionary activities in a Muslim country. The particular Shari'ah ruling which was suitable in a particular time and place regarding mission 'has already been overtaken by technology', argues Usman Bugaje, '[it is] no longer tenable today because we have got newspapers . . . magazines . . . television . . . satellite and people are free to tune into any station . . .'[117] He suggests that the Muslim jurists should decide what the future course of relations between the two communities should be in the light of the new situation.

Muslims, though, have strong views about institutionalized mission; nonetheless they are gradually entering into the same experiment of *Da'wah*. The methodologies of Christian mission, which they have criticized so often in the past, are increasingly enticing them to adopt the 'strategies' and 'plannings', rather than witnessing and stating that 'our task is only to pass on the message'(*wa mā'alayna illā'l-balāgh*).

II
Individuals

Introduction

Six Muslims are the focus of this part of the study. Among others, they responded to the initiative of dialogue between Christians and Muslims. Hasan Askari and Mohammed Talbi were actively involved in the early days of the World Council of Churches and the Vatican's initiative on dialogue with Muslims. Faruqi and Khurshid Ahmad participated in the Tripoli dialogue in 1976 and also in Chambesy the same year. In Tripoli, the main Christian representatives were the Roman Catholics and the Chambesy dialogue was organized by the World Council of Churches. Ayoub participated in Broumana in 1972 and in various organized dialogues. Since then his contribution has centred on the history of Christian–Muslim relations and theological issues, like Christology. Nasr led an Iranian delegation for dialogue to the Vatican in 1978. He wrote with clarity, comparing the two religions on theological issues. In dialogue, his response to Hans Küng has been widely publicized.

Denominationally, they differ. Askari, Ayoub and Nasr are from a Shi'i family background. But their writings and theological approach cross denominational lines. They have used Sunni theological materials extensively in their academic pursuit. The other three Muslims are Sunnis.

Geographically, the selection of the six Muslims under study covers a wide area of the Muslim world. It is interesting to note how the impact of the geographical situation on them has moulded their outlook. Ayoub and Faruqi came from the Middle Eastern countries of Lebanon and Palestine. After the division of Palestine and the creation of Israel, the former Governor of Galilee found himself a displaced person and depicts this phase where he wanted to come to terms with nationalism and religion. His *Urūbah and Religion* is the best example of this inner dialogue. Ayoub was brought up in a country which came into existence on the basis of partnership between Christians and Muslims. He was sent to a missionary school, where he was converted to Christianity. This created tension between him and his family. He came to the West for his higher studies. During this period, he contemplated his roots and finally returned to them. Askari and Khurshid Ahmad were both brought up in undivided India. The political development of the country had a lasting impact on both of them. Askari was born and brought up in the Muslim state of Hyderabad. He witnessed the creation of Pakistan in 1947 and also the annexation of Hyderabad to India a year later. He found himself in a country which accepted 'secularism' as a state policy and it soon dawned on him that his religion was 'one among many'. He began to come to terms with this new situation and looked for the answers in the meaning of religious pluralism. Khurshid Ahmad's situation is the opposite of Askari's. Living in Delhi, surrounded by various religions and beliefs, with the migration of his family to the newly-created Muslim state of Pakistan, he found himself in an entirely new situation where his co-religionists were in a majority. Later he joined the *Jamat-e-Islami* of Pakistan. This eventually led him to focus vigorously on the Islamicization of Pakistan. Nasr's situation differs further. The revolution in 1979 in Iran compelled him to leave the country. Although brought up in a religious family, his and his family's relations with the Shah were enough to make him guilty in the eyes of the new rulers. Nasr took the question of religious pluralism in the light of the 'traditional school'. His writings, like Askari's, have a Sufi overtone. Talbi, from Tunisia, the North African part of the Muslim world, argues the question of religious pluralism, like others under study, on strong theological grounds. His experience of living under colonialism, where his civilization needed to be 're-civilized' and 're-educated' as he puts it, left its marks on him. He questions the need for such re-civilization of his countrymen and its worth. He investigates the question of religious pluralism and dialogue, and the encounter of Muslims and the Western civilization with a critical yet visionary approach.

The Muslims under study have direct access to and knowledge of the West. They studied and lived long enough in the West to understand the undercurrents in Western society. All of them have been in direct contact, as far as dialogue is concerned, with the Churches in the West.

This study concentrates primarily on those Muslims whose writings have appeared in the English language. Those who have written in other languages, viz. in French, German and in Arabic, important as their contributions are, are not included in this study, though they have been referred to in earlier chapters. Talbi, who writes mainly in French and Arabic, has also written in English, and most of his writings on dialogue have been translated into English. They have been included here.

We had an extensive interview with four of the people under study – Askari, Ayoub, Khurshid and Nasr – on the issue of Christian–Muslim relations and dialogue Muslims and the West, *Da'wah* and mission and others. Therefore much of the information supplied here is, perhaps, new. Faruqi died before this study was undertaken. We had correspondence with Talbi on the subject.

Finally, this study concentrates on the writings of six Muslims and their views and opinions expressed on the subject of dialogue and Christian–Muslim relations either through public forums or in interviews. Therefore, their other writings, in some cases their main academic field, are not referred to. For example, Khurshid Ahmad is a trained economist who wrote extensively on Islamic economics, but these writings have not been included. A very basic biography of each of them has been provided in order to put in context the conditions in which they wrote and spoke and participated in dialogue.

4 Isma'il Raji Al-Faruqi (1921–86)

Faruqi was born in Palestine in 1921. He graduated from the American University of Beirut in philosophy. He joined the civil service in British Mandate Palestine in 1945, and later became the last Governor of Galilee. The occupation of Palestine brought him to the United States. There he obtained two masters degrees in philosophy from Indiana and Harvard Universities, and completed his PhD in 1952 'On Justifying the Good: Metaphysics and Epistemology of Value'. In search of the classical Islamic heritage, he studied at Al-Azhar from 1954 to 1958. A year later, at the invitation of Professor Cantwell Smith, he joined the Faculty of Divinity, at McGill University, Montreal, where he studied Judaism and Christianity and produced his major academic work, *Christian Ethics*. For two years, 1961–63, on the advice of Dr Fazlur Rahman, he joined the Institute for Islamic Research, Karachi. On his return to America he joined, as visiting professor, the Divinity School at the University of Chicago. He accepted an Associate Professor's post in Syracuse University in the Department of Religion, where he developed an Islamic Studies programme. From 1968 until his death on 17 May 1986, he was professor in the Department of Religion at Temple University, where he also established an Islamic Studies section. He was the first Muslim scholar in America who devoted himself to the study of comparative religion and Islam.

This chapter discusses Faruqi's understanding of comparative religion and his perspective on Christian–Muslim dialogue. But before we turn to this central issue of Faruqi's work, we should note three general features.

First, his early intellectual life was deeply influenced by Arab nationalism. But his Arab nationalism was unique. His book *'Urūbah and Religion* is the best example. In this book he uses the term 'Arabism' or *'Urūbah*, and not Arab nationalism. Arab nationalism he describes as a product of the last 200 years of Western European political life. But Arabism is much more and much older than the emergence of nationalism in the Arab world. His concept of Arabism is not restricted to Arab-speaking people nor to the Arab race, and not only to the Arab Muslims; rather it includes 'millions of non-Arabic-speaking persons living in territories adjoining the Arabic-speaking lands but stretching as far as Siberia, the Philippines, the Danube, Equatorial and East Africa, who represent comparatively higher or lower degrees of Arabness'.[1] The first part of his book describes Judaism as the first and Christianity as the second moment of Arab consciousness among the Religions of the Book. The consciousness which emerges out of this Arabism is to 'get rid of the injustice they suffer' of any kind and from any power. He also refers to colonial imperialism and Western Christianity's intrusion upon Arab Christians as injustices.

Second, he was critical of the Western Powers not only at the political level, but also at the intellectual level. However, unlike some 'Islamic apologetic' that dismisses all Western thought as decadent and evil, Faruqi admires where admiration is due, and acknowledges his indebtedness to some Western thinkers, e.g. Max Scheler (1874–1928). He credited Scheler in the field of phenomenology where, in Faruqi's words, 'he freed value-theory from the fruitless fixation of seeking the moral in ever more abstractionist constructions of the mind . . . [and] laid open for a rehabilitation of the moral law to its transcendental status'.[2] However, he is critical of their interpretations of Islam and believes that they 'helped destroy Muslims' confidence in Christendom.[3] Faruqi, who was familiar with the methodology of Western subjects and languages, in fact enters into an ongoing dialogue with outstanding minds of the West, be they classical like Aristotle and Plato or modern like Kant and Nietzsche, or contemporary like Tillich and Barth, and comes up with his own answers.

Third, and equally important, he was a man of faith, though he never lost his attachment to the land where he was born, 'nor forgetting the lessons he had learned from the Western philosophy', somewhere along the line as Nasr describes him, he turned away from the Western understanding of 'secularism in all its forms and devoted himself to religious concern – at the heart of which stood Islam, in its relation with both other religions and the secularised modern world'.[4] As he wrote only weeks before his deat, 'After I obtained my doctorate in Western philosophy, I became aware of the state of my ignorance (*Jaahiliyyatii*) and remoteness from the Islamic legacy.'[5]

PRINCIPLES OF COMPARATIVE RELIGIOUS UNDERSTANDING

Faruqi argues that there must be some basic principles 'by reference to which the meanings of . . . systems and patterns may be understood, conceptualised and systematised'.[6] He describes five such principles.[7]

1. The principle of internal coherence. 'No system of any kind', he says, 'is worthy of consideration unless it recognises, as a first criterion of validity, the principle that the elements of which it is constituted are not contradictory to one another. Self-contradiction is fatal to any system'. In the absence of internal coherence he stresses that it not only denies the foundations of comparative religions but also 'the very activity of human discourse, of ideational communion'.

2. 'The system or view presented must cohere with cumulative human knowledge'. Coherence 'with the larger body of human knowledge is a must for all discipline, for all genuine discoveries of truth'. What he is stressing is that if the biblical view is presented, it must cohere with archaeology or philosophy and psychology, history and politics or politics and history. Faruqi points out that 'revealed truth is always *relational* to the human situation. God does not operate in a vacuum.' We shall come later to what he means by 'relational'.

3. He puts forward the principle that 'all revealed truths must cohere with the religious experience of mankind'. He states that if God is the source of revelation, then 'His commands cannot contradict one another'. He points out that the 'content of revelation must reveal the unity of its source, which is none other than the unity of truth'.

4. 'For a system of meanings, a cultural pattern or a system of religious truth to establish its claim to be a system, its 'truths' must correspond with 'reality'. He stresses that no 'theory or view can afford to oppose reality without separating itself, sooner or later, from the life or thought of man. To ignore reality is to be ignored by reality.' Any assumption or data of religious experience, 'either morality, history or understanding of history, if it runs counter to reality' in his opinion 'suffer a revision of theses in the light of the realities they contradict'.

5. 'For a religious system to receive title to systemhood and thus to act as principle of explanation overarching any two contending theses, it ought to be such to serve, in its totality, the upward march of man towards ethically, higher value and Godhead'.

These principles, Faruqi suggests, if applied, should serve as a guarantee for a fruitful dialogue and especially so in Christian–Muslim dialogue. There are other important aspects of Faruqi's principles of comparative religion. He insists time and again that 'revealed truth is always *relational*'. In the field of comparative religion one of the significant contributions remains the principle of evaluation, or meta-religion.

META-RELIGION

Faruqi is critical of methodologies advocated by the comparative religionists. He contends that the system they have adopted puts 'religions in a mere boodle-bag in which religio-cultural wholes have just been put one beside the other in cold juxtaposition'.[8]

He argues that the believers, whose religions were compared, should be listened to by the comparator. He quotes Cantwell Smith in support of his claim that 'no statement about a religion is valid unless it can be acknowledged by that religion's believers'.[9] By doing that, it will create a healthy attitude where a 'continual answer and rejoinder or dialogue, takes place',[10] and believers are ready to listen and be refuted. There is a need to relate and evaluate, and he claims that meta-religion provides the overall principles and it is not 'constrained by any particular religious tradition by which any religious tradition could be judged'.[11] He describes six such principles.

1. 'Being of Two Realms: Ideal and Actual',[12] and 'the ideal and the actual are different kinds of being, they are two'. He elaborates from this standpoint of ethics, and argues: 'Fact and value are two orders of being. If this duality were not true, and fact and value belonged to the same order of being, it would be groundless to judge one 'fact' by 'another'.

2. 'Ideal Being is Relevant to Actual Being'. 'Since the ideal realm acts as principle of classification, of the order and structure of actual being, it provides the standard to judge if the actual is or is not valuable.'

3. 'Relevance of the Ideal to the Actual is a Command'. He stresses the 'whole realm of ideal being is relevant to the whole realm of actual being'. The actual being has to be judged as what it ought to be. Their relationship is not based on this *and* the other, rather their relationship is either/or. In other words, the relevance of 'ideal' is superior and the 'actual' has to strive to attain the 'ideal'.

4. But judging on this basis, i.e. either/or, the actual being cannot become 'bad'. And this is his fourth principle, that the 'Actual Being is as Such Good'. 'The realm of actual', as Faruqi describes, is this-world. 'This-world is good; to enter it, to be in it, is as such valuable.'

5. To 'value' the world, to mould the world and give a direction, so that it could 'embody the structure and content of the ideal, value realization must be possible'. Therefore his fifth principle is that the 'Actual Being is Malleable'. He states that 'man can and does give new direction to the casual, forward push of reality, in order to become something else, something other than he would otherwise be'.

6. 'Perfection of the Cosmos is Only a Human Burden'. He points out that the importance of man is that he is the only creature who holds the key to the 'entrance of the valuational ideal into the actual'. He argues: 'Man is the bridge which values must cross if they are to enter the real. He stands at the crossroads of the two realms of being, participating in both, susceptible to both.'

DIALOGUE

These principles of comparative religion and meta-religion are very important to Faruqi. He stresses that these principles provide a 'guarantee' as well as 'meaningfulness' in Christian–Muslim dialogue. One of his perhaps most systematic presentations on the subject is his article 'Islam and Christianity: Diatribe or Dialogue'.[13] There he reiterates these principles time and again, e.g. he emphasizes that in the absence of the first principle, i.e. 'internal coherence' in dialogue, 'discourses will issue . . . an unintelligible riddle'. Using his second principle, external coherence, he emphasizes that 'the past may not be regarded as unknowable . . . Historical reality is discoverable by empirical evidence', and he leaves the responsibility 'at the door-step of man to develop understanding and reconstruction of his past'.

In dialogue, Faruqi suggests two important points. First, in a situation in which the twin communities find themselves, 'primacy [of dialogue] belongs to the ethical questions, [and] not theological'.[14] On the theological level, he argues, there are a number of areas of 'the wide *disparateness* of the two traditions', e.g. the Bible. Islam regards the Bible as a 'record of the divine word but a record which the human hand had tampered with . . .'. The God of Christianity is another example who *acts* in man's salvation, 'the God of Islam *commands* him to do that which brings that salvation'. Furthermore, 'while Christianity regards Jesus as the second person of a triune God, Islam regards him as God's human prophet and messenger'.[15] Faruqi stresses these and similar other areas where no progress is 'expected without preliminary work' in ethical areas. Here one detects that he finds some sort of prospects possible even in an area as difficult as theology. The other areas, he points out, are that 'the two communities should rather first establish a mutual understanding, if not a community of conviction, of the Muslim and Christian answers to the fundamental ethical question, what ought I to do?'[16] And that is the ethical area where both religions command their followers to act. Difference in theological

perception either hereticates, creates intolerance or begins conversion
and compromise. 'Difference in ethical perception', he argues, 'is that
of the brother who does not see as much, as far or as deep as the
other'. This is a situation which calls for the involved 'midwifery of
ethical perception'. He stresses tolerance and midwifery – which 'are
precisely what our small world needs . . .'.[17]

Faruqi claims, and this is his second important point, that 'dialogue
presupposes an attitude of freedom *vis-à-vis* the canonical figuration'.[18]
Explaining the term 'figuration', which he uses frequently in his writings, he shows: 'Jesus is a point at which the Christian has contacted
God. Though God has sent down a revelation, just as this revelation
had to have its carrier in Jesus, it had to have a space-time circumstance in the historical development of Israel. Equally, Muhammad,
the Prophet, is a point at which the Muslim has contact with God Who
sent a revelation through him. Muhammad was the carrier of that revelation, and Arab consciousness and history provided the space-time
circumstance for its advent.'[19] 'Once the advent of these revelations
was complete', and men confronted new problems 'calling for new
solutions', there arose the 'need to put the revelation into concepts for
the ready use of understanding in precepts and in legal notions. Thus
the revelations were figurized'. Simultaneously different minds created
different 'figurations' in varying environments and historical circumstances. Obviously there were a multitude of figurations, some with
adequate, others with inadequate, accuracy of conceptualization and
perceptions.

In the case of Christianity, after many centuries of contention, Faruqi
argues, 'it became evident that one of the figurations surpassed in the
mind of the majority all other figurizations'. The community decided
to accept its revealed content and declared it holy. 'Community reasoned,
all other figurations are "heresies" . . . Slowly "other" figurations were
suppressed and the chosen figurations stood as "the dogma", "the Catholic
Truth".' 'In the case of Islam', he says, 'the general religious and
ethical principles revealed in the Qur'an were subjected to varying
interpretations and a large [variety] of schools produced differing
figurations of law and ethics . . . each school projected its own thought
onto his own person. Consensus finally eliminated the radical figurations
and preserved those which, in the judgement of the community, contained all the essentials.' Later 'Muslims sanctified this figuration of
the fathers, [and] solemnly closed the gates of any creative interpretation.' Theoretically, they did not hereticate every departure from their
canon, but they observed it in practice.[20] Faruqi reminds both com-

munities that there is 'no wholesale condemnation of any figuration' even one that is accepted as 'the Catholic Truth'. He finds 'every figuration is capable of growing dim in its conveyance of the holy, not because the holy has changed, but because man changes perspective'.[21]

In addition to these two points he remarks that 'no communication of any sort may be made *ex cathedra*, beyond critique. No man may speak with silencing authority.' He further stresses that God's 'command is not whimsical . . . [God] argues for, explains and justifies His command, and is not offended if man asks for such justification'. 'Divine revelation', he argues, 'is authoritative, but not authoritarian'. In this spirit poignantly he reminds his Christian friends 'that no question may henceforward be declared out of bounds, not even the questions which the tradition has so far declared once and for all at Nicaea in AD 325'.[22] Faruqi emphasizes that a Muslim is obliged by his faith to present Islam to others. But a Muslim should also be prepared to listen to others' account of their faiths. It is a two-way affair – 'freedom to be convinced as well as to convince, of the truth'.[23] He argues that it is 'only natural that if the Muslim is entitled to present his case, that the non-Muslim be equally entitled to do so'.[24] He emphasizes, that it 'cannot take place except in a free dialogue between two convictious person or parties'.[25] In the process of *Da'wah*, 'to bear anything extraneous to the argument would be to vitiate the process'.[26] Describing the Shari'ah point of view of such a process, he claims that bringing such converts, in what he calls an 'illegitimate manner', is a 'prosecutable crime' and the person's decision to accept Islam by such a process 'is null and void'.[27] Any change with the process, he believes, will go against the spirit of the Qur'an and hence is unIslamic.

COMPARISON WITH ARAB (OR SEMITIC) RELIGIOSITY

The religious traditions, beliefs and patterns of figurations may differ between Islam and Christianity, yet the core and essence of Arab religiosity binds these two religions and the third, Judaism. 'It is these moments and movements that united into one stream and marks the stream as a whole from the other streams, notably the Ancient Egyptian, the Indian and the Chinese.'[28] Faruqi's study highlights four points in evidence of the common base of the two religions.

1. 'Reality is dual and consists of two quite distinct and separate beings, Creator or God, and creature and nature'. He argues that Ancient Egypt and Greece, Hinduism and Taoism identify God with nature,

whereas Semitic religions do not. Pointing out the ancient Arab position, which associated God with many of His creatures and therefore was 'rightly called "associationists" (*Mushrikin*), others who resisted and stood firmly behind the absolute unity and transcendence of divine Being, these were the ancient *Hanifs* who served', as Faruqi puts it, 'as a springboard for the religious reform (revelation) of the succeeding cycle'.[29]

2. 'God the Creator communicates with His creatures through revelation. The content of revelation is the law, or His will, which is the ought-to-be and ought-to-do of the creature'. The purpose of the creation is to fulfil 'His will', which, he argues, 'must be built into the creature precisely because it is creature'. Therefore the ought-to-be and ought-to-do in the creature take place by reason through analysis of this innate pattern in nature.[30]

3. God must have built into human beings 'the capacity to realise His purpose' and place it in the universe, which is equally His creation, where 'such fulfilment is indeed possible'. He further emphasizes that both 'the creature and its environment must in themselves be good, for the Creator cannot be conceived to have started the world in deficiency, weakness, or with an ulterior motive which assumes Him to be in debt or liability to any other being'.[31]

4. 'Since all creatures have the will of their Creator which is His purpose and their *raison d'être* embedded within them, they must be equipped with the ontological efficacy required for its fulfilment.' This efficacy in his view 'constitutes the laws of nature, whose validity is universal but whose necessity cannot go beyond or override the divine will. It stops at that will because it is its very instrument. Thus it applies to all men as it applies to the stone, plant or animal.'[32]

It would not be out of place to mention that Faruqi stresses that the Old Testament should not be seen as only a Hebrew or Christian scripture. 'It is also Islamic scripture, inasmuch as it is the partial record of the history of prophecy, and hence of divine revelation.'[33] He suggests that the Islamic version may differ from the Jewish or Christian version, but should be accepted as 'another version'. He stresses 'for just as Christianity is "a new Israel", Islam is "another Israel", legitimately giving a version of Semitic origins which are as much, if not more, its own as that of the Hebrews'.[34]

CHRISTENDOM AND MISSION

Faruqi contends that there is a clear distinction between Christianity and Christendom. He invites Muslims to be very clear about the two. Christianity, he argues, is God's religion and cannot be indicted under any circumstance. But Christendom is different from Christianity. To be able to distinguish between the two, he finds, 'is a great intellectual achievement'. Christendom, which emerged in the West, developed its own way of understanding Christianity, and sent missionaries along with the colonialists to the non-Western world. He argues that it is Christendom which is culpable of 'two arch-enemies of the contemporary Muslims; colonialism and mission'.[35] Colonialism was responsible for the displacement and dispossession of Muslims both physically and psychologically. Missionaries, Faruqi claims, played 'the role of colonial governor, trader, settler, military, physician and educator'[36] and in some cases 'missionaries were caught doing the workings of the colonial power, and used by the latter to [their] advantage.'[37] He encourages both Muslims and Christians to work together 'to lift this Satanic burden',[38] as he puts it. He is optimistic and finds hope in the Church's statements such as *Pacem in Terris* and *Populorum Progressio*, the Pope's encyclicals of 1963 and 1970.

On the question of mission, Faruqi argues that 'Western Christian mission to the Muslim world was never a mission of Jesus, but a mission of the Western figuration of Christianity arrogantly asserted in words, hardly ever exemplified in deeds'.[39] He accepts the duty of mission as a divine duty both in Islam and Christianity. But he points out first, the perception of Christendom of non-Christians where 'the majority of mankind are declared enemies whom it is the duty of the faithful to "convert"'.[40] Second, the missionary's 'home [i.e. the Western countries] is increasingly secularised'. On these two points he finds it is difficult to accept that mission to non-Christians is a genuine mission.

Faruqi suggests two ways to overcome this problem. First, since missions are financed and carried out by organizations and Churches, the Vatican and World Council of Churches, are in a position to cease such activities. However, the work of Orientalists, 'being individual in nature and often financed by autonomous colleges and institutions cannot be commanded to stop'. Alternatively, both Muslim and Christian scholars can jointly produce accurate and honest works on Islam.

He appreciates the difference Christian theologians draw between *Kerygma* and *diakonia*; however, he asserts that even in *diakonia* the Churches have never come forward to explain what criteria they are

applying. He considers that one essential element in such an endeavour is the consent of the people the Churches want to serve.[41]

Second, he suggests that to learn about others' convictions, to analyse, criticize them and share with 'one's own knowledge of the truth',
is a noble task. 'If this is mission, then Islam and Christianity must
missionise to the ends of the earth.' He points out the equivocation of
the term 'mission' and suggests the word should be dropped from the
'vocabulary and the term "dialogue" be used to express the man of
religion's concern for man's convictions'.[42] 'Dialogue then', he says,
'is a dimension of human consciousness . . . It is the fulfilment of the
command of reality to be known, to be compared and contrasted with
other claims, to be acquiesced in if true, amended if inadequate, and
rejected if false.' Dialogue, then, becomes the removal of all barriers, . . .
and disciplines our consciousness. 'Dialogue in short', he argues, 'is
the only kind of inter-human relationship worthy of man!'[43]

DIALOGUE AND AUTHORITY

Dialogue, Faruqi remarks, lacks authority. He invited the Tripoli conference 'to pick up the banner of the common man of the world . . .
representing the religious and moral conscience of Christendom and
Islam', and encouraged the development of a spiritual front and the
constitution of much-needed authority. Authority based on 'Islam and
Christianity . . . would speak in the world for the ethico-spiritual base
of all existence . . .'.[44] Authority in dialogue is a recurring theme in
his writings. In his article 'Islam and Christianity: Diatribe or Dialogue', he insists that dialogue should not remain on the level of theological discourse alone, but rather should recruit support to enable it
to assume an international authority.

Such international authority, Faruqi emphasizes, will only be effective when and in so far as all parties are equal. Dialogue cannot succeed, 'where one party is "host" and the others are "invited guests".
Every party must be host and feel itself so.' He stresses that there can
be no 'upper hand' and 'lower hand' in dialogue; all 'hands' must be
equal.[45] In the absence of such equality dialogue is 'struggling desper-
ately to survive'. He emphasizes that Christians who participate and
organize such dialogues are perhaps doing so because of 'the guilts of
colonialism and mission, and loyalty to their countries,' continuing
ascendancy in world power. The Muslims, for their part, 'were always
the invited guests of the Christians and felt it. Neither did any other

Muslims elect them to participate, nor did they appoint themselves to do so. Rather they were selected by the church authorities in expectation of collaboration with their host.'[46]

THE SECOND VATICAN COUNCIL AND PROTESTANT THEOLOGIANS

Is Faruqi convinced of the progress made by the Second Vatican Council and leading Protestant theologians? He appreciates the stand taken by the Second Vatican Council on social justice, moral values and peace, etc., and seems happy to cooperate on such issues. But he is not convinced of the approach of the Council, especially *Nostra Aetate*. In one of his papers, 'Islam and Other Faiths', he finds the attitude of the Decree is 'paternalizing'. He comments:

> twenty centuries after Jesus, that Judaism is religiously acceptable as a preparation for Christianity, and fourteen centuries after Muhammad, that Islam is a tolerable approximation of Christianity, it asserted that outside the Roman Catholic Church no salvation is possible, thus withdrawing with one hand what is granted with the other.[47]

To Faruqi, *Nostra Aetate* is successful in that it stopped 'the calling of non-Christians by bad names', but 'it is too modest a contribution'. Faruqi finds that the document is a clear indication that the Roman Catholic Church has kept the exclusive right of salvation to itself. 'As regards the issues taken up by the foregoing dialogue', he points out that 'Catholic Christianity is still to be heard from'.[48]

Unlike the Catholic Church, yet similar to the Sunni Muslim position, there is no decisive authority for Protestants. 'As to Protestantism', as Faruqi puts it, 'we have still heard nothing regarding Islam except rumours and hearsay from individuals.' He notes that the World Council of Churches did not accept Libya's invitation to join in Tripoli's Islamic–Christian dialogue, and remarks sarcastically, 'it participates only in dialogues held under its own auspices . . . under its own terms and with Muslim representatives of its own choosing'.[49] In stating the Protestant position, he examines the role of some of the leading Protestant theologians, and especially Paul Tillich. He analyses Tillich's *Christianity and the Encounter of the World Religions* where he repudiated the neo-orthodox approach, which refuses even to acknowledge the existence of such a problem as 'man's religion pose[s] for Christianity'. He finds hope in Tillich's suggestion of the possibility of 'self-criticism in the light of difference with other religions'. But Tillich disappoints him when he comes to the issue of the criterion of self-criticism. The criterion for Tillich is the 'appearance and reception of Jesus of Nazareth as the Christ',[50] and of this criterion, Faruqi contends: obviously, 'the basis is not God, nor the will of God, but the Christian figuration of God. But loyalty to figuration produces footnotes and commentaries, not knowledge . . .'.[51] Here one finds Faruqi judging Tillich on one of his principles, i.e. freedom *vis-à-vis* the canonical figuration.

Faruqi wrote to Tillich, and in fact he sent his article 'Islam and Christianity: Diatribe or Dialogue', and seemed surprised by a positive response, which he says, 'recaptures my lost optimism'.[52]

5 Mahmoud Ayoub (1935–)

Mahmoud Ayoub was born into a devout Muslim family in 1935 at Ayu Qana (South Lebanon). He grew up in an environment where Christians and Muslims participated in each others' daily life, in weddings, funerals and festivals. As a child, his parents sent him to a British Presbyterian missionary school, an experience which changed his whole life. As he remembers, 'at the school I had a Christian upbringing, so my life was kind of influenced by both my parents' deep piety and the missionary zeal of my school . . . the school authorities did not really have an educational programme for us, what they wanted to do mainly was to make us Christians and of course they did and that created a lot of tension between me and my family and particularly my father.'[1] The upbringing over the years in the Presbyterian Church convinced Ayoub that he needed to save the souls of his parents. In return they 'wanted to make sure that I was a Muslim and part of the family, and also to save my soul'.[2] It was the spiritual insight of his mother that looked beyond these immediate complexes; she understood that her son was going through 'an experience and he will return'.

Ayoub's missionary zeal convinced him that the people in the school were not 'Christian enough', so he joined an American Southern Baptist group. As a convinced Christian he was involved in various missionary activities. This active participation continued until the late 1950s. From the late 1950s till the mid-1960s Ayoub began questioning his faith. He studied theology at the University of Pennsylvania in 1964, and in 1966 went to Harvard. The constant questioning in Ayoub's mind finally convinced him, as he says, 'I knew that I could no longer fit into this emotionally-charged expression of faith of the Baptist',[3] and he left the Baptist Church.

His childhood teachings and instructions in Islam prompted him to return to Islam, but he was aware that he could not; he was deeply involved in Christianity. He found a half-way house and joined the Society of Friends – the Quakers. What encouraged him was that 'they are an open and sensitive society and their principle of the spirit of God in every human person gives . . . a great deal of reverence for other people's faith'.[4] Perhaps that is what he needed. It was through

97

his interaction with Muslim students on the university campuses and studying with Wilfred Cantwell Smith, who encouraged him to re-examine his own roots, that he finally returned to them,[5] as his mother had anticipated. It was under Professor Smith that he completed his PhD in 1975. He later published his thesis, *Redemptive Suffering in Islam – A Study of Devotional Aspects of 'Ashura' in Twelver Shi'ism* (New York: Mouton, 1978). He was a Research Associate at the Centre for Religious Studies at the University of Toronto (Canada). Currently he is a Professor of Islamic Studies at the Department of Religion, Temple University, Philadelphia.

Ayoub's Christian upbringing has left a lasting influence on him. He speaks about Christianity 'in ways that Christians can recognize and understand, more so than most Muslims I know.' He says, 'I grew up in it and then I studied it thoroughly in my adult years and you can't completely ignore your past, it somehow becomes part of your life.'[6]

This deep-rooted influence of Christianity has caused some doubts amongst Muslims, something he is very much aware of. 'I hear in the U.S.', he says, 'that so and so thinks you are Christian, they don't know you are a Muslim!' His reply: 'I am very much a convinced and practising Muslim – as much as I can practise.' But, he says, 'I also feel again [that] because from my own social background as well [as] in Lebanon where there is a mixed population [of Christians and Muslims] and my upbringing and my knowledge of Christianity, I want to take it [Christianity] seriously and study it and that is what I do.'[7]

Ayoub acts as a bridge between the rich and classical knowledge of Islam, which is mostly in Arabic, and the non-Arabic, especially English-speaking, students of Islam. His two-volume work *The Qur'an and its Interpreters* (State University of New York Press, 1984, 1992 respectively) could be cited as one of the best examples in this direction. He has published a number of articles on various themes. But for our purpose we shall concentrate mainly on those that deal with aspects of Christian–Muslim dialogue.

DEFINING DIALOGUE

Ayoub argues that people who are involved in dialogue hope most of the time, though they do not admit, 'that through dialogue the truth that I seek will be seen by the other'.[8] The question of salvation even if it is not acknowledged takes the centre stage in dialogue. Ayoub points out that whether Muslims would like to choose 'to be plural-istic or exclusivistic' they will find verses in the Qur'an to support their position.[9] But this is possible only if they ignore the context of the revelation of the verses. Giving an example of the verse that 'there is no compulsion in religion: truth stands out clear from error . . .'[10] (al-Baqarah 2:256), he argues that the occasion of the revelation shows clearly a way of dealing with other faiths. The occasion[11] he describes as follows: 'group of oil merchants . . . came from Syria and they were Christians, so they convinced a young man to become a Christian and go back with them. His father came to the Prophet and said: "What can I do? Should I let part of me go to the fire?" This verse was revealed, and the Prophet said let him go.'[12]

Giving this example Ayoub argues that in this increasingly plural-istic world, 'whether we want it or not, [it] is something which we have to live with. We also have to learn to live with the idea that we have to be selective within our own traditions.'[13] To live in a pluralistic world, the important thing, he suggests, is that 'we have to get to know one another'.[14] This implies a presupposition. 'To recognize the integrity of each other's traditions, on the one hand, and to recognize the freedom for people to make choices on the other . . .' and therefore not to 'engage in', what Ayoub calls 'point scoring'.[15] In dialogue 'in which I remain open to share my faith and for my Christian brothers or sisters to share their faith with me, we would not use enticements'.[16] As a Muslim, 'I have to take seriously', for example, 'what Christians mean by the word Gospel, that is what' for Ayoub 'dialogue means', the search, how the others describe themselves. In the process of dia-logue, presenting each other's converts as a 'victory', to Ayoub, is not only a wrong attitude to dialogue, but also cheap.[17]

DIALOGUE – WHAT WENT WRONG?

Ayoub argues that the question of dialogue is not a late twentieth-century development. It has an ancient pedigree. He suggests it started with the writings and thought of St John of Damascus. He claims that 'St John of Damascus's purpose was not so much at the time to make converts to Christianity from Islam, but rather to protect Christians from Islam.'[18] This need 'to protect Christians from Islam created a need to show Islam as an inferior religion *vis-à-vis* Christianity'. In other words, it generated polemics and in return it created a desire for war rather than for dialogue. Gradually, as the Western Christians sent missionaries to the Muslim countries, polemics played its role. Keeping this factor in mind, Ayoub argues that there were two other important factors responsible for keeping the tensions between two communities alive. These were that the Church 'professionalized missionary activities and, secondly, they tied it to political agendas'. The whole missionary enterprise, he argues, 'went hand in hand with the colonial [expansion] and often the success of the one depended on the other and therefore many times conversion was not to Christianity alone but to Christian cultures and to Christian political motivations and ambitions and so on'.[19]

The second important area he identifies was the Crusades against Muslims. The justification for the Crusades was essentially the interpretation of the Scriptures and the command of the Pope. It was internal strife and warfare in Europe, Ayoub argues, that provided the setting for both the 'civil and ecclesiastical authorities to find other avenues to channel the energies of their warring subjects'.[20] Ayoub quotes the proclamation of Pope Urban II, made on 27 November 1095, who exhorted his subjects, 'in the name of Christ to hasten to exterminate this vile race from our lands',[21] by which he meant the Holy Lands, 'and to aid the Christian inhabitants in time'. To add greater stress to this exhortation he cried out 'Deus le volt' (God wills it). Similar views expressed by the ecclesiastical authorities and carried out in practice, helped to deepen the division between the followers of the two religions.

Ayoub also sees an anti-Western Crusade amongst the Muslims. Emotionally-charged books and pamphlets have been published, like 'Western Leaders Say: Destroy Islam and Exterminate its People'.[22] This pamphlet quotes the conquest of Jerusalem by General Allenby during the First World War who said, 'today, the wars of the Crusades have come to an end'. Such statements have provoked a counter-attack amongst Muslims despite the sober teachings of their religion. Muslims in the Middle East, especially after the creation of the state of Israel, have become more suspicious of Western domination either directly or by proxy. They link this domination with a 'new Crusade' and the more it is linked with Christian history the more it becomes a Crusade against Christianity too. Doubts and mistrust are further aggravated by the statements and writings which Ayoub quotes in his articles.[23] This, he says, is unfortunately detected by the Muslims in 'every sphere of Western activity in their society'. These 'anti-Islamic sentiments which often translate themselves into anti-Arab sentiments is still playing an important part'. Ayoub cites the Gulf War: 'I believe', he says, 'that the devastations that were done in Iraq would not have been done to another country if the country was a Christian or predominantly a Buddhist or a Hindu or whatever'.[24] He remarks that it was possible because of history which played its part in the psyche of the Western mind against the Arabs and Islam.

A third important area which created barriers between the two religions is colonialization, evangelization and Orientalism. Ayoub does not go into the detail of their history as such, but points out the spirit that it nurtured and sustained. He describes how for 'many Orientalists, Islamic civilization is an imperfect residue of Byzantine civilization. This idea was born out of the nationalistic and ethnic ideologies of the nineteenth century. Among these, Aryanism, or the "master race" theory as applied to white Europeans, has played a major role in shaping Western attitudes towards Islam as a faith and a civilisation.'[25] Giving examples of Sufism, which attracted Western thinkers a great deal, Ayoub argues that it is difficult for them to accept that it is Islamic. Therefore, Western thinkers and writers tried to prove that it is 'an expression of a primitive Aryan religious phenomenon which is foreign to Islam'. Since there is no good in Islam and it lacks the spiritual heritage of Semitic religions, it is 'the mission of the West to save Muslims from Islam'.[26] Ayoub cites in this respect several examples from the writings of Temple Gairdner, Laurence Browne, Hendrick Kraemer and others, and points out Muslims' doubts about the sincerity of Western scholars on Islam and Muslims. He cites Omar Farrukh's book *Evangelization and Colonialism in Arab Lands*, in which the author draws a distinction between what he calls 'official colonialism', which is political, and 'actual colonialism', which is intellectual, social and economic.[27] Farrukh's analysis encompasses almost all aspects of community life. In brief, anything that comes from the West has been viewed with suspicion, doubt and, at times, with an element of plot and conspiracy.

Ayoub describes how, in his experience, two things went against the true spirit of Christianity: that missionary activities were professionalized and, secondly, they were tied to political agendas. But he notes that the situation is changing. The 'Christian political motivations and ambitions . . . have been replaced by a genuine desire for a better understanding and better co-existence which came in Christianity out of two things'.

First, he argues that 'Christians began to realize that the world cannot be any more divided into Christian and pagans and obdurate Jews'. He stresses that the validity of other religions has to be recognized, and he finds that Christians are realizing 'that there are profound religious faiths and traditions and they have to be taken seriously outside Christianity'.[28] This recognition of other religions as on a par with Christianity helps for a better understanding.

Secondly, he describes how 'many Christians began to see the wrong approach, the insensitivity of the whole missionary activity and therefore there were feelings of guilt that the Christians had to deal with politically, religiously and economically and socially'.[29]

Ayoub argues that Muslim–Christian relations are no longer on the 'battlefield and around the conference table'. A 'better understanding, peaceful co-existence, and the establishment of a fellowship of faith among people of faith', which, he stresses, is the purpose of dialogue, 'is only possible among people enjoying the same standard of security, economic well-being and social equality in all respects'.[30] This equality, he says, does not exist between the 'rich and technologically advanced West and the Muslims of the Third World'. He says that it is only possible in 'Europe and North America where Muslims and Christians share the factory workbench, the school, community centre, and even the cemetery'.[31]

Ayoub stresses that Muslim migrants in Europe and America today are different from those who migrated in the last century. 'Many people', he notes, 'came to North America and South America during the last century, in the second half of the 19th century, and largely were assimilated because they came without an education, either poor farmers or workers and finally they just melted into the society. If they thought they were Muslims, their children did not.'[32] He finds this has changed. The immigration that has taken place since the Second World War, the new immigrants 'to North America and other Western countries [are] professionals . . . who are very much rooted in their faith and at times actually fleeing religious persecution at home'. They are, he says, coming 'to North America and Europe where they can have religious freedom'.[33] These people, he stresses, are not going to be assimilated into the majority culture in the sense that they will give up their religion. Neither are they small in number. He argues that 'there is now the feeling that Western society is not going to be any longer culturally and religiously Christian and Jewish', and he stresses that it 'has to be Christian, Jewish and Muslim'. He cites the Christian argument which often 'speaks of the Judaeo-Christian tradition', by which an impression has been given that the tradition is somehow one. This of course has not always been the case. He points out that in 'the Middle Ages Christians even burnt Hebrew Bibles. The Bible is their Scripture, but because it wasn't in Latin, they burnt it'. The 'idea of the Judaeo-Christian tradition is a recent phenomenon'; now there is a level where we can speak of the Judaeo-Christian-Islamic culture. The Muslims are a part of whatever made the 'culture of the West', which means that Muslims are 'as much a part of Abraham and Aristotle as are the Jews and the Christians'.[34]

From the point of view of interaction between Islamic and Western civilizations he hopes 'that it would never become a kind of mish-mash of the three religions, they are distinct in some ways'; and he stresses that 'it is best if they do remain distinct'. This he finds very important for a meaningful dialogue. One cannot become a Hindu, Buddhist, Jew, Muslim or Christian all at the same time. He says, 'I am a Muslim and only as a Muslim can I meaningfully dialogue with people of other faiths who would become my fellow travellers, my sisters and brothers in faith'. It could be possible, he remarks, and be done meaningfully 'and in a challenging way only when I speak from my own roots'.[35]

On the process of ratification and enhancement of dialogue, Ayoub has two important suggestions for Muslims. At a practical level he finds that Muslims have yet to be accepted. This is because we are also 'different in certain habits, customs, dress, codes and so on' and 'somehow there is still mistrust and fear, say of the veil on women or of the Muslim who may stay aloof from parties where alcohol is consumed'[36] or of Muslim dietary habits. These are very practical problems.

Western society is increasingly pluralistic, in terms of religion and culture, but the migrant Muslim society is 'culturally pluralistic' too. Even if the Muslim community had been culturally monolithic, 'not characterized by Egyptian or Pakistani cultural traits', Ayoub argues, 'there remain elements of difference and separateness', simply because of the community's religious needs and requirements. He finds the dialogue of two cultures and the level of day-to-day problems 'could be more immediately fruitful because the points are fairly tangible and can be worked on'.[37]

Theologically, he notes some difficulties too: 'there are times when we on both sides can go so far and no further'. He points out, 'whatever is the understanding that Christians have of the Trinity and whatever we say about the Trinity as in the final analysis, Islam would have to insist . . . that we can only accept Jesus as a Prophet, a human Prophet of God, however miraculous his life and birth have been, but nonetheless he is still a human creature of God'.[38] He emphasizes those certain differences where both communities can and cannot go any further. 'I must say for me', he argues, 'often when I hear liturgically or otherwise the Christian proclamation of divinity of Jesus, somehow I cringe, I can tell you, because to us that does violate *Tawhid*'.[39]

THE CHURCHES AND DIALOGUE *VIS-À-VIS* MUSLIMS

Ayoub claims that the progress made by the Churches in dialogue came about because 'they are aware of a long history of no dialogue but [a] sort of missionary fight'. In many ways Muslims are now left behind. 'Perhaps', he says, 'we are not under the same constraints to make the same kind of progress',[40] especially if one takes into account that 'Islam has recognized Christianity much more than Christianity has recognized Islam'. And from the Qur'anic principles, he points out, 'one could work out an Islamic theology of world religions. There is not a parallel in the New Testament in that way or [in] the early fathers'.[41] He stresses that Muslims with the World Council of Churches and the Roman Catholic Church have 'had a history of dialogue because of its international character'. There are very few people, he points out, amongst the Muslims, even those who are living in the West, 'who know really anything in any profound way about Judaism and Christianity and other faiths, and often when we dialogue, we are dialoguing with people . . . who know far more about Islam than any Muslims'.[42] He finds an imbalance which needs to be corrected. He suggests that Muslims should study other religions seriously and 'not simply from the Qur'an . . . the Qur'an has a view of Christianity, but we must also know what the Christians think of themselves'.[43]

Referring to the Declaration on the Relation of the Church to Non-Christian Religions (*Nostra Aetate*) of the Second Vatican Council, he points out that 'it is important because it speaks for so many Catholic Christians and represents a clear departure from the Church's classical stance with regard to people of other faiths'. In the Council's declaration he finds the 'earlier attitude is recognized and rejected'.[44]

Ayoub is however critical of the Declaration; the Declaration, as far as Muslims are concerned, has taken an 'absolute minimum' approach. 'Muslims', he points out, 'do much more than merely venerate Jesus, but they do so not to please the Church, or show a spirit of ecumenism, but because God in the Qur'an demands of Muslims to accept all the prophets and messengers of God who came before Muhammad'.[45] He referred to this point in the Secretariat in the Vatican, 'they said at least the Vatican Council made the initiative which could be carried further',[46] and he agrees with that view. But recent developments in the Roman Catholic Church make him critical of the Church's stand on mission. He is critical of Pope John Paul II's encyclical, *Redemptoris Missio* (1991), which he argues 'is not . . . in the spirit of Vatican II'; things always have a context 'Why now?' In the midst of the crisis between the West and the Middle East in the Gulf War. To say that the Catholic Church is not involved is not true. It is very involved. There are Catholics in the Muslim world. The Catholic Church is a Western institution, at least the Latin Church, why now has the Pope felt the urge to call upon Muslims to 'open their doors to Christ?' And what does it means?[47]

Ayoub is in favour of opening a Unit or Section that will deal with other faiths, by a Muslim organization like the Organization of Islamic Conference (OIC). But the problem, he points out, is 'who will lead such a Unit?' Muslims are much more attuned to people who are polemicist. If such people occupy the Unit, then its purpose is killed.

DA'WAH AND SHARI'AH

Da'wah to Ayoub is not essentially *da'wah* to a religious community, but *Da'wah ilā Allah*, a call to God. Ayoub believes that he is involved in *Da'wah ilā Allah*, in a way, but should this be measured in terms of conversion? He questions the wisdom of it.[48] Giving an example, he explains his position. In Trinidad, some Muslims brought a young Catholic man to him who wanted to become Muslim. Ayoub remembers well that he talked to him and told him that his decision would not be an easy one, it would change his life in many ways, and he asked him to go back and think about it and come back the next day. The people who brought the young man to him were not happy and said, 'What if he dies?' Ayoub replied, 'If he dies he is fine because his intention is good', and the next day that man came again and still wanted to be a Muslim. In such circumstances, Ayoub notes that the group around the new convert would say welcome to Islam but, 'I would say welcome back to Islam'. He believes that 'we are all Muslims in this ultimate sense and then the problem becomes accepting the implication of this, when and if we join the Muslim community with its Shari'ah and religious dispensations and so on'.[49]

Ayoub finds invariably that people who accept Islam or Christianity through conversion 'create a personality problem because a person then has to justify his conversion and it would take an attitude that sometimes is far harder than those taken by born members of the tradition'. Human beings, Ayoub argues:

> cannot easily be defined as being Muslim, for me it has many meanings, even without dialogue. Outwardly, I am comfortable being a Muslim and I want a culture. But of course inwardly it is something that you have to work on all the time ... Every time I pray I affirm my Islam anew to me and in my heart and in my faith and so on ...[50]

As far as the Shari'ah is concerned, it defines itself, argues Ayoub, 'it is the way to God'. A person may live in some ways in accordance with the law, but inwardly his life may be far from it.[51] Ayoub suggests that Shari'ah has many meanings, both social and individual, and we have to see it also as a dynamic set or system of moral imperatives rather than as a strict law in the strict sense. He contends: 'Shari'ah is not law it is a moral system.' He suggests taking seriously 'the argument some people advance that severe punishment in accordance with the Shari'ah cannot be applied until the society is fully Islamic'.[52] He does not differentiate between the crime of a ruler and that of an ordinary subject of a country where either full or partial Shari'ah is implemented. 'You cannot apply the law of cutting off the hand of a thief who may steal [a few pennies] ... from somewhere and yet operate on the fact that a certain privileged group of the population has the right to abscond and misuse their wealth, ... for their own pleasure'.[53] He cites the examples of Abu Bakr and Ali who used to keep constant checks on their income and who used to take from the public treasury much less than what was allowed. In such circumstances he sees some justification for rigorous implementation of Shari'ah. Shari'ah to Ayoub becomes 'part of the Islamic ideal' which, he argues, 'must remain an ideal but which cannot be fully realized on this side of things',[54] meaning perhaps in this world.

Ayoub finds in the demand for Shari'ah by Muslims in Nigeria, the Sudan and Pakistan more of a political issue than a religious one. He suggests that Muslims 'have to re-examine how Shari'ah would be implemented and to what extent it should be implemented on non-Muslims'.[55] He points out that Shari'ah cannot be imposed on a non-Muslim because many things which the non-Muslims do is because 'his Shari'ah allows him to do this', or not to do it. He cites examples from the Prophet's traditions. 'The Prophet', he describes, 'condemned the Jewish adulterous men and women, [but] he did not condemn them on the basis of the Qur'an. He said, what does the Torah say?'[56] Since the Torah prescribed stoning adulterous men and women, he judged them according to their Book. He stresses that Muslims 'cannot say Islam prohibits drinking, then, therefore if I hear a Christian has alcohol in his home and drinks alcohol I would go and flog him as though he was a Muslim',[57] as this is not the right way for the implementation of Shari'ah.

Ayoub has some suggestions for Christians too: 'I believe', he says, 'that the Christians now have come to appreciate the Jewish attachment to the law and even going against the condemnations of Jesus of the Pharisees and have begun to see the Pharisees as playing a very important and positive role in the development of Rabbinical Judaism and so on. I hope that Christians would appreciate also our attachment to the Shari'ah'[58] as well.

ON CHRISTOLOGY

Ayoub contends that the Qur'an presents a Christology of the human Christ, empowered by God and 'fortified with the Holy Spirit'. He emphasizes that 'it is fully Islamic Christology based not on borrowed distortions of early Christian heresies, but on the Islamic view of man and God'. The similarities and resemblances of Islamic Christology and early apocryphal literature like the *Infancy Gospel of Thomas* and the *Protoevangelism of James* are 'similarities of framework and story, not of theology or essential view'.[59] The Muslim view of Christology, he emphasizes, 'Christians must take as a Muslim view and accept as such, at least as the methodological basis for their research and study.' 'It is no longer profitable', he finds, 'to take Qur'anic statements about Jesus simply as distortions of, or borrowings from, the Gospels. Rather, they should be accepted as authentically Islamic statements and as expressing an Islamic view.'[60]

Ayoub describes the various views expressed by the Muslim commentators of the Qur'an on the subject of Christology. He argues at length on the question of the death of Jesus. Despite the differences of opinion amongst various commentators, he points out two areas where all Muslims agree. First, Islam denies the divinity of Jesus 'without denying his special humanity'. Second, Islam denies the sacrifice of Jesus on the cross, as an atonement for sinful humanity. But the point of disagreement which Ayoub highlights is that the Qur'an 'denies neither the actual death of Christ nor his general redemptive role in human history'.[61] Ayoub argues that the very early commentators of the Qur'an:

had some knowledge of the Christian insistence on the crucifixion
as a historical fact. They did not, however, grasp the implication of
this fact for Christianity, and therefore tried to harmonize the Qur'anic
denial with the Christian affirmation. They accepted a crucifixion as
an historical fact, in agreement with Christians, but denied it of Jesus,
in agreement with the Qur'an. They adopted not a docetic position
in interpreting the words *Shubbiha Lahum*, but a substitutionalist
one.[62]

Ayoub, refers to the verse of the Qur'an which states: 'but they killed
him not, nor crucified him, but so it was made to appear to them . . .'
(Surah Al-i-Imran 4:157). He suggests that the commentators 'have
not been able convincingly to disprove the crucifixion. Rather they
have compounded the problem by adding the conclusion of their
substitutionalist theories.'[63] He stresses that the mistake has been made
by the commentators by taking 'the verse to be an historical statement'. This statement, like the other statements concerning Jesus in
the Qur'an, 'belongs not to history but to theology in the broadest
sense'. Giving an example, he emphasizes that 'it is similar to the
Qur'anic assertion that Mary, the mother of Christ, was the sister of
Aaron'.[64]

Ayoub argues that the Qur'an is not speaking about the man Jesus
but 'about the Word of God, who was sent to earth and who returned
to God. Thus the denial of the killing of Jesus is a denial of the power
of man to vanquish and destroy the divine Word, which is forever
victorious'.[65] The substitute theory, he claims, passed through various
stages of development. In the process of the Qur'an's commentary,
the commentators, he stresses, 'did more than indulge in an exercise
of textual analysis'.[66] He points out that initially the commentators
thought that 'whoever bore the likeness of Jesus, and consequently his
suffering and death, did so voluntarily'.[67] At subsequent stages, Ayoub
suggests, the commentators were increasingly interested in the 'historical accounts and gospel materials and hagiography' and gradually
a preference developed for what he calls this 'punishment substitutionism',
where God is 'completely absolved from the responsibility of injustice
or wrongdoing'.[68] A man with a likeness of Jesus was killed in spite
of his protests. Finally, by the sixth century Hijrah or twelfth century
CE, he argues, 'we witness . . . [an attempt] to interpret the entire passage in one complete story'.[69] Of the many narrations, which went
through various stages, Ayoub finds some of the materials came from
Christian converts to Islam. For example, he points out a narration

which he finds in the writings of Ibn Ishaq, supposed to have been related to him by a Christian convert.

Ayoub suggests that the Muslim commentators 'indulge' in a somewhat 'excessive textual analysis'; he claims the commentators were very open and expressed themselves in an uncompromising manner 'letting God be God', even at the cost of 'denying man the privilege of being man'. On the other hand, he points out that the Christian position is equally uncompromising and serious 'on letting God be man in order for man to be divine'. This gap he finds vast, even though he stresses the difference is in 'one of theological terminology rather than intent'.[70]

Ayoub constantly reminds all Muslims and Christians that the Qur'anic Christology, Christology of the human Christ, needs to be taken seriously in its own right. Equally he challenges that the Muslim perception, developed through the ages, needs re-examining. By shifting the whole argument from the historical to the theological, which, Ayoub believes, is 'not an impenetrable wall' if Muslims take this divine challenge, in the Qur'anic spirit of 'fair exhortation'. In his recent writings investigates two relevant terms: '*Ibn*' and '*Walad*'. The former has been used in the Qur'an as 'son', which Ayoub argues signifies 'filial relationship', 'understood metaphorically to mean son through a relationship of love and adoption'. '*Walad*' refers to the more intense relation of 'offspring' and this, Ayoub stresses, signifies 'physical generation and sonship'.[71] Here he finds the Qur'anic commentators took the latter term and 'argue against the Christian concept of Christ's divine sonship'. Ayoub finds that the early Christian theologies are equally responsible in providing the meaning in which Muslim theologians took '*Walad*' for '*Ibn*'. The Christian theologian Abu Qurra in particular, Ayoub points out, 'leaves no doubt in the mind of a Muslim reader that Jesus is the son of God, engendered by Him from eternity' (the verb '*walada*' means to engender, to give birth). Abu Qurra fixes on 'God the father and Jesus His son'. This direct language, Ayoub finds, still remains in the 'language of Syrio-Arabic liturgy'.[72]

Ayoub encourages further debate on the issue of Christology. Jesus provided a great bridge of piety and spirituality between the two communities and equally has been a great theological barrier, which Ayoub seems to be denting effectively.

6 Hasan Askari
(1932-   )

Hasan Askari was born in Hyderabad (India) in 1932. He received his MA and PhD in Sociology from Osmania University and later joined the same department in Osmania as a lecturer. He became a Reader in 1957 and remained in that post until joining Aligarh Muslim University in 1975. He worked there for a couple of years, after which he left India for Europe and eventually settled in England. During his stay in India, he wrote extensively on the question of modernity and faith, multi-religious society and dialogue, to name just some of the various areas of his work.

Askari's perspective of dialogue and the various dimensions he proposes for understanding a multi-religious society is the focus of this study. But first, we look at the two significant factors that shaped Askari's insight and ideas.

First, young Askari witnessed two important changes in India during 1947 and 1948. After years of turmoil, India was divided and Pakistan was created in 1947. A huge migration took place, millions of people migrated to both sides of the newly-created border. During this transitional stage, a further development occurred. Askari's home state, Hyderabad, was annexed to India in 1948 and Askari found himself in secular India. His religion was one among many. In his own words:

> this was a very fascinating challenge, at times painful . . . within the Indian context, I discovered that my religion was one among many and I had to come home spiritually and theologically within a multi-religious India. So I had to go beyond the requirements of secular acceptance of culture and religion in India, beyond tolerance of each other. I had to understand the mystery of more than one religion.[1]

Second, it was his early writings – especially on inter-religion – that brought him closer to various theologians and thinkers like Cantwell Smith, whom he met in India in 1962. This meeting had a lasting impact upon Askari. He follows him, as he puts it, 'through and through' in ideas and in thought. He is greatly influenced by his distinction 'between faith and belief, between the personal and subjective and cumulative traditions'.[2] He came into contact with one of the influential Indian theologians, Stanley J. Samartha in 1967, who was then very much involved in ecumenical consultations on dialogue. Samartha has had a profound influence on Askari and their friendship has continued ever since. The friendship with Smith and Samartha provided him with opportunities to participate in inter-religious consultations in Europe and America. These visits to Western countries provided him with an opportunity to understand the meaning of a multi-religious society. 'When I visited Europe', he says, 'I was amazed at the amount of interest shown in matters spiritual, from the occult to the paranormal'.[3] He saw the West as a great powerhouse of spiritual revival, especially in the light of the changes and development in Christian theology, which hitherto had quite obstinately rejected all understanding of religious traditions other than Christianity. When the opportunity came to contribute to the process of dialogue, he did so with enthusiasm and even made the West his home.

DIALOGUE AND MUSLIMS

Askari is well aware of the Muslim suspicion of dialogue, as a 'marked attempt at conversion'. He argues this 'suspicion is not always without basis'. He points out four main reasons for this:

1. A Muslim mind fails to understand 'the deep and vast changes the Christian faith, in its interpretation and expression, has been undergoing in almost every century. The notion of an evolving and expanding faith is somehow alien to the Muslim mind.'
2. The 'political experience of Christianity recently in the form of Imperialism, hampers on both sides the openness and trust necessary for an informal encounter.'
3. The 'cultural experience of Christianity, particularly in the form of science and technology, is usually looked upon as a threat to Islamic civilization. The Christian-Western influence is held responsible for secularization of culture and institutions.'
4. The 'intermingling of academic and religious traditions by Muslims is another aggravating factor. One often comes across and intriguing mixture of fantasy with fact, inquiry with apology.'[4]

Muslims' mistrust and misunderstanding of dialogue, in Askari's view, lie not so much in theological or dogmatic differences, as in Muslims' cultural and political experience.

He also points out two equally 'grave' features in the Christian situation:

1. Christians have modelled 'the speech of religion' on the model of 'the speech of science'. The process of secularization has already taken command, paving the way for the priority of the 'word of man' over the 'Word of God'.
2. He is concerned about the discovery of the unity of 'communication and control' in the West, where communication in practice is one-way traffic. It generates a kind of monologue in society, which in his view 'is a monstrous existence that sweeps the social and the cultural worlds, without conditions, without limits'.[5]

'Under the impact of [the] monological era', Askari is concerned that 'religion might also attempt to imitate the preoccupation of science with general and abstract truth'. He fears that this may lead to a false position in which religion becomes 'a rival to science'.

In dialogue, Askari disagrees with some Muslim views, which suggest that it is better to avoid the difficult theological areas of the Trinity, *Tahrīf*, etc. By avoiding these issues, he stresses, we are not following 'our own Islamic tradition in that field'. Citing Ibn Hazm (994–1064 CE), he disagrees with Ibn Hazm's views, but gives credit that he was the 'first one in the entire history of religions I suppose who took texts other than his own', and took the Bible very seriously,'and he was the one who established the rules and methods of textual and historical criticism which Europe followed later'. Askari finds that all these 'theological constructs', as he puts it, 'are human constructs. Therefore, in dialogue all these areas need further discussion and elaboration.'[6] The theological agenda 'is not exhausted', what he calls 'the traditional list of themes'. He emphasizes that, 'in the 20th century [Muslims] should evolve [their] own agenda of theological mysteries, [they] can't go on repeating'.[7]

In dialogue Askari likes to expand the agenda for Muslims from what we have pointed out earlier. In his opinion, there are two 'important areas' that need to be explored. First, he suggests Muslims should read the Qur'an without embroiling themselves in theological arguments. In other words, the Qur'an needs to be read in its own context and all the theological developments in the early history need to be set aside. He contends that Muslims 'took the Qur'an in evidence of reference to buttress and strengthen one position or the other'. Secondly, he considers his own situation and asks 'why it took twenty-five years or twenty years for me to come to a point where I said yes to more than one religion because if God is transcendent, if He is *Subhan* (Glory), then His mystery cannot be exhausted in one religious form.' As in nature there are varieties in human language, and also there are various cultures. In Askari's opinion, there 'should be a variety in religion, not an artificial variety'; rather 'spontaneous variety' needs to be explored.[8]

Askari points out three major approaches still unstated in Muslim scholarship of the Qur'an and inter-religious dialogue:[9]

1. *Change of methodology*: He warns Muslims that they should be careful of the 'usual approach' of selecting certain passages from the Qur'an and applying them to a given situation. He agrees that one should see 'the context and also recall how these verses were understood in the Islamic tradition [and] Islamic scholarship'; this is 'vital'. But he finds that 'this has not been done properly'. He encourages future scholars 'to develop a new hermeneutics, that means to recontextualize those verses'. This is a 'very critical task'. In this he expects opposition from those Muslims who oppose dialogue.

2. *Change in concept*: Muslims must be very clear about 'the concept of the entire, the semantics of the word dialogue'. When we bring the word dialogue close to the Qur'an what one finds is that Qur'an in fact invites Jews and Christians to reflect on the Islamic invitation 'to rethink the understanding of Prophethood' of the Prophet Muhammad. In the 'actual semantic field there is no more dialogue'. Therefore, Muslims have to be very careful before choosing one verse and applying it to the whole issue of relation between Christianity and Islam.

3. *Change in the mode of understanding*: The Qur'an, he stresses, is 'through and through dialogical', not one part, or another, but the entire Qur'an is dialogical. 'The Qur'anic form of revelation is dialogical, it is this form which the Prophet lived', which is *Sunnah*. What he emphasizes by *Sunnah* is the personality, *Shaksiyah* – the entire personality of the Prophet, which is available to us 'to understand, to communicate with, to relate to'. Muslims have developed, academically, a method 'which invokes the totality of the Qur'an'. He notes and suggests that the only acceptable method is 'to live the Qur'anic movement', not only to practise 'the parts of the Qur'anic imperatives or commandments to be a good Muslim or a pious Muslim but to live the Qur'anic moment of dialogical mode of understanding of God and man'. Therefore, a Muslim has to read the Qur'an in 'close intimacy

of the *Sunnah* . . . then we can see what the Prophet recited, then we can see what the Prophet is doing'.[10]

Askari argues that the Qur'anic critique of Christianity should be taken seriously by both Muslims and Christians. 'The Qur'an is not saying', he points out, 'that what you believe, X believes and what we believe Y believes are to be exchanged for the other. The Qur'an is saying that whatever beliefs you have you should not commit the ultimate sacrilege of absolutizing your belief.' He points out in reference to this the Qur'anic critique of the sonship of God (Al-Tawbah, 9:30–31). 'The Qur'an is bringing to the Christians a warning.' He reminds us that we are talking of the Word of God and we should be very careful. He also reminds Muslims that the 'Word of God' is also saying the same thing: that if Muslims commit the same mistakes or make their words more supreme than the Word of God, then they are equally facing the same Qur'anic injunctions. That is why the Word of God 'is not the word of man'.[11]

On the methodological level, the Qur'an's approach, he points out, is of a real transformation of the individual. 'We have to apprehend', in Askari's analysis, that the 'Qur'anic totality is dialogical and then we should identify the specific moments of Qur'anic encounter with other belief systems.' Here, the Qur'anic interest is not to change one belief for another, as we have noted earlier, 'but to transform the consciousness of all beliefs'. He reminds us that 'those are two different things'. One may have an Islamic belief, a Jewish belief or a Christian belief, or other religious beliefs. For Askari, there are 'preferences on a universal criteria; on a national criteria, how broad [these] beliefs are, [whether they are] wrong or right, how they are articulated and what are the social and political consequences, we must all examine this, but the Qur'an is transforming the consciousness of man about religious beliefs including the Islamic beliefs – that is why the Qur'an outlasts every school of theology.'[12]

THE TRANS-RELIGIOUS DIMENSION

Compared to Faruqi's meta-religion, Askari's trans-religion is more radical. It provides for various levels of communities across the traditional boundaries of religions. In Faruqi's meta-religion principles have been provided, where religions can be tested without breaching their boundaries. In Askari's trans-religious dimension, the boundaries of religion becomes irrelevant and various levels of belief create communities.

Askari warns the followers of any religion, and especially Muslims, that religion should not become a god in their life. Therefore there is a need for a high degree of alertness and a greater need to 'proceed beyond religion as a concept, as an identity'.[13]

Against this background, we shall discuss briefly his unique view of communities. He argues that 'only four communities evolved throughout history', and stresses that 'they are going to remain forever'.

In his analysis, those millions of people who are unconscious and concerned about daily life and are least likely to talk about any ultimate questions are the majority and exist in every religion, culture and country. They may differ politically and culturally or in any other way, but they are all one community.[14]

The second community is of those people 'who are a little awake and who call themselves religious'. They are 'immersed in the outward forms of the religious practice'. But they can't go beyond those forms – visible, mental, institutional or others – and they are found across the national and cultural boundaries. In Islamic terminology we call these the people of *Ahl al-Zahir* – the people of outward forms. In Askari's analysis they form one community; whether they are Jews, Christians or Muslims they belong to one *Ummah*.

The third community is of those people 'who move from the letter to the spirit, from the outer to the inner'. They are fully awake and 'look beyond the outward and reach for the inward dimension of what they believe and practise and of what others believe and practise'.[15] Askari points out that 'they are very strange people ... they may appear as Muslims, Jews or Christians, or whoever they are, they stand and dwell in houses in which they belong', but 'they speak the same language as their faith, but inwardly they are different people ...'. To Askari they are the *Hizb-Allah*, the people (Party) of God. 'In this group are people of all religions and times because they are the people and from these people are drawn the people who later become the Prophets and Messengers of God in history.'[16]

The final category in Askari's community analysis are the people 'who have gone beyond the outward and the inward and are the elect and they are the *Mursalin* and *Anbiyā'* – the Messengers and Prophets – or the people of *Haqīqah* – the people of truth.[17] 'They are both known and hidden. They are both present and absent. They guide without appearing, and influence the word without going from place to place, wherever they are, they radiate compassion, serenity, peace, love and joy.'[18]

Stressing the importance of this analysis, he describes how wherever he has spoken, and whoever he has spoken to, about these categories, 'people have accepted [it] very well'. But, if one accepts these categories, then the question of dialogue becomes irrelevant and becomes instead a question of 'encounter'. He well remembers that, on various occasions, he faced problems of encounter with others. Stressing the people who belong to the second group, the people of outward forms – *Ahl al-Zahir* – he finds he has 'no connection with [them]. How can I connect? Of course I am sympathetic to him . . . but if I meet a Hindu or a Christian or a Jew or any other person who belongs to the third group then I have a connection.' Putting himself into the third group, he claims that 'the calculation is not that paramount to recognize the other'. But the difficulty is that a dialogue between the first and the second community is meaningless because 'they already know each other'. A dialogue between them would be a dialogue 'to confirm each other's mirror image', and they give 'auto-suggestion to each other'. The third group, in Askari's opinion, 'becomes the transformer and therefore when they speak they speak a different language'. But the people of outward forms (*Ahl-al-Zahir*) convert the message of this group into 'their own form' and the 'ball is thrown back into the same situation'.[19]

THE CONCEPT OF TRANSCENDENCE AND IMMANENCE

Transcendence and immanence are central concepts in the writings of Askari. He points out, without naming them, certain Christian scholars, implying obliquely that the Islamic concept of God is 'too transcendental or too above or too far away from the human predicament', compared to the Christian understanding of God. In Christian theology God is at the 'human level . . . closer to man [and] almost becoming man or participating in human suffering or human predicament'.[20]

He finds the reason for such thinking among Christians is a lack of understanding of Muslim spirituality and the Qur'an. Referring to 'a basic component of all religiosity . . . in all religions', he finds 'awe' is at the centre of it. He warns that it should not be translated 'into abstract terms like distance or such derogatory terms as a gulf between God and man'. The concept of nearness – *Taqarrub* – or intimacy with His loving kindness with every person has been ignored by such scholars, although it is clearly articulated in the Qur'an. For example, 'wherever you turn you will face God' (Al-Hadid 57:4) or 'wherever you are, God is with you', etc., indicate His 'presence, immutable, eternal, the universal presence of Divine Reality and that presence is an indivisible unity'.[21]

In a logical primacy of transcendence Askari contends that 'whatever is truly transcendent is truly immanent'. Giving an example, he argues: 'one who transcends time and space' and all 'limits is then alone or [is] accessible to everything in the cosmos, in the world'.[22] What he is stressing is that if somebody is praying on one side of the planet and another is praying on the other side, they are nevertheless praying to the same God at the same time. Giving examples from Islamic devotional prayers, he reminds us of a prayer of the fourth caliph Ali. Ali used to counsel people going on a journey and leaving their homes and their relatives behind. He shows it is a 'beautiful prayer resting on two words used in Arabic, one is *Sāhib*, and the other is *Walī*. *Sāhib* means companion and *Walī* means guardian, protector'. The prayer is: 'O God! You are the only one who can be both my companion here in the journey and also my protector of my family back home.' *Sāhib* and *Walī*, two attributes, can be attributed to God alone. He reminds Christian scholars and others that 'throughout Islamic piety, Islamic orthodox literature and mystical reflections and poetry', one can find this nearness of God as in Christianity and Judaism. Therefore, he argues, the 'polemical distinction between Transcendence and Immanence – using Transcendence as a basis to become critical of Islam – is absurd'.[23]

Askari claims this implicit theological understanding is rooted in the mainstream, 'the Western philosophies and theologians'. This he sees as 'a great loss of Transcendence' where the 'West is imprisoned in one particular history ... geography and one particular ideology'. Pointing out the Muslim situation, he argues that the Muslims too have 'lost their sense of Transcendence making it imprisoned in their own ideological and religious self-consciousness', which Askari, stresses is 'un-Qur'anic'.[24]

THE QUESTION OF ABSOLUTE TRUTH AND REVELATION

The question of Absolute Truth is a central point in Askari's approach to dialogue or dialogical relations between the religions. For him, 'all religions and all approaches within each one of them, are relative to the Absolute Truth – they all are just approaches, and the only conviction common to them all is that there is an Absolute Truth'.[25] For Askari, it is not enough to say that all religions point to the same Truth, for the truth as such is 'not given for easy perception but is interwoven within each religious matrix, interlocked with all other religions, and yet not completely within them'.[26] He points out that more than one religion in history is in fact a 'form of witness of the Absolute which cannot be exhausted in only one religion'.[27]

But what about the religious claims of finality – 'Muhammad is the seal of Prophets' or 'I am the Way'. Askari looks at this question at various levels. At the political and psychological level at which the concepts operate, so that the community possesses the whole truth, the final truth and a blueprint of how to conduct one's life,[28] Askari finds that the believer 'achieves a very deep psychological security . . . there is no doubt about that'. This provides 'a stable foundation to stand upon as we are told'. Then Askari points out that as soon as one moves from the psychological to the political level, 'we enter', as he puts it, 'into the most problematic zone event at this superficial level'. Here 'superficial' refers to the theological, not the philosophical level. He stresses again the positive aspect of this principle of confidence, but it generates 'another psychological need', 'a negative need of denying the same validity, the same order of validity to another teaching before' or after 'one's own'. That psychological need generates, in his opinion, a 'polemical claim', which turns into a political need of 'suppression and oppression'. Whosoever disagrees with that particular claim and interpretation is liable to be punished or even eliminated. This position, to Askari, is 'morally, spiritually and philosophically invalid and even subhuman', because, it elevates 'one's self to a position where one possesses the monopoly of truth and therefore is superior'.[29]

Askari describes the question of finality further at the phenomenological level. He reminds us that Muslims are not alone in this claim; others claim it too. He poses the question in dialogue: 'Should we close our eyes and start having a moral unity of religious or only a political unity against some common enemy?' In his opinion, it cannot solve what he calls the 'theological enigma'. He points out that the 'word finality is [only] applicable in any meaningful sense, theologically speaking, to God. Its use for any other finite earthly historical manifestation, or for a person or for a book or for a word or for a sign is to be theologically invalid'.[30] Therefore a 'very substantive question' – the claim of finality – 'does not stand theological scrutiny'. He argues, on the basis of the Qur'an, that if the One God has given to all communities and in all times one and the same message, and the 'message remains one throughout history until the end of the world, it cancels from within itself any idea of artificial historical finalities'. He further asks: 'When the whole message is one, how can one other message become more true and completely true compared to others?'[31] He accepts the possibility of the message becoming distorted, corrupted, deleted. In which case a fresh revelation is required. But the fresh revelation does not mean a new revelation. It happens, he argues, not only in the 'life of the nations but in the life of the individuals' as well: 'to wipe out the rust from our hearts, we need to be reminded, we need to be corrected'.[32] He takes the new revelations as correctives and not a separate message or entity. The *Al-Dhikr* (the reminder) is the most important weapon to clear the mind of an individual and society, and the Revelation, is the reminder. It is a Mercy and Love of God. God is free to reveal in any way He wishes (as he has said elsewhere, there are three books of God available to human beings at all times and places – nature, history and man himself); if one accepts this principle *Mashi'at Allah* – whatever Allah wishes – then one is in direct conflict with contrary views. This, he argues, was the Prophet's contention about the Jews of Madinah. 'It was in this perspective that the Qur'an is critical of the Jews and Christians. When they objected to the revelation of the Prophet. . . .'[33]

Muslims, he finds, adopted this theology from the Christians – exclusivity – and have applied it to the finality of Islam and to the Qur'an almost in a Christian sense, which to him is an 'undoing of the Qur'anic perspective'. But is he looking for a religion after Islam? In his understanding there is no need. Because, 'there is always Islam after Islam . . . What we mean by Islam is both wholly understood [in a proper] context'. Since Islam is a continuity, 'in the beginning was Islam, in the middle was Islam and in the end is Islam', as he puts it. He does not see any need for a Prophet, a teacher, a sage to come to substitute the Qur'anic understanding of *Tawhīd* (unity of God) and *Subhāniya* (glorification).[34]

THE OUTER AND THE INNER DIMENSIONS OF DIALOGUE

Unlike Faruqi, Askari believes that the concept of Christianity and Christendom is 'a formulation which rarely works out in reality'. He suggests that one should 'distinguish between Christian faith, Christian vision and Christian history'. He discusses what those who distinguish between Christianity and Christendom really mean by Christianity. 'If Christianity is what is Christianity then Christendom follows from it'. He prefers and encourages that clarity should be reached 'to make a distinction between the collective and the personal, the outer and the inner dimensions of one's spirituality'. That to him is a vital issue.

Moving from the outer to the inner dimension of dialogue remains Askari's personal *Jihād*. One can sum up his whole work as a struggle 'primarily to move from the outer to the inner, from the collective to the personal dimension', because he argues:

> as you move from the personal to the collective, as you move from the inner to the outer, you are going to divide it, you are going to discriminate, you are going to pre-judge, you are going to excessive bias and prejudice. You are moving on a slope towards the physical confrontation towards plunder and towards murder – mentally and culturally and psychologically by pre-judging the other.[35]

Askari does not consider a denominational dialogue or confessional dialogue between Christians, Jews and Muslims to be the real purpose of dialogue. For him, the 'real dialogue is to create a perspective where I could see the other as a person, as a seeker, an *'Abdullāh* (servant of God), [a] *Makhluq* (creation)'.[36] He stresses more a personal (inner) dialogue compared to the institutional (outer) dialogue towards this end. The institution more or less represents a type, whereas personal dialogue looks at the other as a person. He explains this elsewhere in an article in a different context, but it is suitable here to explain his point. 'If I introduce Mr. Smith to Mr. Ahmad, the latter conditioned as he is by his own closed self-understanding as a Muslim, he will see Mr. Smith as a Christian, a type which embodies all what Mr. Ahmad's Islam equates with Christianity.'[37]

Here Islam could be represented as an institutional or outer dimension of dialogue, or vice-versa. In dialogue, in his opinion, encounter between persons and not between types matters more. He finds that the WCC has moved from its original commitment to an inner dialogue of faiths, between people, and has started looking more towards institutional representations from Islamic organizations:

> In 1968 and 1970 we met as individuals, as individual scholars and seekers and students of dialogue and we created a good departure, later it became a political dialogue and once the dialogue became political between communities, between nations, then it has also its own dynamics.[38]

Askari is not against an institution of dialogue where people can work, write, publish, promote or propagate. These things are important to him.

OTHER CONCEPTS IN ASKARI'S WRITINGS

The Concept of Lag

Askari compares the New Testament and the Qur'an, in a response to Hugh Goddard's 'Each Other's Scripture', and makes a comparison from a phenomenological point of view. The difference between the theological and phenomenological approach, he points out, is one of 'claims' and of 'phenomena'.[39] Though he compares the two Scriptures, phenomenologically, yet he argues, they 'are not phenomenologically comparable. Their *origins* as phenomena are quite different.' He stresses the words 'their origins as phenomena', where he points out that it is not a 'judgement upon their claims, authenticity and finality'. In his comparison he claims that 'the New Testament is a reference to Jesus while the Qur'an is an event in the life of Muhammad. As such there is a time lag *vis-à-vis* the New Testament, and there is an immediacy *vis-à-vis* the Qur'an.[40]

Concept of Minority/Majority

Askari opposes the idea of a minority or a majority defined merely by the large or small numbers of a faith community. 'It is not the number but the character', he argues, 'not the quantity but the quality, which determines the religious description of a group'.[41] If it rested on numbers, it would never have been possible to raise voices in favour of rights and against injustice. 'It is', he stresses, the 'confidence in faith that lonely individuals or small groups can confront and withstand the challenges of larger and stronger groups . . . In other words, a numerical and quantitative mode of self-awareness and awareness of the other is the very antithesis of the mode of awareness in terms of faith.'[42]

Keeping in view the present-day situation, the question of 'minority/majority' has created considerable unrest in both the First World and the Third World. He explains his position with an example:

> When a blind man is waiting to cross a street, those who are blessed with sight, unless they are blind in a far more profound sense, help him to cross to the other side. The blind man has thus a right over his fellow man, and the fact that he is handicapped and that he is just one person has nothing to do with this right that he has over others. Both rights and the responsibilities that go with them are a matter of human response to a human condition.[43]

But if the right of a blind man waiting to cross the road is determined by his colour, class, race, religion or nationality and we refuse to help him, then, Askari argues, 'something very seriously wrong has entered the human situation – an abnormality or sickness which is too familiar to comment upon'.[44]

7 Khurshid Ahmad (1932–)

Khurshid Ahmad was born in Delhi in 1932. He had a traditional Islamic education at home and completed his secondary education in an Anglo-Arabic Higher Secondary School in Delhi. At the time of India's partition, his family moved temporarily to Lahore and later settled in Karachi. He enrolled at the Government College of Commerce and Economics and graduated in economics. In 1955, he took an MA in the same discipline; in 1958 he became a Bachelor of Law; and in 1964 he took an MA in Islamic Studies. He proved to be a brilliant student. His formal training in these disciplines was to have a decisive influence on his later, public life. Through the study of economics and law 'not only did he develop a propensity for empirical and sociological analysis (something that is very rare among active Muslim workers), but he also acquired that uniquely "practical" bent of his personality, the ability to give a concrete, institutional form to vague dreams and visions . . .'[1]

Delhi provided him with a multicultural environment. He describes how from 'a very early age I was in contact with Muslims, Hindus, Christians and Sikhs in particular'. This encouraged him, in later life: 'when I was working', he says, 'for my Masters in Islamic Studies, one of the subjects was Comparative Religions. That further increased my interest in the comparative study of Islam, Christianity and other religions.'[2]

During his student life he had an obsession – to have command of the English language. This led him to read Jawaharlal Nehru's writings, which guided him, gradually, towards 'secularism' and 'atheistic thought'. Through Nehru's writings he discovered N.M. Roy, whose writings further developed and deepened atheistic roots in him. Later, he says, he read Bertrand Russell, John Stuart Mill and others, whose writings inspired scepticism and doubts about various aspects of human life, especially about religion and God. He was searching for a direction. During these years of intellectual wandering he sought the advice of a close friend, who advised him either to read the literature of the Communist Party or Mawdudi's writings and to understand the system of *Jamaat-e-Islami*. Although Mawdudi was a close friend of his father, Aziz Ahmad, Khurshid discovered him through *Tanqīhat* (lit. Evaluation), *Tafhīmat* (lit. Explications) and *Khutbat* (lit. Orations or Sermons). The writings of Iqbal – *The Reconstruction of Religious Thought* – and Mohammad Asad's *Islam at the Crossroads* attracted him to Islamic thought in general. These proved to be the turning point in his life.[3]

Khurshid joined *Islami Jamiat-e-Talaba* and became its national President from 1953 to 1955. Then he joined *Jamaat-e-Islami* in Pakistan in 1956, was elected to its Central Executive Council in 1957, and is currently one of the four *Na'ib Amir* (deputy leaders) of the organization. As editor and translator into English of Mawdudi's thoughts, he became one of the best communicators of *Jamaat-e-Islami* outside Pakistan.

He is an activist. His very mission in *Jamaat-e-Islami* is to establish Islam in all its totality in Pakistan. This brings out the whole question of Shari'ah – its meaning and implementation, as well as its relation to other believers. This makes a discussion on him more significant. How does an activist, and not a theologian as such, understand dialogue in its wider context? Secondly, his experience of living in the West, especially in Britain, and maintaining a continuous connection with various Islamic organizations and institutions in the West, provides an added dimension to his views on dialogue. Furthermore, during his stay, he has actively participated in and organized dialogues, mainly with Christians, but also with Jews, at regional, national and international levels.

Khurshid first came to England in 1966. From 1969 to 1972 he joined the University of Leicester as a research scholar. This was a period for encountering questions dealing not only with the challenges that come from secular ideologies or from Western civilization as such, but also with the challenges that come from the Christian and Jewish religions. He argues that there are major areas where Islam and Christianity cannot meet, but he stresses that 'there is also a vast area where our approach is common'. But he points out the approach of the Churches is much more accommodating of 'the Western civilization and culture', rather than realizing that the Church 'has a much higher role to play in the future of mankind . . .'.[4]

His direct involvement in dialogue began when he decided to live in England for a longer period. He established the Islamic Foundation in Leicester in 1968, but began functioning in 1973. Through the activities of the Foundation, he was exposed to various national and international dialogues, especially with Christians. He also took the initiative to have a multi-religious dialogue involving Jews. This step, he notes, had 'some political risk element, but somehow', he stresses, 'I didn't give that much importance and I thought that as a man of religion, we should try to rise above immediate political interests'. He further says, 'if there is a possibility of developing some kind of faith-based approach to the problems with which humanity is confronted today, this is worth trying'.[5] Once this multi-religious dialogue had developed he was elected Vice-President of the Standing Conference on Jews, Christians and Muslims in England (JCM), 1974–8. He became a member of the Advisory Council of the Centre for the Study of Islam and Christian–Muslim Relations (CSIC), Selly Oak Colleges, Birmingham, 1976–78. He was invited to give a series of lectures as a Visiting Professor on 'Islam', 'Christian–Muslim Dialogue' and 'Islam and Orientalism' by the Free University of Amsterdam and the Catholic University of Nijmegen in 1976. In the same year, he was invited by the Pontifical Institute for Arabic and Islamic Studies, in Rome, to give a series of lectures on Islam.

DEFINITION AND BASIS OF DIALOGUE

For Khurshid the definition of dialogue is simple: 'instead of talking about each other, we should start talking with each other'. He claims that this is 'the real spirit and ethos of dialogue'.[6] He finds, as a Muslim, the basis for dialogue with other religions to be in the teachings of the Qur'an. It is the unity of divine revelation which, he argues, gives one the strength and encouragement to involve oneself in dialogue. The 'element of divine message' in all religions must encourage us all to engage in a meaningful dialogue. He contends that the Muslim 'approach is not exclusivist, our approach is not isolationist'. A Muslim, he argues, by definition, 'belongs to the whole family of divinely guided people'. As a Muslim all 'faith-based communities have some relationship to my faith, my community and my approach to the world'. Therefore, a natural consequence 'is contact, conversation, dialogue, amongst men of faith in particular'.[7]

Secondly, Islam is by nature a religion of *Da'wah* or invitation. Once a Muslim accepts that what he believes has an 'outward direction', 'an invitation open to all', and is not limited to blood-ties and political and economic interests, then he will share his faith with everybody and anybody. For Khurshid this is also a part of dialogue, which involves 'knowing, learning, reaching, talking, discussing, persuading each other'.[8]

Thirdly, he emphasizes, God has given people the right to choose and freedom of choice, 'even the right of a man to refuse to accept God as his Lord'. This shows, he claims, that 'variety [and] plurality is not abnormal, it is not an aberration . . . it is not something to be eliminated, it has to be accepted.' Khurshid stresses this is only possible 'through dialogue, through contact, otherwise we would go for either a strategy of isolation where everyone lives in his own world or a strategy of elimination where there would be a perpetual struggle and warfare . . .'.[9]

Fourthly, he stresses that the Qur'an has laid out in clear terms that a Muslim is not allowed to abuse the gods of others. 'While we do not subscribe to them, we do not regard them as right and just, which means a state of co-existence'. He calls this 'a state of pro-existence, where you respect each others' position without agreeing to it or subscribing to it'.[10]

Fifthly, he argues that the Qur'anic critique of Christianity and its encouragement and invitation to Christians to share in a common cause should be taken seriously (Al-i-Imran 3:64). This is the verse that he calls '*Ayatul-Hewar*'[11] (verse of dialogue), which makes it 'incumbent upon the Muslims to invite the Christians and Jews and by implication to all to a dialogue, to a discussion that if there is some area of agreement then the area of disagreement should not hold us from at least co-operating as far as the area of agreement is concerned'. He stresses that in dialogue there has to be some common ground, otherwise, as he puts it, 'it would be a dialogue between deaf and dumb'.[12]

He finds that even within the area of difference there is a point where we can share with others. He points out, though, 'our concept of *Tawhīd* may not be shared by others', somehow we all 'claim to believe in that God. Look toward Him as the Guide, the Lord, believe that [our] return is towards Him [and] . . . look towards Him for salvation, for guidance, for light, for grace, whatever that be'. In this approach to God he finds an area 'which can provide a basis of commonality, of co-operation, of co-existence'. Along with that, 'there can be an area of differences where we can continue to discuss and differ and live with our differences and that is what dialogue is'.[13]

Finally, Khurshid traces in the Qur'an two fundamental needs of human beings – survival and procreation. In both these areas he argues that Islam has 'opened the gates of a perpetual relationship' between Muslims and Christians and Muslims and Jews. He stresses that Kosher meat is also 'Kosher for me'. He has some hesitation, though, about eating meat slaughtered by the Christians because 'when Christianity was proposed in Europe [it] somehow moved away from the Judaic-Christian tradition of the credulous civilization that was the Middle East, [and] they departed from the manner of slaughtering of the animals too'.[14] Yet he finds a valid basis for meeting at the dining table, at least with the Jews.

He also points out that Islam has given permission to Muslims to marry a Christian or Jewish woman, and she can remain a Christian or a Jew and be the 'wife of a Muslim, a member of its family and responsible for the procreation of humanity'. Khurshid argues these are two major 'dimensions of human conditions and in both there is a contact between the three religions, their co-existence, their perpetual dialogues have been institutionalized'.[15]

DA'WAH/MISSION AND DIALOGUE

Khurshid suggests *Da'wah* is a 'built-in mechanism' in Islam. *Da'wah*, he argues, 'keeps the community as well as individuals who compose it, active and upright, ensures the moral health of the individual and the community and acts as a corrective force and a blessing for the whole of mankind'.[16] Islam's primary concern, and therefore the purpose of *Da'wah*, is 'to build correct relationships between God and man, between man and man and between man and society'. The central issue, according to Islam, he stresses, 'is not man's need to know the person of God and to extricate himself from a vicarious predicament by seeking the grace of a Saviour, but his need for *Hidāyah* (Divine Guidance) to enable him to know the will of God and to try to live in obedience to it'.[17] Here one can find a profound difference of approach between Islam and Christianity towards life, its mission and purpose.

Da'wah, in his opinion, has to be given in an atmosphere of freedom, where individuals have choice. Islam, he argues, 'does not believe in forced uniformity which is against the demands of nature'. Islam, in his view, 'accepts differences as authentic'. This acceptance provides 'a *modus vivendi* for different individuals, societies, cultures, religions and civilizations to live side by side with each other, competing in what is good, tolerating where they differ and as such able to work for seeking what is good for mankind and what brings man nearer to God'.[18] He further argues that just to turn towards God is not enough, cooperation 'in society and its organization to achieve *Adl* (justice) and *Ihsan* (moral excellence and benevolence) is a Divine imperative'.[19]

Can dialogue be part of *Da'wah* or mission? Khurshid has no qualms about it. As we have seen earlier, dialogue to him is a part of *Da'wah*. He is prepared to accept dialogue as a part of mission. 'I have no quarrel with it', he finds, 'as long as it is a religious mission . . . as long as it is dialogue, as long as it is an invitation, as long as it is an effort to share. I welcome it.' One must not try, as he puts it, to 'cheat' or 'masquerade', and he stresses the importance of not allowing 'such methods as will imperil the morality, the spirituality and the religiosity of the whole effort' either by the Christians or by the Muslims.[20]

Khurshid has articulated the areas of mission which Muslims feel unhappy about. He points out that, in the past, some missionaries who arrived in Asian or African countries 'might have been motivated by the best of spiritual intentions' and he emphasizes this is not among the points in dispute. The Churches' emphasis on *diakonia* (service), he says, 'is a laudable objective and effort, no one can be opposed to that'. What he opposes is 'when *diakonia* becomes an instrument of proselytization, conversion and influences a person not morally, intellectually, ideologically, reaching a person not through dialogue or discussion but trying to exploit his weakness, whether he is a child . . . sick or under strain, poor . . .'.[21]

Khurshid, writing as guest editor of the *International Review of Mission*, sums up the Muslim critique of Christian mission in the following four points:

1. Gross and flagrant misrepresentation of the teachings of Islam and of the life and message of the Prophet Muhammad (peace be upon him). Instead of examining Islam as it is, a totally unreal picture of Islam was concocted and used to denigrate Islam and Muslims. Although the high watermark of this type of approach to the study of Islam has passed, the effort still persists, even though low in profile and under many a disguise.

2. The methodology of Christian mission concentrated upon influencing the object in a state of weakness and helplessness. Instead of direct invitation, approaches were made to those who were disadvantaged, exploiting their weaknesses for the sake of proselytism. The poor, the sick and the immature were made special targets of economic assistance, medical aid and education. Many a Christian mission acted as an organic part of colonialism and cultural imperialism. All this was a very unfair way to bring people to any religion.

3. Whatever the ultimate aim, subversion of the faith and culture of Islam seems to have been the prime target of the Christian mission-

ary enterprise. Nationalism, secularism, modernism, socialism, even communism were fostered, supported and encouraged, while the revival of Islam and the strengthening of Islamic moral life among the Muslims were, and even now are, looked upon as anathema.

4. Muslims were treated as political rivals and as such subjected to overt and covert discrimination and repression. Their just causes fail to evoke any significant moral response from the Christian world . . . Muslims are puzzled when they compare the relative lack of Christian concern over the increasing de-Christianization of the Christian world with their obsession to what amounts to de-Islamization of the Muslim world.[22]

In later dialogues he pursued this line of argument.

THE CHURCHES AND DIALOGUE

The initiative of the Churches especially the Second Vatican Council and after, and the World Council of Churches, Khurshid points out, has been very encouraging. But whereas dialogue began with enthusiasm and hope, now he finds 'stalemate or simple repetition of what was said earlier'. A position where 'we are moving', he says, 'in blind alleys and the breakthrough is not around'.[23] He claims the WCC 'made a good beginning, but somehow midway they realized that the way things had unfolded did not enable them to achieve the objective they had in mind'.[24]

Refering to the Second Vatican Council's appeal 'to forget the past', he notes, 'the message that I get from the . . . Council and what I myself believe in is that the past should not become a shackle'.[25] He suggests that in the past there were many things which had been very good, 'reassuring' and 'rewarding', yet others were 'obnoxious', 'disturbing'. He argues that both are important today. It is 'only through learning from the past that the present and the future can be protected'.[26] He suggests that the past should not be allowed to become a 'bottleneck', neither should the difference be 'exaggerated'. One cannot ignore the past; ignoring the past, Khurshid argues, is 'a positive disadvantage'. He stresses the need to recognize the differences, but these should not become a hurdle in dialogue.

Khurshid describes the last 40 years of the Churches' initiative and experiment in dialogue as a 'positive' step. He reminds us that 'four decades . . . are not sufficient time to make final judgement'[27] on the issues of dialogue. He notes that despite the 'degree of coolness', compared to earlier dialogue, 'the chapter is not closed' and it would be better if both Christians and Muslims 'leave it open'.

MUSLIMS IN THE WEST AND DIALOGUE OF CULTURES

Khurshid's recurring theme is Islam and the West. He looks at the whole encounter between the two, Muslim minorities in Europe, and religious plurality and democracy from Islamic resurgence perspective. He describes the West as a 'concept and a culture'. He places much emphasis on the forces of history and civilization.[28] Therefore, the West is not purely a geographical entity, and he describes Western culture as being 'in its late phase of maturity'.[29]

He compares the West with Islam – Islam being faith and a civilization – and argues that the West did not perceive Islam as a civilization or religion, but 'merely as a rival political power'. Describing the popular image of Islam (of 'Arabian Nights' and 'Anti-Christ') in the West, he argues, 'these images were blown into existence to serve specific purposes', and claims that 'they were inflated or deflated to suit the shifting sands of politico-religious relationships between the world of Islam and the West'.[30] He notes that although these images have now begun to fade, they 'pollute the public mind and constitute an obstacle to the growth of a correct and sympathetic understanding of Islam and the Muslim life'.[31]

In the contemporary situation, he finds that the Islamic resurgence in the West is seen as 'fanaticism' and 'militant'. Khurshid believes the resurgent Islam or Islamic movements 'have their roots deep in the society of the Muslim people, medieval as well as modern'. He remarks that these 'movements have mostly been conveniently ignored by the Western observers of the Islamic scene, who have confined their gaze to the ripples on the surface of the water, never caring to understand the currents and cross-currents beneath the surface'.[32]

The urge, that the West should understand what Muslims are saying, is ever more alive in his writing and speeches. He reminds the West again: 'Muslims do not constitute a threat to the West.' He describes how there 'is no indication or even a remote possibility of any Muslim armed incursion into any Western country or even a threat of sabotage of their political system'. He emphasizes that 'Muslims are only trying to set their own house in order. They want the right to order their individual and collective lives and institutions in accordance with their own values and ideals'.[33] He argues that the Islamic resurgence is not against modernization, but Muslims want to do this 'in the context of their own culture and values'. What they disapprove of is 'impositions of Western culture and values' upon a people 'who have their own distinct culture and civilization'.[34] He emphasizes that there is a possibility of coming closer and having a closer relationship between Islam and the West. 'If China and the United States and Russia . . . and India can have friendly relations without sharing [a] common culture and politico-economic system, why not the West and the Muslim world?' *Much depends upon how the West looks upon this phenomenon of Islamic resurgence and wants to come to terms with it*'.[35] (Khurshid's italics). He urges passionately that differences should be resolved 'peacefully through dialogue and understanding, through respect for each other's rights and genuine concerns'.[36] In a long article on the subject, he points out that the disagreement between France and America in the GATT agreement on cultural issues is a good indicator. A completely free trade policy may put Europe, and France in particular, at risk from American cultural invasion. Khurshid asks, 'Is it too much if Muslims expect the same sensitivity to be shown to their own cultural concerns and religious sensitivities?'[37]

Describing the Muslim situation in Europe, and referring to the educated elite, Khurshid argues that this small percentage of Muslims have wielded a considerable influence in community affairs, they can articulate the community's case to the local and national social and political bodies. But their involvement within the community is often minimal. The bulk of the community consists of unskilled or semi-skilled labourers. 'Their commitment', he finds, 'to religion is more traditional and less rational.' Referring to the community's elders, or the first-generation immigrants, in most cases, it has been seen, they have a limited knowledge of the indigenous languages, English, French or German, and they 'find it difficult to develop a dialogue on religion or ideological matters with the local people'. 'Psychologically', he argues, 'also most of them are primarily interested in the wage nexus. This has naturally affected their outlook and areas of interest.'[38]

Khurshid points out that the most important problem Muslims in the West are facing is 'to maintain and strengthen their distinct religious and cultural identity while participating positively in the national life of their homeland'.[39] Muslim culture, he stresses, is a 'value-oriented culture and the Muslim community derives its identity from its religion. That is why religion is not regarded as a personal affair.'[40] The behaviour of the community takes shape and pattern in dress, food, marriage and family life. This may not be very important from the Western perspective, but it is of crucial importance for Muslims. Lack of full appreciation of this culturally important area of Muslim behaviour, in his opinion, is at the root of many tensions.[41]

Democracy, which is supposed to bail out this situation, Khurshid finds completely inadequate. 'The basic problem with the Western democracy', he contends, 'is that it has been developed as primarily a political system. The idea of cultural and social democracy is still undeveloped.'[42] He argues that the recent developments in communications and technology in the world of commerce and tourism, etc., are forcing upon us the ideal of a 'multi-cultural' and 'multi-religious' society. He contends that the idea of a multi-cultural and multi-religious society cannot be an abstract idea, and points out the change not only should reflect 'attitude', but also 'institutions and laws'.[43] Here he suggests a dialogue of 'Muslim experience', which accepts 'plurality of cultures, religions and life-style', could be of great help. This, he emphasizes, is not merely an idea but a historical reality.

Although Muslim experience could be very useful, Khurshid finds that Muslims in Europe are in a state of 'unpreparedness' and are 'ill-equipped for the task ahead'. He points out the 'old groups and loyalties' persist amongst Muslims and lack of 'enlightened and committed leadership' makes the matter worse.[44] To overcome this state of 'unpreparedness' Khurshid suggests that the Muslim community should evolve 'a new pattern of Islamic life and culture in the context of the Western society'. He stresses that they 'should live as full participants and not as pseudo-citizens. They have to develop a new mode of life, in consonance with the values and norms of Islam and in the context of local conditions'[45] and not transplant it from their country of origin. They have to leave behind their nomadism. Once this 'nomadism' has been uprooted or even faded from memory, Khurshid states, 'Muslims in Europe can make a significant contribution by developing the vision of multi-cultural, multi-religious and multi-racial societies'.[46] In the past the minorities, he argues, were instrumental in evolving 'political democracy', and he suggests that Muslim experience can help in evolving a socially and culturally rich democracy.

But did the issue of *The Satanic Verses* in Britain and the head scarf issue in France help towards cultural understanding? Khurshid suggests that both issues have been blown up out of proportion 'due to the media or due to human failing'; 'things which are of marginal importance quite often' affect 'the relations between Muslims and Christians or Islam and the Western world'.[47] He stresses that the relationship between Islam and Muslims in the West, as well as with the Christians are more 'fundamental issues'. He finds that, as in the past, both Muslims and Christians will be able to live in harmony and understanding 'without risking the whole fabric of relationships on issues' like these.[48] He points out that there is variation within Western culture as far as dress is concerned from 'bikini to evening dress', and this variation is accepted as natural. But what is unnatural in this spectrum, the colour of *Hijāb* (scarf), immediately becomes obnoxious and unacceptable, and threatens relations between Muslims and Christians and local culture.[49] Khurshid suggests future dialogues should address issues like *The Satanic Verses*, which have been described and protected as 'freedom of expression', and the scarf issue in France,, which has been perceived as a threat to local culture.

SHARI'AH – ITS MEANING AND PERSPECTIVES

Khurshid has been one of the chief protagonists of Shari'ah. Since his days as a student he has been active in the movement to implement of Shari'ah in Pakistan as well as helping and encouraging the efforts made by others in the Muslim world. In various dialogues in Tripoli, Chambesy and Colombo, he has emphasized that 'Christians should not object to the Muslim effort to build their society on the basis of the Shari'ah',[50] rather, Christians should help Muslims in this process. He writes: 'Shari'ah means, literally, the path and in Islam it stands for the path that has been spelled out in the Qur'an and *Sunnah*. So Shari'ah is defined as the Qur'an and *Sunnah*.'[51] He points out that it has a number of dimensions in the areas of commands and commendations. Commands (*Ahkam*) relate to what is prohibited (*Harām*) and what is made obligatory (*Fard*). Commendable means one that is disliked (*Makrūh*), the other that is preferred or advised (*Mustahab*) and the rest is permissible (*Mubāh*). Khurshid argues that the 90–5 per cent of *Shari'ah's* areas come under the list of permissible or *Mubāh*. He suggests that 'within the legal framework there is a vast area of flexibility, innovation, change, evolution'. He stresses that it is only the 'framework which has to be protected' and within that framework there is plenty of room for 'change and evolution'.[52] But Shari'ah is not mere legality, 'there are also moral imperatives' and 'spirituality', which help to fulfil the injunctions of Shari'ah. This is what Shari'ah is.

   Khurshid disagrees with the suggestion that Muslims are not defining Shari'ah properly. This suggestion, he argues, is due to the fact that their outlook is Western and secular, where the law can be enforced through the law courts only. In Islam, law has a wider view. The injunction (*Ahkam*) of Islam also deals with areas like prayers, fasting and *Zakah* (poordue). The Anglo-Saxon legal perspective is inadequate to understand such a wide concept of Shari'ah. A second difficulty from the Christian perspective, Khurshid points out, is in the approach to the Old and the New Testaments. The two were not looked upon by the later Christians as complementary; rather the New Testament was seen in isolation. In that perspective Shari'ah considers Christians as something 'non-spiritual' or 'non-religious'. He suggests that 'the Christians should be happy to see that Muslims demand for Shari'ah to be the basis of their individual familial and collective life' and argues they 'should not look upon these as either encroachment of their rights or as a defeat for the value system which some people think would mean a loss to Christianity . . . and to think that Westernization is helpful to Christianization' is incorrect.[53] He emphasizes that Muslims are asking that Shari'ah be introduced for Muslims only. Or where it has been introduced, introduced only in Muslim majority areas, even in a country where Muslims are in the majority.

Christians are caught in a situation where, in countries like Pakistan, the Sudan or Nigeria, they have been able to find not only freedom from colonial rule but are also trying to sever their relations with whole systems of the colonial legacy, so the Christians are trying to respond in a way which dissociates them from the former colonial systems. That problem in itself is enough to be faced. The other much more serious matter is the Muslim insistence on Shari'ah with the confidence they have found in Islam. Christians find themselves, perhaps unwittingly, on the side of past colonialists in opposition to Shari'ah. Khurshid insists that Muslims have to make sure that Christians have 'full protection of their rights, giving them the opportunities in whatever fields, religion, education, culture, they want to protect and develop and perfect their identity . . . [including] all the human rights'.[54]

Referring to Pakistan's Christian population, which is about 1 per cent of the population, Khurshid argues that in the contemporary political climate of Pakistan it would have been 'very difficult for them to get elected to the Parliament, yet we have developed a system of election where non-Muslims elect their own representative', whether Christian, Hindu or Parsee. Describing his own participation in parliamentary committees he claims that 'we had threadbare discussions with both the Roman Catholic as well as the Anglican bishops in Pakistan, we invited even Parsees, we invited not only the Members of Parliament but the Bishops were invited to the Parliament to come and discuss with us their rights in the country'.[55] Khurshid is now a Senator in Pakistan's Parliament, finds an opportunity of dialogue with other religious representatives and finds a worthwhile role in that capacity.

The introduction of the Shari'at Bill, moved on 13 July 1985, has generated an emotional debate in the country. The Christian press was unanimously opposed to it. Khurshid argues in one of his earlier works: 'the true position is that the representatives of the Christians in the First Constituent Assembly of Pakistan and some of the leaders of the scheduled castes, who form the most important minority, have demanded the establishment of an Islamic state, for they hold that their rights can be better safeguarded in such a state . . .'[56]

8 Mohammed Talbi (1921–)

Mohammed Talbi, was born in 1921 in Tunisia, and is the eldest son of ten children – five brothers and five sisters. He was brought up in a traditional Muslim home, which left an indelible mark on his life. Under the guidance of his grandfather, the family prayed the daily prayers together in the courtyard of their home. *Du'a* (supplication) and committing to memory parts of the Qur'an by heart were an accepted form. Unlike his uncle, who preferred to send his children to a traditional school and later to al-Zaytuna University of Theology, Talbi's father sent him to French primary and secondary schools. This experience of coming out of a traditional environment and entering an entirely new system provided a great deal of opportunity to compare the two systems. Talbi reflects this experience in various writings. Coming in contact with the French education system was the beginning of an encounter with believers of other religions. 'Abruptly', he says, 'I was immersed among many Christians, and some Jewish children. It is so that, in the long run, I became what is called a "Western-educated scholar".'[1]

Talbi's immersion in the French education system took him, in 1947, to Paris for further education. 1947 to 1966 was a shuttling period between Tunis and Paris. He used to earn his living as a teacher in Tunis and spend it as a student in Paris. In 1966, he completed his doctoral thesis on *L'Emirat Aghlabide 184–296/800–909 Histoire Politique*. Finally, he returned to Tunis to join the Faculty of History at the University of Tunis, where he taught Islamic history until his retirement in 1986.

In Talbi's life we can identity two important developments. The period between graduation and the completion of his PhD was the formative period of this thought. This was also a period of contacts with other believers, including atheists and Marxists. This period in his life was also a period of comparison between the two cultures, one which he belongs to and the other which he is learning from, but at the time he was bitter about the occupation of his country. He says:

> ... in a 'protected' country – Tunisia – I experienced the suffering of being a second zone citizen in my own land. We were then called

'indégines' (natives). The dignity of being a nation, with an old and valuable civilization was denied to us. We had to be civilized afresh. Among our protectors it was commonly felt, sincerely and offendingly at the same time, that this was a sacred duty which a superior civilization owes to populations which were less advanced.[2]

Giving an example of the writing of E.F. Gautier, *The Islamization of North Africa: The Dark Ages of the Maghreb*, Talbi notes: 'To say the least it is evident that the Islamic civilization was not highly appreciated. [And] . . . little has changed since then.'[3] This educational and learning process in and with the West provided Talbi with the necessary tools to point out the path to be selected for a better understanding between Islam and the West, and Christianity in particular, which we shall discuss later.

This encounter with the West also provided Talbi with an opportunity to look deep into his own tradition, consider it afresh and identify the country's ailment. Whether it is a question of the *Ummah* and its role, or women, or opening up to other cultures and civilizations and the encounter of the revivalist movement at home and abroad, these are a few highlights which he addresses to Muslims. Basically, he encourages Muslim intellectuals to practise *Ijtihad*.

THE CONCEPT OF THE *UMMAH*

Talbi reflects on the situation of the *Ummah* – its development and challenges within, and in relation to, other communities. The Muslim *Ummah*, he stresses, is no longer a 'geographical entity'. The *Ummah* 'is no longer one nation and there is no longer a nation whose citizens are all Muslim'.[4] Considering the emerging scenario of the Muslims, he describes the term *Ummah* comprehensively: 'there is a community every time there is an assembly of people who have things in common and are aware of it, whether these be physical or moral concerns, worldly or spiritual goods, or concrete or abstract aims to be achieved'.[5] He urges the Muslim community to be open-minded so that one can be receptive yet maintain commitment to one's roots in one's milieu and tradition. Talbi's view on the *Ummah* can be briefly summarized under the following seven broad sub-titles:

Confused Boundaries

The *Ummah* within secure geographical boundaries, with a Caliph at its head, no longer exists. For economic reasons, Muslims have to leave their homes in large numbers and now they live in their millions in the West. He points out these 'unwelcome guests' in the Western countries are 'confused [about] their boundaries'. 'Islam as a cultural phenomenon, which is rooted deeply in authenticity, is still alive and widely in demand', but he finds, on the other hand, Islam as a faith, 'as a living conviction, a commitment and metaphysical certainty, as well as a religious observance, is at crisis point . . .'.[6] He cites Lebanon as an example, and points out that the concept of the *Ummah* has been 'manipulated for all kinds of ends . . . In spite of the deliberately confusing nature of the vocabulary used' in Lebanon 'neither Christianity nor Islam, as religious convictions and communities of living faith, are truly responsible for the happenings there'.[7]

A New Meaning of *Ummah* is Taking Shape

The term *Ummah*, which is associated so closely with the term '*Arabiyyah*' and interlocked with the 'unitary political structure', Talbi finds 'is undiscovered and unrealised'. The Arabs, who use this term so exclusively to identify with nationhood, are losing their grip on the term. He proposes that the Arab nations – now divided in various boundaries and at the moment independent in their behaviour – should use the term *Sha'b* (people). The constant use of the term *Ummah* may raise false assumptions. He argues that the new situation which has emerged is irreversible: 'the frontiers of the *Ummah*', he stresses, 'are no longer extended over the earth. They are now exclusively in the hearts of those who pray, whether in Sweden, China, Cairo or anywhere else. The Germans or Malaysians can be part of it, while Tunisians or the Egyptians can be excluded from it by their free and conscious choice'.[8] The motivating force which keeps the hearts of Muslims and the sense of community, he argues, remains in the Qur'an, and not in the culture of a country. He stresses that the great change that is taking place is not a bad thing. He describes that 'the concept of *Darul al-Islam* had perhaps become a stifling ghetto and an obstacle to progress. The *Ummah* could no longer be contained with its limits.' He emphasizes the need to redefine the *Ummah*'s laws, which could extend beyond the geographical boundaries. He claims that:

Islam as a faith is not a nation, but it is part of a nation. It is a religious community. The thinking of Muslims is therefore called upon to reconcile his/her loyalty to the faith with his/her many other loyalties. On the national, or one might even say universal scale, in a world which is very complex and diverse and where there are other groups based on faith in God or some other force, with which exchanges are necessary.[9]

Ummah and other Communities

Talbi argues that in today's changing world isolation is suicidal. He stresses that the *Ummah* 'must construct a necessarily pluralist universe in conjunction with others'. But is this contrary to the spirit of Islam? 'Not at all,' he claims. 'Islam is certainly a unified totality, but it is open-minded. It accepts and respects diversity.' He finds a significant example of such coexistence in the Constitution of Madinah.[10]

Talbi has apprehensions too. The era of civilization comprising various communities – will that be a facilitating force for individuals? Or will it be a 'crushing machine', suffocating the much needed development of 'personality' and 'individuality'. That remains to be seen. The only thing, he suggests, that this generation can do is 'to redefine the nature of their internal links in order to save their respective identities',[11] and this should be done whilst respecting the freedom of individuals and groups, and without becoming an obstructive force.

Circles of 'faithful' and those of 'no faith'

The circles of faithful, in Talbi's writings, include Muslims, Jews and Christians – the People of the Book. The people who have 'no faith' he describes as those who believe that a religion and all its aspects are irrelevant in today's world.

Talbi argues that although, historically, Islam covers two communities – Jews and Christians – as the People of the Book, the Qur'an mentions that there were messengers sent by God to various people. He points out, on the basis of the teachings of the Qur'an, that 'in terms of faith, the circumference of an even wider community is evident, extending beyond that of the people of Abraham'. This he terms 'the community of Service to God', despite the different perceptions of God in many religions they received the revelations and they are 'the community of those who pray with pure and sincere hearts'.[12]

The second group, those who have 'no faith' or 'at least believe they do not', Talbi deals with from an existential point of view. Both groups with 'faith' and 'no faith' are sharing this world together. None of the group would like to 'rock the boat, the space ship of our diverse, mutual humanity' and fate are linked together by 'earthly ties'. So far as the earth is concerned, God has no preference. Pointing out the Qur'anic imperative – the earth will be the inheritance of those who serve Him well (Al-Anbiya 21:105) – he stresses that 'religious communities can easily lose their way, misinterpret the Word of God, allow themselves to become blinded by their passions and appetite and cease to be "good followers"'.[13]

Ummah **and its Mission**

Talbi distinguishes the mission of the *Ummah* at two levels – that of ideal and theories, and that of commitment and action. He urges that this distinction should be treated with care. As we have seen earlier, the *Ummah* at a spiritual level is alive and active, but at the geographical level, the *Ummah* is tied up with various regimes – or manipulated by them.

At the first level – ideal and theories – Talbi finds the mystery of God. God commands the *Ummah* to preserve and transmit His Word – 'the most precious confidence (*Amānah*) it has received. The Word is Universal, it is aimed at all people' (Al-A'raf 7:158). All people are therefore urged ultimately to be part of the one same community of brothers' 'loving God with all their heart and loving each other in God'. But 'God in His infinite and unfathomable wisdom did not wish . . . it must be earned'. In this pattern of God's plan, the role of the Muslim community, must be to merit and accept the mission bestowed on it, which consists of avoiding extremes and acting as a witness.[14]

The area which is less clear, Talbi argues, is the area of commitment and action. Unlike the principles, the 'process of action is always confused and its results are uncertain'. At a political level, he argues, faith should not be allowed to be compromised. He stresses that a Muslim cannot leave the political domain, but to make the 'community a state', he contends, 'has never succeeded . . .'. He encourages Muslims to participate in politics through a political group without jeopardizing their affiliation to the religious group. He suggests that a Muslim should not involve his faith as such by siding with one regime or an other.[15] He encourages Muslims to *Ijtihad* in matters of such political and social transition.

A Community of Trust

The *Ummah*, along with other communities, Talbi argues, should 'reconcile their right to be different with mutual understanding and collaboration, on all levels, spiritual and material'. It is 'respect for all that is to be respected'. Arguing a seemingly contradicting situation – bearing witness and the rights of others – Talbi describes as 'loyalty to oneself and to one's community, receptivity and keenness to bear witness and to give freedom of passage and respect for the opinion of others; these are not contradictory but complementary notions or attitudes'.[16] He argues that Islam is different, and it 'must defend its right to be different'. But Muslims should also afford the same right to others. If a community is behaving differently – in their politics, profession, etc. – and does not recognize Muhammad as Prophet and does not accept the Qur'an as the Word of God, then the gulf certainly is wide, but, as Talbi argues, 'there is always room for harmony where there is mutual respect'.[17]

What the *Ummah* is not

Talbi describes Islam as of this world, but at the same time it is of the other world. He links the two worlds, as Islam does, and further points out that the *Ummah* which is rooted in Islam has only one authority to answer. 'Caesar is not above God, and does not have at his disposal any private domain of which he is the sole independent Lord.'[18]

TALBI AND DIALOGUE

Definition of Dialogue

Dialogue for Talbi is a 'state of mind, an atmosphere, an opening. . . . an attitude of friendship or of comprehension'.[19] This comprehension and opening, he feels, is much more urgently needed by Islam. Islam, in his words, has long lived within 'safe boundaries', but in today's new circumstances it can no longer afford to remain isolated. He finds Christianity has a lead over Islam, as it has never lost its contact with other religious beliefs. 'Thus dialogue for Islam', he argues, 'is first and foremost a necessary and vital re-establishment of contact with the world at large'.[20]

Conditions and Difficulties of Dialogue

Talbi states clearly that dialogue should not be looked upon as an 'art of compromise'. He views dialogue seriously and demands in it sincerity and freedom of expression, without hostility. He states quite clearly that the lack of equal partners in dialogue is a serious drawback. Referring to a situation which we have briefly touched upon, that Christian theology was in constant touch with other religions, compared to Islamic theology, he argues that after the twelfth century, Islam 'progressively lost its contact with the world'. He cites the examples of a number of Christian scholars who are equally knowledgeable in the development of their religion as in Islam. But he finds no parallel in Islamic tradition. He suggests that in such a situation Muslims 'must expose the things which give [rise to] mental reservations and distrust . . . in public in all frankness and serenity'.[21]

Secondly, in a situation where Christians and Muslims find themselves 'unequally prepared for dialogue', dialogue is 'possible between partners who make no secret of their own convictions'. He contests Mohammad Arkoun's suggestion that Christians could take over and assure the religious future of Islam, with the same determination, total commitment and the same depth of conviction with which they serve Christianity. It seems to Arkoun that this is the best way of preparing Muslims for future dialogue, since when one strives to set others free one frees oneself at the same time.[22] Talbi argues, 'one should never await passively to be liberated by others, but one should set about freeing oneself'.[23]

Thirdly, Talbi points out that the polemical spirit of the Middle Ages gave rise to the spirit of 'caricatures and falsifications by spreading lies in the name of truth', what he calls the spirit of adventure in new circumstances has no place in a serious dialogue. He suggests that the way of guaranteeing that such a negative influence is eradicated from the avenues of dialogue, 'is to remove any idea of using dialogues, either openly or in one's own mind, as a means of converting the person we are talking to'.[24]

Fourthly, the duty of witness – what Talbi calls 'the duty of the Apostolate' – is so important in Islam as well as in Christianity that it could become a hindrance if it takes the form of polemics or proselytizing. Witness, he emphasizes, must be 'an attentive openness towards our neighbour, an incessant seeking for truth through a continuous deepening and assimilation of the values of faith, and, in the final analysis, pure witness'.[25] This pure witness he stresses is *Jihad*.

Finally, the question of salvation could become an obstacle for dialogue. Talbi, without losing the central idea that Islam is The Way of Salvation for the whole of mankind, stresses that every religion claims that God is Justice, Mercy and Love. This is the very area where he suggests 'we need a real theological renewal and a radical change of mentality'.[26] He refers to the changes that took place in the Christian outlook about other religions, viz. the Second Vatican Council. He argues that Islam too has a similar attitude in the classical and modern theologies. With Ghazali, 'Abduh and Mahmud Shaltut, he believes 'when some parameters are worked out, it is not impossible to admit the plurality of the paths of salvation, outside the Islamic tradition for sincere and righteous people'.[27]

Risks in Dialogue

Talbi finds an 'excessive politeness in dialogue' and 'utopian hope', which makes people believe 'that ecumenism will be there in the very, very near future' not only inter-Christian but also inter-religious ecumenism. He warns that this 'tendency, generous in itself, leads us, if we do not watch out, to the illusion that very soon our people, our communities, will fall into each other's arms. This is a delusion stemming from an excess of optimism.'[28] He suggests that our hopes should not anchor themselves on convergence of our faith and the colloquia that we organize, but rather we should have faith in the Creator.

A second important risk he finds is the 'risk of situation'. Non-Muslims find themselves in Muslim countries and vice-versa. A very contentious issue is the question of *Dhimmī*. He argues that this problem is not only philosophical but also practical in nature. He finds the question of *Dhimmi* is like 'the old story of a bottle being described as half-full or half-empty'. Muslim historians paint a rosy picture of the status of *Dhimmī*, whereas the Jews and Christian historians see it differently. However, he suggests approaching this 'historically contentious question . . . with much realism, departing from our respective traditions'. He argues: 'today we live in a world, where *Dhimmī* no longer should exist. It has become imperative and absolutely indispensable to shelve this notion in the cupboard of history.'[29] This, he contends, is possible from an Islamic point of view.

A third risk is the 'temptation of proselytization'. 'Whoever believes in a truth, also has the tendency to communicate it. Something which is quite normal.' What he points out as a risk is mission 'conceived of as one-way traffic'. He detects the same tendency amongst Muslims too. This, he argues, creates difficulties where one partner in dialogue 'accuses the other of using less than honourable means'. He suggests that holding 'some colloquia with the purpose of defining the deontology respectful of the freedom of the other, respectful of God and respectful of human rights'[30] is essential.

Finally, Talbi points out, 'the obsession with insecurity' is another problem in dialogue. A community, when it finds itself in a minority, feels insecure, and this magnifies the 'risk of intolerance'. As an example he cites the state of Israel surrounded by Arab states. He suggests that Muslims and Christians should enter into 'a three-way dialogue' between the Abrahamic traditions.

The Purpose of Dialogue

Talbi finds a free exchange of ideas is beneficial to all. He points out the primary objective of dialogue is 'to remove barriers and to increase the amount of Good in the world by a free exchange of ideas'.[31] Having found inspiration in the declaration of *Nostra Aetate*, he feels quite confident in using the list suggested by the Second Vatican Council, e.g. 'What is man? What is the meaning and purpose of life? What is goodness and what is sin? What gives our sorrows and to what intent?' Each of these questions, he suggests, should be developed into a theme for dialogue inviting representatives from 'all religions, whether they have their scripture or not'.[32] But he stresses that the question should be a question for understanding and learning and not for interrogation.

Talbi argues that the purpose of dialogue could be unlimited, though its scope may not. The unlimited purpose perhaps is that the Muslims' participation in dialogue with non-Muslims may yet generate another dialogue within the Muslim community at various levels. 'By creating . . . a fertile climate of tension, which has so dramatically been lacking in Islam for centuries', he argues, 'dialogue could play the role of shaking Muslims out of their false sense of security and could make their hearts and ears once more attentive to the Message of God . . . in our present day understanding, listening to Him in the here-and-now or the present moment.'[33] He is against those who dissociate themselves from their past heritage, what he calls the 'wealth and positive advances' made by the *Ummah*, yet he is not in favour of clinging to the past. 'The precise purpose of dialogue, whatever the circumstances, is to reanimate constantly our faith, to save it from tepidity, and to maintain us in a permanent state of *Ijtihad*, that is a state of reflection and research.'[34]

DIALOGUE – THE CHURCHES AND MUSLIMS

Talbi, who showed enthusiasm for and found inspiration in the declaration of *Nostra Aetate*, finds that the Churches are taking a 'step inward' on the question of dialogue. He points out that both The Holy See and the World Council of Churches (WCC) have tried to link 'more clearly and more tightly the Mission with the Dialogue, in order to make more explicit their intrinsic relationship'.[35] He finds the reason for doing so is 'to ease the indoor criticisms'. Referring to the document promulgated by Pope John Paul II on the occasion of Pentecost (10 June 1984), 'exactly two decades after the creation of the Secretariatus Pro Non-Christianis', dialogue, he stresses, 'is clearly and emphatically subordinated to the Mission and embodied in it'.[36] The purpose, he argues, of dialogue as an independent vehicle of 'a respectful medium of peace, friendship and communication without intention to evangelize and convert has [been] lost'. Instead, he finds its 'declared aim is hence to be the first step on the way to evangelization and conversion'. He argues that once the aim and purpose changed, dialogue became no more than 'a tool adapted to the intellectuals'; 'in brief, a sophisticated equivalent of the bowl of rice and the healing pill used to attract, trap and convert the poor and the sick'. This dialogue, which he calls 'a fish-hook dialogue', he stresses, 'is not mine, and I am not ready by any means to swallow the bait'.[37] More recently, he has confirmed his position: 'for me', he says, 'at least as a Muslim it is not acceptable at all to divert dialogue from its goal – peace between religions and mutual comprehension – and to make of it simply a tool to reach another purpose, to transform it . . . into a mission endeavour'[38] is unacceptable.

He argues that to bear witness is an 'unquestionable human right and duty'. One cannot help 'trying or at least desiring to share with another person in a spirit of love'.[39] But the question of witness, he suggests, should not be confused with 'blind proselytism'. Witness to a faith, he argues, must come from within. Talbi finds this spirit missing in today's dialogue; rather there is an element, what he terms 'besiegement', in current dialogues. He finds the reason for less enthusiasm on the part of Muslims in dialogue is because they are 'tempted to see in it a kind of scaffolding for mission agencies'.[40]

Talbi has some suggestions for Muslims; 'first and foremost', he argues, 'to make it very clear that . . . the mission – or its equivalent, *Da'wah* on the side of Islam- is one thing, and the dialogue is another . . .'. He finds no benefit in mixing them. For the Muslims, he emphasizes, to do so is to put the 'Mission-Pill' into the 'Dialogue Box'.[41]

Dialogue to Talbi is a means of uprooting the spirit of polemics. He argues that to use dialogue 'either openly or in one's own mind, as a means of converting the person we are talking to' is not only harmful, but also a restoration of the age of polemics. In fact, he stresses, if dialogue is 'conceived as a new form of proselytism, a means of undermining convictions and bringing about defeat or surrender, sooner or later, we shall find ourselves back in the same old situation as in the Middle Ages'.[42]

Talbi emphasizes that as far as the doctrine of Islam is concerned, there is no justification. Islam 'in fact owes itself for the deepening of its own theology' and does not need external support to explain the status of non-Muslims. It needs to deepen its own theology. Despite this advantage on the side of Islam, Talbi argues, Muslims have given the impression of 'being reticent at least at the level of its representative organizations, such as the *Rabitat al-Alam al-Islami* [Muslim World League] and the theological University of al-Azhar in Cairo, for example'. He hopes that the Organization of the Islamic Conference (OIC) will work in this direction and urges them to include dialogue among their activities.[43]

Despite the various obstacles in dialogue, Talbi is confident that in the end dialogue will succeed. Because, in the absence of dialogue, what is left is 'confrontation' and 'fighting'. To make dialogue succeed – in his words, the 'cornerstone to avoid the failure' – 'we have to respect fully [a person's] free choice as our equal brother in full dignity and in full liberty. In a word, we have to respect the right to be different as a basic human right, without interfering in what must be considered as the most sacred matter of conscience'.[44] This theme occurs in another place in his writings where he argues: 'faith is a choice, and a choice is only a choice if it is a free and reasonable one'.[45]

DIALOGUE WITH THE WEST

As we have seen, Talbi distinguishes between Islam as a 'cultural phenomenon' and Islam as a 'faith'. This distinction also applies to the West. There is 'the West of faith', 'the mystical Occident which continues to exert its attraction, which can inspire humility and silence the purest devotion – and this is too often forgotten'. The other West he calls, 'the West which produces to consume and consumes to produce, evoking both fascination and revulsion',[46] which is both admired and derided. As in the case of the cultural phenomenon of Islam, Islam cannot be said to be truly represented, as is the case of the West's consumerism, where Christianity, which is one of the most important elements, is not truly represented. But in the case of 'defamations and anathemas', Talbi finds a difference. The 'Qur'anic veneration for Jesus', he argues, 'prevented Muslims from letting any of their indignations extend to the founder of Christianity. The reverse has not always been the case, nor is it, concerning the Messenger of Islam.'[47]

Talbi describes three areas of 'distinctly divergent' and 'diametrically opposite' views of the two civilizations, which, he emphasizes, 'have only become more pronounced with time'. First, he shows that in the 'Western scheme', the 'separation of two very distinct realms: that of Caesar, and that of God, is the norm'. This, he says, is because when Jesus declares his Reign, he had little choice but to note the very 'definite and indelible frontiers of Caesar's empire'.[48] After Jesus, he contends, that was not always the case. 'The West, secular today, has not been innocent of theocratic forms of power in the past.' In the case of Islam, Talbi points out, 'the ground was initially virgin, so to speak', meaning there was no empire like Rome which brought some sort of homogeneity within the empire by implementing its code of law and practices. Compared to this the Arabs were run by tribal and clan loyalties and this meant religion did not become a private affair but rather was the main player in society in constructing the law and implementing it. In brief, 'Muhammad did not find himself confronted with any Caesar at Madinah . . .'.[49]

A second area of divergence, Talbi finds, is the Shari'ah. In Christianity, he argues, there is no parallel to Shari'ah with the exception of a very restricted area of canon law. But he finds this to be more inspired by natural law and falls within the aegis of Caesar. 'In Islam, one must judge matters in the light of Revelation.'[50] He points out that originally the West was transformed by Christianity and has placed its emphasis on law 'outside of its theological and cultural aspects', whereas Islam, 'which is law-oriented, is at the same time a religion, code, ethical system, society and culture. It is a whole.'[51] He argues that if Islam and the West are to profit from each other's differences, then Islam, in his opinion, 'has to realise that there is an ineradicable Caesar-side to every person that is indisposable for the creative dynamics of history'. On the other hand, returning to his earlier theme, he stresses, 'the West must realise that Caesar is also only a human being and that, as such, he is in the final analysis subordinate to God, the true ruler of everything that exists (*Malik al-Mulk*), who is the source of all being and all power.'[52]

The third area of divergence, Talbi finds, is the role of women in the two societies. Islam opted from the very beginning for sexual segregation, whereas 'Western society, for integration'. The Iranian black *Chador* has made these differences much more visible. Talbi argues that the difference is equally visible in the family model too. 'Unlike Christianity', he contends, 'Islam has no prejudice against sexuality'. He also points out the difference in the attitude to marriage: Islam does not consider a contract between two partners a sacrament, and allows the option of divorce. He points out the areas, which most Islamists stress, of 'freedom in management and disposal of all [women's] personal property without any control by their husbands contrary to Western women'.[53] The difference between the two civilizations, in Talbi's view, are of the 'contradictory social options' available to them. He finds both Muslims and the West are in fact 'playing with mirrors'. But what is the way out? He claims that until 'each one has accepted th other as he is', there is no way out. In the process of such dialogue Talbi makes it clear, it is 'not a question of tolerance but of respect and acceptance'. Talbi, like Ayoub, believes that the West needs to see itself as a Judaeo-Christian *and* Islamic tradition and should be sympathetic not only to Athens and Rome, but to Baghdad and Cordova as well.

9 Seyyed Hossein Nasr (1933–)

Seyyed Hossein Nasr was born in Tehran, in 1933 into a Shi'i family of *Ulamā* and educators. He received his early education in religion and literature in his native city, Tehran. Later, he chose to study physics and mathematics in the United States, where he received his BSc with Honours in physics from the Massachusetts Institute of Technology in 1954. In 1958 he gained an MA and PhD in the history of science and learning with special emphasis on Islamic science, from Harvard. He returned to Iran and was appointed Associate Professor ⸱f the History of Science and Philosophy at Tehran University. He ⸱came a Professor of the Faculty of Letters and Humanities at the me university in 1963. He was appointed Vice-Chancellor of Tehran niversity (1970–1) and Chancellor of Aryameher University (1972–5). Ie returned to the United States during the Iranian Revolution of 1979, where he was appointed Professor of Islamic Studies at Temple University (1979). He has taught at the George Washington University since 1984.

Nasr has a distinct approach to religion. He associates himself, quite strongly, with the 'traditional school'. This emerged in the West some 70 years ago with the writings of René Guenon. His writings influenced a group of contemporary and later writers like Titus Burckhardt, Martin Lings, Leo Schaya, Marco Pallis, A.K. Coomeraswamy and W.N. Perry, as well as Nasr. But above all, Frithjof Schuon remains the outspoken representative and centre of the school. This school does not accept 'the historicism of the academic approach to *Religionswissenschaft* developed in Europe in the nineteenth century'. Nor does it accept the phenomenological approach to religion, which should not be confused with 'the traditional perspective of religion'. Furthermore, it should not be 'identified with either sentimentalism that sees all religions as being the same', or that of 'the neo-Vedantists'.[1] What is this 'traditional school' then?

> It is a knowledge that lies at the heart of religion, which illuminates the meaning of religious rites, doctrines and symbols and which also provides the key for the understanding of both the necessity of the plurality of religions and the way to penetrate into other religious

universe without reducing either their religious significance or our own commitment to the religious universe to which we who wish to study other religions belong.[2]

Nasr defines the tradition as

truths or principles of a divine origin revealed or unveiled to mankind and, in fact, a whole cosmic sector through various figures envisaged as messengers, prophets, *avataras*, the logos or other transmitting agencies, along with all the ramification and applications of these principles in different realms, including law and social structure, art, symbolism, the sciences, and embracing of course Supreme Knowledge along with the means for its attainment.[3]

The 'traditional school' has provided Nasr with a tool to explain the various differences of religion in an entirely new light. With this background information in mind, we shall look in some detail at Nasr's comparison of Christianity and Islam, and dialogue in general, and his dialogue with one of the contemporary Christian theologians, Hans Küng.

CHRISTIANITY AND ISLAM – A COMPARISON

In Christian and Muslim relations Nasr emphasises that the central issues are metaphysical and theological rather than social and political issues. Here we find a distinct departure compared to Khurshid and Faruqi. He argues that these issues need to be confronted 'in a sincere and serious manner' by both the communities. Here all sorts of 'diplomatic platitudes and the kind of relativization'[4] need to be put side. Nasr compares Islamic beliefs which are central to Islam *vis-à-vis* Christianity. The purpose of the comparison is to make believers understand the nature of the Islamic perspective, especially the Western mind. It is also important to note that when Nasr compares Christianity and Islam, it is the Western understanding of Christianity which he confronts. In Nasr's writing the mystery and nature of God are prominent. He explains that in Christianity God is 'essentially a mystery which veils the Divine from man'. In Islam, however, it is man who is veiled from God. It is human responsibility to 'rend this veil asunder' and know God. God has given human beings faculties such as intelligence to reach Him.[5] Despite the major differences between the two religions, especially when we enter into the Trinity/Unity debate, he contends that it is not difficult to 'reach an accord' on the reality of God as One. In this respect he cites early Muslim and Christian theologians – Muslims such as al-Ghazzali, Rumi and Ibn Arabi, and Christians such as Nicolas of Cusa, whose theological work provides a good ground to formulate a necessary 'doctrine of the nature of God'. He suggests that Muslims and Christians need to make greater effort 'to provide further formulations of traditional and orthodox doctrine in a contemporary context'.[6]

Nasr's approaches other Islamic concepts and beliefs with the same clarity as his approach to the concept of God. Here we shall focus on three principles of Islam, viz. Revelation, Prophethood and Shari'ah.

Revelation

Nasr examines the concept of Revelation and its two broad aspects:

Sacred Scripture

Nasr argues that Christians have approached the Quranic revelation in the same way as they approach the Bible and the way it has been understood by them. Western 'rationalism and empiricism' have been employed to understand the Qur'an. In the name of 'objectivity' and 'scholarship' a conclusion has been communicated which implies that the Qur'an is not the 'Word of God', and therefore, in their eyes, must be the word of the Prophet. Links have been made to the Christian monks in Syria and the Jewish community in Madinah, from whom the Prophet learned and produced the book called the Qur'an. Nasr suggests that in this respect some Christian theologians are also guilty, which he finds strange, as these rejections come from Christians and Jews who accept that their religion is a revealed truth.[7] The influence of rational and empirical criticism is largely responsible for diminishing the sense of the sacred of the Bible for both Christians and Jewish believers. In many quarters the Bible is considered to be simply history or literature. The same elements, Nasr argues, are keen to apply 'their own findings' to the sacred scriptures of Islam.

Sacred Language

Nasr finds that the lack of understanding amongst Christians about the significance of the sacred Arabic language of the Qur'an stems from the fact that Christianity does not have a sacred language of its own. Rather, there are several liturgical languages which are used in the Christian mass. Insufficient theological attention been given by Christians to differentiate 'between sacred, liturgical and vernacular languages'.[8] He points out that there are different types of tradition in the religious world. One is based upon the founder, who is considered to be of 'Divine descent', such as in Hinduism, the *avatara*. Tradition such as this has no sacred language as such; rather the body of the founder 'is an external form', i.e. the body 'itself is the external form of the word'. In Christianity, he argues, Christ himself is the Word of God and therefore it does not matter whether one celebrates mass in Greek, Latin – or for that matter in Arabic or in Farsi. What matters is participation of the worshippers in 'the blood and body' of Christ. 'Latin in the Catholic Church', he reminds us, 'is a liturgical language not a sacred one'. In traditions like Islam and Judaism, where the sacred language is directly connected to the message and is the chosen vehicle to communicate with the people, then the 'very sound and words' of such a sacred language are part of the revelation and play the same role in such religions as 'the body of Christ does in Christianity'.[9] Therefore, the Islamic tradition and the Jewish tradition perform their religious rites in their sacred language and cannot be performed other than in these languages, whereas in Christianity the body of Christ plays the central part in the Eucharist and prayers can be said in any language.

The comparison of Revelation, so Nasr argues, should not be compared book for book and the Prophet for prophet. Comparison between Revelation, rather, lies in the Qur'an and in Christ:

> The Word of God in Islam is the Qur'an, in Christianity it is Christ. The vehicle of the Divine Message in Christianity is the Virgin Mary, in Islam it is the soul of the Prophet. The Prophet must be unlettered for the same reason that the Virgin Mary must be virgin. The human vehicle of a Divine Message must be pure and untainted. The Divine Word can only be written on the pure and 'untouched' table of human responsibility. If this Word is in the form of flesh the purity is symbolized by the virginity of the mother who gives birth to the Word, and if it is in the form of a book this purity is symbolized by the unlettered nature of the person who is chosen to announce this Word among men.[10]

The Prophet and Jesus

Nasr contends that it is difficult for a non-Muslim to appreciate Prophet Muhammad's role 'as the prototype of the religious and spiritual life'. It is difficult for Christians to understand the socio-political and spiritual life of the Prophet, especialy where politics and religion are separated. He suggests a comparison between the Old Testament prophets Daniel, Solomon and Abraham may resolve a lot of misunderstanding. They were 'at once spiritual being and a leader'; such characters are rare in the West and a combination of such a functions 'appears [an] impossibility'. Western Christianity often quotes Jesus that 'My Kingdom is not of this world' in order to emphasise his spiritual life.[11]

Prophet Muhammad's multiple marriage has been seen in the West as a weakness towards 'the flesh'. Nasr argues that Prophet needs to be understood 'not as a saint who withdraws from the world but as one who sanctifies the very life of the world by living in it and accepting it with the aim of integrating it into a higher order of reality'.[12]

Nasr is in favour of opening up the debate on Christology 'in an intra- as well as inter-religious context'. He claims that 'theological Christology is not an acute problem as his historical life'. There is a resemblance with Islamic Christology in early Christianity. If that could be allowed to continue, then perhaps we would have less difficulty to explain each other's problems. Problems, in acceptance of the life of Jesus as 'recorded in the Gospels and accepted in Christian tradition'.

At the same time accepting the Quranic account of Jesus the Son of Mary, and Jesus not crucified, Nasr argues that if the modern epistemologies are to be applied to find a way out then we all are at loss. Traditional epistemologies need to be applied. This, in his view, may provide a solution. 'One could say', he remarks, 'that such a major cosmic event as the end of the earthly life of Christ could in fact be "seen" and "known" in more than one way, and that it is God's will that Christianity should be given to "see" that in one way and Islam in another.'[13]

SHARI'AH

Nasr believes that in relation to Shari'ah Muslims are focusing their attention 'more on religion than law'. The attitude of 'secularists and Christians', as well as some Muslims, 'is based on the general attitude taken towards law in Western civilization derived mostly from the particular nature of Christianity as a "way of love" without a divine law'.[14] He shows that 'the conception of Divine law in Islam and in Christianity can be seen in the way the word canon (*Qanun*) is used in the two traditions'. He points out that, in Islam, 'it has come to denote a man-made law in contrast to Shari'ah or divinely inspired law. In the West the opposing meaning is given to this word in the sense that canonical law refers to laws governing the ecclesiastical organization of the Catholic and Episcopal Churches and has a definitely religious colour'.[15] Nasr suggests that the meaning of the well-known saying of Christ, 'Render therefore unto Caesar the things which are Caesar's', should be looked at in two different ways. One, as it is commonly interpreted, 'as leaving all things that are worldly' and therefore having nothing to do with the secular authorities or secular domain of whom 'the Caesar is the outstanding example'. The other, which Nasr seems to favour, i.e. since 'Christianity, being a spiritual way, had no Divine legislation of its own, it had to absorb Roman law in order to become the religion of a civilization. The Law of Caesar, or the Roman law, became providentially absorbed into the Christian perspective once this religion became dominant in the West, and it is to this fact that the saying of Christ alludes.'[16] Nasr argues that even if 'Roman law had a divine aspect from the point of view of Roman religion, it was not an integral part of the Christian revelation', and he points out that this 'is the basic reason why Westerners cannot usually understand the meaning of Shari'ah'.[17] He states that the situation in Islam differs completely. 'Islam never gave unto Caesar what was Caesar's. Rather, it tried to integrate the domain of Caesar itself, namely political, social and economic life, into an encompassing religious world view.'[18]

Emphasizing the Islamic position and nature of Shari'ah, Nasr remarks that the Shari'ah 'corresponds to a reality that transcends time and history'. To conform to the teachings and application of it he suggests that 'religion should not be reformed to conform to the ever-changing and imperfect nature of men but men should reform so as to live according to the tenets of revelation'. It is 'the human that must conform to the Divine and not the Divine to the human'.[19] But this emphasis on Shari'ah, as some critics argue, destroys human initiatives. Nasr believes such 'criticism, however, fails to understand the inner workings of the Divine law. This law places before men many paths according to his nature and needs within a universal pattern which pertains to everyone. Human initiative comes in selecting what is in conformity with one's needs and living according to the Divine norm as indicated by the Shari'ah.'[20]

Nasr finds the absence of a sacred law in Christianity is responsible for various social ills in the society, especially unrestricted desires and 'unlimited exploition'. He sees that the development of capitalism away from the divine domain is at fault.

DIALOGUE

Nasr calls the term dialogue, 'a very honourable term', especially 'in the West and in philosophical traditions'. The meaning of the term, he points out, in 'Platonic and Socratic' discourse is understood 'as a means of discovering the truth'. But 'as used since the Second World War', in the religious sphere, it 'has come to mean discussing various aspects of religion among followers of each religion with the aim of a better understanding of the two sides'.[21]

Nasr argues that dialogue with Christianity and the West are two different things, although they are interrelated. He points out that the Muslim world's mistake is in equating the West with Christianity. He claims that in every dialogue between Islam and Western Christianity 'there is a third partner which is secularism in the modern secular West'. To him the 'major problem is that the West is not the Christian West' and that makes 'dialogue much more difficult'.[22] He is in favour of carrying out a religious dialogue with Christianity. He is aware of Christian criticism of 'Islam for not having undergone the same secularist and diluting influence' which Christianity has undergone in the last five centuries. He contends that 'there is no reason in the world whatsoever why Islam should do so'.[23]

'Islam must be able to have a dialogue with the West in its totality.' But this dialogue, in Nasr's view, would be different from dialogue with Christianity. Because dialogue with the West 'is not so much dialogue of reaching a single truth because there is no common truth between Islam and secularism in contrast to Christianity and Islam which are based on a common truth which is God Himself'.[24] The purpose of such dialogue, in his view, would be a 'better understanding'. But even in this dialogue of Islam and the West, Nasr points out, 'there is an element [of] Christianity present'.

Nasr's earlier writings suggest that he sees dialogue between Christianity and Islam as an opportunity to counter atheism, humanism, secularism, etc. He proposes in a reflections on one of Hans Küng's articles, 'to place all the religions, including Christianity, in one world or camp before which stand the forces of agnosticism and secularism'.[25] This is reflected in his earlier participation of dialogue. Nasr led an Iranian delegation to the Vatican in December 1977, where he proposed the following five areas as possible fields of dialogue and collaboration between Christianity and Islam:

1. How to confront atheism and contemporary agnosticism.
2. How to confront the danger of technocracy and ecological ruin.
3. How to intervene profitably in the problem of the energy crisis.
4. The youth problem.
5. The future of faith and hope.[26]

The core of dialogue, Nasr suggests, 'is that if you want to talk to another person and get meaningful results, you must see what he is, right now, in himself, not what you would like him to be in order for you to talk to him'.[27] The basic element in dialogue, for Nasr, is 'faith in God', which 'unites and gives to the Christians as well as the Muslims a similar vision in various aspects on man, his obligations and the ideas which he should obtain'.[28] He finds solace in the various problems that humanity is facing in such collaboration.

There are three other purposes of dialogue, in Nasr's view. Dialogue 'plays an important role in buttressing our own faith'. In dialogue a person encounters another person from another religion 'in whom he sees the mark of authentic faith and piety and wisdom and even on the highest level sanctity. To reject that as being untrue or unreal causes a danger for that person to lose his or her own faith'.[29]

Secondly, Nasr argues, there are many Christians in the West, whose 'faith has been attacked by nineteenth-century secularist philosophies or the Age of Englightenment before that', but who when they discover living traditions 'outside of Christianity in which faith is very strong and wisdom and divine knowledge have not been lost', in such encounters they discover their 'own religious universe'.[30] This in his opinion is another important purpose of dialogue.

Thirdly, Nasr stresses that

all religions are in a deeper sense interrelated and therefore instead of fighting against each other, for them [to discover] . . . their transcendent and divine ground or principle or origin of all religion is the best answer to those who make use of the diversity of religion in order to destroy religion which has been done by so many people like Feuerbach and Marx and a lot of the grandfathers of anti-religious philosophy in the last century.[31]

The political events of the last two centuries, Nasr emphasizes, aroused suspicions in the Muslim mind. Although the colonialists were secularist, their policies had double standards. Giving examples from France, Nasr points out that 'after the French Revolution, they killed a large number of Catholic priests'. But he finds 'there was support for the nuns and Catholic missionaries in North Africa'. The relationship 'between missionary activity and colonialism left a deep mark upon the minds of many, many Muslims which has not been totally eradicated'. He finds that this practice has not been suspended, but exists in a new form. 'In certain areas of the Islamic world such as Indonesia and [in] parts of Muslim Africa, black Africa, that type of wedding between Christianity and in fact not the land of Christ or the message of Christ, but modern civilization through which . . . they tried to propagate the religion [is] still very strong'.[32]

In relation to the West and Western Christianity, until today, he argues, the West has not considered anything Islamic 'to be of any intellectual or spiritual significance for Western man'. He stresses that Muslims see 'dialogue with the West is a kind of opportunity for Westerners to solve some of their own problems rather than those of Islam. . . . They . . . think that dialogue is a political smokescreen in order to prevent the Muslims from thinking about more important issues.' But, importantly, Nasr believes they are not 'wrong in this assessment'.[33] The fear could be lifted, Nasr suggests, if the Muslims could have an assurance that they will be 'treated as Christians were treated by Muslims, let us say, in Spain, or in many other episodes throughout Islamic history – not in all episodes by any means, but in the vast majority of them – that they would be able to collaborate together'.[34]

Nasr points out two other factors that mould the Muslims' perception of dialogue – one, he shows that there is a significant change in the attitude of Muslims towards the West. He compares the younger generation of Muslims today to the generation of 50 years ago. He finds the younger generation to be less tolerant. He argues that though contact with the West has opened some new vistas, it has 'created a closed door policy' amongst the younger generation. This is because they 'have been totally disillusioned by the machinations that have gone on'. Other factors, Nasr suggests, are the 'over-emphasis by Western scholarship and mass media of the most fanatical', the 'most disoriented elements of contemporary Islam as being normative Islam'. They pushed aside the 'moderate and normative Islam as being something blasé and passé'. This attitude, he argues, 'pushed to the side more and more' those who are really interested in dialogue.[35]

Finally, the question of human rights. Human rights, which have been referred to in various dialogues, and their purpose for Christians, Nasr finds, are more dominated by the secular outlook and secular view. To adopt a proposal for human rights as promulgated in the West, he stresses, 'could represent a trap for some religious men'. He considers that the theory of the rights of man has been built outside religion and emphasizes that 'Islam does not recognize such ideology. Man for Islam does not possess inborn rights, rather he has a radical obligation toward God; the rest is only the consequences of this relation.'[36] Referring to the question of the rights of an atheist under Islam, he argues, 'Islam has not developed a law for atheists.' But because of this, 'Islam is not going to change its worldview simply because another civilization has decided to disband religion and has put human rights above divine rights.' Referring to *The Satanic Verses* affair, he describes this as a 'great contention between the Western civilization and Islamic civilization'. To Nasr, 'it is a question of priorities' – which rights are more important, 'the rights of individual human beings or the rights of the sacred'. He answers: 'each civilization has a right to answer itself and before God and before its own destiny and its own people, so it cannot dictate to another civilization as the West is doing today'.[37]

DA'WAH/MISSION AND DIALOGUE

Nasr defines *Da'wah* as an opportunity 'to present the message of Islam and the message of *Tawhid* wherever possible'. The condition, in his opinion, is to present Islam 'without coercion'.[38] In *Da'wah* and mission, he argues that both religions 'should have the freedom to present their religion'. The religion, he emphasizes, can be presented 'provided it is only that', that is, it should not go beyond presentation. For Nasr, Christian missionaries overstepped the acceptable norms. Today 'Christianity is sold with the help of Louis Pasteur and hospitals . . . and scholarship and getting jobs and so on'. Christian missionaries at times become instrumental in spreading humanist and secular ideas. Citing the example of the American University of Beirut, he points out, that Western civilization got a 'foothold through Christianity', which to Nasr is unacceptable. He also detects inequalities between the Muslim and Christian situations, for when Americans say 'we do not mind if you come and preach to us', the 'advantages . . . money and the . . . power' of 'Muslim missionaries' in New York State are at a disadvantage compared with New York missionaries in Indonesia'.[39]

In relation to *Da'wah*/mission and dialogue Nasr finds 'some clash' between the two. In 'order to have dialogue', he suggest, one 'must transcend the idea of trying to convert everyone to your religion'. Rather, he prefers to use the term 'witness', and through witness of one's religion 'someone may receive the call of God and embrace Islam'.[40] This, he suggests, is a far stronger position for Muslims than any other thing.

In Nasr's view, dialogue in a wider sense is a part of *Da'wah*. He suggests that Muslims 'have to reach a level of understanding . . . of the doctrine of *Tawhid* and the role of Islam in the world as a whole'. This, he argues, 'will provide a wider vision where they will be happy if they have good Christians amidst them who understand them without becoming Muslims, as in fact has been the case between most Oriental Christians and Muslims, and Jews and Muslims over the centuries.' He believes that today many Muslims 'have lost the universality of their own past', simply because, in his view, they have lost the wider perspective of their religion. If Muslims today 'went back to the best' of their 'own traditions' then *Da'wah* would not be understood in the sense of 'bitter enmity against Christianity, Judaism and other religions; 'much of that is political'.[41]

HANS KÜNG AND NASR

As we have seen, Nasr associates himself quite strongly with the 'traditional school', a school which rejects the historicism of the academic approach or the phenomenological approach to religion. He finds it equally difficult to accept Hans Küng's[42] ten guiding principles for contemporary theology, which he formulated in his book *Existiert Gott?* (Does God Exist?).

But before we discuss the 'guiding principles', let us see how Nasr sees theology itself. He takes the word 'theology' in its literal sense – 'the science of God' – and stresses that it 'should explain the temporal with reference to the Eternal and not the Eternal in the light of temporality, which is made to sound very real . . .'. He agrees with Küng's two important elements of survival of theology, viz. a 'return to the sources' and a 'venturing forth on to unchartered waters', or, as he quotes from Küng, 'a theology of Christian origins and center enunciated within the horizon of the contemporary world'. 'This means', Nasr remarks, that 'God is at once the origin and the center, the beginning and the now'. Therefore 'theology must obviously be concerned with origins and the "now" which is the only reflection of eternity in time which binds humankind to the eternal.'[43]

He challenges Küng's agreement with Schillebeeks' 'two sources' for the creation of 'scientific theology'. The 'two sources' are the Judaeo-Christian movement and the contemporary human experiences of Christians and non-Christians. He points out that there are three groups of 'sources' to consider. First, the Judaeo-Christian tradition, second, the other religions, and third, modern secularism. He remarks that the 'West has to take cognizance of the religious and metaphysical significance of other religions', but he rejects the notion that modern secularism could be a source of religion. Rather, 'theology must seek to explain in the light of its own principles. It is not theology which must surrender itself to modern sciences and its findings. Rather it is modern science which must be critically appraised from the metaphysical and theological points of view and its findings explained in this light.'[44]

Regarding the guiding principles Nasr has responded to each principle Küng has discussed in his book *Existiert Gott?* Here we shall summarize Nasr's views on these principles. He suggests that to make a theology intelligible to non-believers, theology should not 'lead believers to unbelief in its attempt to be intelligible'. He finds 'the current scholarly methods' of theology are not sufficient to defend 'the truth as revealed in God's religion'. He states that adopting only the 'current scholarly methods' will lead to humanistic and rationalistic scholarships, but will not lead to a mechanism or 'in each religion for the protection of the truth'. He agrees with Küng that the views of opponents should not be 'ignored or hereticized', but he argues that the 'truth is one thing and charity is another. We must love other people, but that does not mean that we must be indifferent to the truth.' He finds Christianity, and for that matter all religions, have to face the very 'delicate problem' of other forms of truth, other than 'a particular form of truth which we call our religion'. He also agrees with Küng in that it is good 'to practise an inter-disciplinary approach . . . [and] a constant dialogue with related fields'. Nasr suggests that it should not be 'carried out from a position of weakness and with an inferiority complex and thereby remains faithful to its own nature, mission and genius'. He stresses that dialogue with other disciplines should be 'among equals or those nearly equal'. 'Theology', he argues, 'has as much a right to study nature and the mind as do science and philosophy.' In the present day, Küng suggests, 'problems of the past should not have priority'. Nasr disagrees, 'It is mostly as a result of neglecting the past as a source both of tradition and of experience for humankind that so many problems face present-day humanity.' Küng argues that the 'criterion determining all other criteria of Christian theology can never again be some ecclesiastical or theological tradition or institution, but only the Gospel, the original Christian message itself.' Nasr points out how 'this Holy Book', that is, the Gospels, 'could serve as the source for the truth of the Christian faith without the church, the oral teachings, the traditions and all that in fact connect a human being who calls her or himself Christian to the origin of this religion'. He also strongly disagrees with Küng on the issue of the Gospel, which 'should be expressed in the commonly understood language'. He finds the 'so-called commonly understood language of contemporary humanity is itself no more than a debased jargon, influenced by the mass media and often deprived of the beauty of the language in question'. Nasr remarks, 'Why should the Word of God sound like the outpourings of a football announcer?' Nasr comes back to his favourite theme when commenting on Küng's guiding principles – having an ecumenical vision is one thing, 'but joining world religions and contemporary ideologies, which are the products of a secularized West, is really an insult to those religions'.[45]

In a much later, face-to-face discussion with Küng, Nasr contests the very basis of Küng's celebrated premise for dialogue, i.e. peace.[46] He argues, 'truth comes before peace and peace follows from the truth . . .'.[47] He appreciates that Küng has 'taken a step toward the understanding of Islam', a step further than various Christian theologians, both Catholics and Protestants, before him. Yet he finds that the theological problems remain the same. Dialogue has not crossed the boundaries in more than goodwill or good gesture. The theological issues – the Prophet, Revelation, God and His Mercy, History, Christology – remain under the constraint of 'polite diplomacy'.

Nasr stresses that 'at the heart of Islamic–Christian misunderstanding is not only doctrines, which can be theologically and metaphysically regarded, but a thousand-year heritage of the hatred of Christians for the founder of Islam'. He contends that even today, 'with all the platitude, diplomatic declarations, and even humanitarian gestures towards Islam, and even in the Vatican declarations of 1962, the Prophet of Islam is always left aside'.[48] He emphasizes that the relation of the Prophet to the Qur'an is central. Describing the various views within Islam, he finds that the fact that the Prophet of Islam receives 'the Qur'an verbatim from heaven' is central to Islam and in dialogue. Küng's reference to Fazlur Rahman's view that 'the Koran as the Word of God be regarded at the same time as the word of the human prophet', Nasr describes as 'an isolated case'. One cannot 'overlook the beliefs of a billion Muslims concerning the nature of the Qur'an and its relation to the Prophet'. Furthermore, 'non-Islamic Western analysis based on the separation between the Qur'an and its traditional commentaries over the centuries is not going to help dialogue with Muslims', simply because the development of various apects of the traditions throughout the centuries is based upon the Qur'an.[49]

The very important question of Christology, Nasr links directly to the concept of Word of God. As we have seen, in his earlier comparison of Jesus and the Qur'an, he states that the Muslim beliefs are that 'the Qur'an, the whole Qur'an, and not parts of it, is the Word of God'. Hence its Christology is part of the Qur'anic Christology, and to perceive it as a 'wrong Christology makes absolutely impossible any dialogue with Islam'.[50] He stresses, as in the point we have discussed earlier, that it is possible that 'God waited for two humanities on earth to understand a very important event in two different ways . . .'. He contends that it is not possible to divide the Word of God, of which one part could be rejected and the other accepted. He raises the question: 'What good would it do if a person like Hans Küng were to spend his efforts for the next ten years trying to develop a model for dialogue with Islam which does not correspond to any reality on the Islamic side?'[51]

Küng disagrees with Nasr. Referring to the Qur'an, in his reply to Nasr, he seems to suggest that the influence upon the Qur'an of various ideas from its immediate surroundings cannot be denied. Muslims have not accepted this, as have the Jews and Christians, who have held this stance quite adamantly for some time. However, Küng believes that it is only a matter of time. He argues, that just as Spinoza used historical methods to question the Hebrew Bible and Oratorian Fathers in Paris, so Richard Simon questioned the New Testament using the same methods. Muslims, under the influence of Western scholarship, cannot avoid historical questions for much longer. Referring to the question of the Crucifixion and its denial in the Qur'an, Küng points out, 'let us say that the Gospels are wrong, and that the whole New Testament is wrong, that Jesus was not crucified. To say this from a source which comes from the seventh century is for an historical thinking man, I think, personally impossible'.[52]

Finally, Nasr emphasizes that 'the only religious dialogue worthy in the eyes of God is one which does not sacrifice in the name of any expediency on the human level, be it even worldly peace, that which He has revealed in each religion.'[53]

10 Discussion

Part II has discussed six Muslims, each prominent in dialogue with Christians, all of whom come from different backgrounds. Their social, cultural and political environments have moulded their vision and appreciation of dialogue. They have all lived long enough in the West to understand the nature of the encounters and issues involved, especially in Christian–Muslim relations. Though their denominational differences, Shi'i and Sunni, and their approach to the religions are responsible for differing emphases in their approach, nonetheless there are remarkable similarities in their overall approach to dialogue with Christians.

1. The principles developed by the Muslims under study, for comparing and finding a basis for relations with other religions, have many similarities. For example, Faruqi's 'meta-religion' and Nasr's 'traditional school' both refuse to accept the phenomenological approach as well as the historicism of the academic approach, which compares events and incidents without reference to people and their beliefs. The thrust of their argument is that comparison of religion is meaningless unless it is acknowledged by that religion's believers. Both Faruqi and Nasr in this respect are not the original propounders of the principle; they merely articulate what earlier academics and theologians spelt out. Faruqi, for example, appears to be heavily under the influence of the Spanish Muslim theologian Ibn Hazm, he calls him 'the first comparativist of religions and the greatest Muslim comparativist'. As Ibn Hazm remarks, the essence of humanity, religious experiences and their expressions cannot be mutually contradictory or essentially different. Faruqi's 'meta-religion' also points in that direction. Furthermore, Faruqi subscribes to Ibn Hazm's view that in so as far as the scripture or religious text should make a coherent whole, this should not be self-contradictory and should not contradict the essential principles of mankind's religious experiences. Again, we find that this reflects Faruqi's 'meta-religion'. Ibn Hazm's efforts to study and compare religions stem from his belief that a student of religion should be a seeker after truth. Faruqi's whole argument alludes to that. While Faruqi argues for the search for truth, Nasr's traditional school searches for the universal metaphysical truth underlying all religions. Religions are illuminated by the presence of the knowledge, in the shape of symbols and rites, associated with various religions. The presence of such knowledge in all religions

makes it possible, and easier, to relate to each other. Nasr deals with the contradictory claims of each religion and the claim of absoluteness in each. He suggests the very presence of *knowledge* in all religions and its Origin is One. Therefore, despite the differences and emphasis, each religion is certain of that Origin. Nasr praises in this respect his mentor, Frithjof Schuon. He regards him as the greatest figure of the traditionalist school in the field of religion. Since knowledge lies at the heart of all religion, Nasr argues, this will give a greater degree of ecumenism.

In contrast to both, Askari's 'trans-religious' dimension places followers of religion in different categories. He maintains a distance between inter-religious dialogue and inter-religion. For him, inter-religious dialogue is one of many ways in which inter-religion becomes a conscious process. Inter-religion, Askari believes, has been ignored by those who study religions, simply because inter-religion does not fit into their psychological or social principles, or into their categorization. Askari's view of 'trans-religion' finds little support within the Orthodox Muslim view. But Askari pursues this method of comparison even when his is a lone voice, and with remarkable consistency, in his writings.

Though these principles can help individuals to develop their understanding, they have neither been of major help nor hindrance for a non-academic person to engage in dialogue. These principles, at the intellectual or academic level, may provide some clarity, but for an ordinary person trying to relate in the social context to his or her situation with the rest of the community, these principles seem irrelevant.

2. Our study of the six Muslims shows that past encounters and their impact upon the two communities play a substantive role in contemporary relations between the followers of the two religions. Ayoub traces the problem to the very early Christian writings. John of Damascus, writing on Islam, was motivated by a strong desire to prevent Christians from becoming Muslims. Instead of explaining Muslim beliefs and practices to the Christians whom he addresses, he chose to portray Islam as an inferior religion to Christianity; and, by implication, there is no need to accept an inferior religion. Talbi points out that in the writings of twelfth-century Christians during the Crusades, the priority was to demonize Islam and especially its Prophet. Muslims were labelled the 'anti-Christ' in order to motivate and recruit Christian soldiers and to gain support from various Christian constituencies. The colonial period, they all agree, had a devastating effect upon Muslims; it is one of the major factors of distrust in dialogue.

Missionary activities, carried out mainly during the colonial period, are invariably associated with the colonialists' agenda in the eyes of Muslims. Today, any dialogue with Muslims is bound to reflect the issue of colonization and mission. All these aspects of academic writings — the impact of the Crusades, colonization and mission — have been a long-standing grievance for Muslims. Muslims believe the academic writings of the West, popularly known as 'Orientalism', as well as the Crusades and colonization, in some ways have influenced contemporary Western writers and as a result they are suspicious of writings by Christians, no matter how well-meaning they may be. Even if a book is presented fairly by a writer on Islam and Muslim history, the Muslim tendency seems to be to look into the deeper 'intentions' of such publications and search for sinister motives. Mission is, equally, a serious issue in dialogue, which we shall discuss later.

In this respect the step taken by the Second Vatican Council towards Muslims, all six Muslims believe, is a courageous one. However, they also point out that the Council took an 'absolute minimum approach' towards Islam. Faruqi sees in *Nostra Aetate* a 'paternalizing' attitude. Ayoub remarks that this document is a clear departure from the Church's 'classical stance'. He finds that the document's pronouncement that Muslims 'venerate Jesus' simplifies the importance of Jesus, who is a prophet to Muslims like other prophets before him. In Khurshid's view, *Nostra Aetate* sends a clear message to both Christians and Muslims that the past should not become a 'shackle' in the pursuit and building of better relations. Talbi, an enthusiastic supporter of *Nostra Aetate*, however, like Ayoub, believes that the Roman Catholic Church, especially under the current Pope, has taken a 'step inward' on the question of dialogue. The Churches are far more concerned now with tightening relations between 'mission' and 'dialogue'. Talbi includes the World Council of Churches in this respect. They believe the small opening made by the Second Vatican Council in relation to Muslims has been blocked by heavy mission concern. Although Nasr appreciates the spirit of *Nostra Aetate*, he finds that the Roman Catholic Church in particular and Christianity in general have been 'diplomatic' about accepting Islam as a religion. They have accepted Islam as a 'religion' but not as a complete step. He wants the Churches to make up their mind about Islam as a religion, as another aspect of God's authentic revelation, and deal with it accordingly.

3. Study of the six Muslims shows that though each of them defines dialogue differently, the spirit remains the same. They all recognize the importance of dialogue, but differ in their emphasis.

In the present-day situation, Faruqi argues, the primacy of dialogue is an ethical question and he would like to postpone theological issues until considerable progress has been made at the ethical level. Much the same view is expressed by Khurshid – what he calls dialogue for 'pro-existence'. In this ethical area, '*Adl* and *Ihsān* should be the co-objectives. Askari disagrees, and is prepared to enter into a dialogue which many Christians and Muslims perhaps would like, at this stage, to avoid, viz. on Revelation, Crucifixion, Trinity and others. Ayoub and Nasr do enter into these critical areas, albeit differently. Ayoub, for instance, explains Christology in an 'unconventional' way and criticizes the Qur'anic commentators who have not been able convincingly to disprove the Crucifixion. He points out that commentators have mistakenly taken the Qur'anic verse 4:157 as an historical statement. He emphasizes that it belongs to theology in the broadest sense. Nasr enters into these areas with an explanation of meanings and of finding parallels between the two religions. He compares aspects of revelation, prophethood and others. Talbi is in favour of openness, at both ethical and theological levels, towards other religions.

4. To some degree, all six Muslims express some hesitation and doubts about the way the Churches have handled the issue of dialogue. Askari, who participated in the very early stages of dialogue especially with the World Council of Churches, emphasizes the importance of the individual and is suspicious of 'institutional dialogue'. At the individual level, personal dialogue and spiritual quest between Christians and Muslims, in Askari's view, should be the purpose of dialogue. Any 'institutional' level of involvement is dominated by the consideration of pleasing a particular section of a community. This 'institutional' consideration, in Askari's view, itself becomes a hurdle in dialogue.

Faruqi expresses doubts about the way the Churches choose Muslims to participate and to 'represent' the community. He implies that Muslims who have been invited to consult and discuss the issue of Christian–Muslim dialogue by the Churches largely lack credibility in the Muslim community and seem 'liberal' and inclined to compromise on various issues. Askari, for example, would not compromise the basic belief of Muslims, and perhaps Faruqi is also signalling this. However, Askari wants to challenge the position that an individual has to be a 'representative' in dialogue.

Khurshid expresses concern about certain aspects of proselytism – *diakonia* and dialogue. He argues that while proselytism and misuse of *diakonia* continue, dialogue will remain an ineffective means of bringing about a better understanding between the two communities. He finds that the 'missionary enterprise' has targeted the Muslim faith and culture and anathemizes the revival of Islam. Under such circumstances, for a meaningful dialogue both Muslims and Christians must review their position.

Ayoub and Talbi express reservations regarding recent encyclicals and statements of the Pope. In their view these statements suggest that dialogue has been used as an instrument of mission; in Talbi's words, 'scaffolding mission'. Both are attracted first to the 1984 'Dialogue and Proclamation', document which identifies dialogue as 'one of the integral elements of the Church's evangelizing missions', and by the Pope's encyclical *Redemptoris Missio* (1991), which again confirms their fear that the Church is taking a step backwards in relation to Muslims when it makes inter-religious dialogue a part of the 'Church's evangelizing mission'. Compared to the 1964 Second Vatican Council's statement, this encyclical, in their view, is not an improvement. Perhaps they have in mind a part of the encyclical which points out very clearly that the Church alone 'possesses the fullness of the means of salvation'. Talbi, who is not prepared to put dialogue in the category of *Da'wah*, is also not prepared to accept dialogue in the mission's service.

5. All six Muslims raise the question of relations between Islam and the West. Theological encounters and at times military clashes took place during the time of the Prophet and the *Khilāfa* (caliphate). The early contacts with Europe were mainly through the trade routes and, by 711 CE, Muslims had gained a foothold in Spain. Other parts of Europe, too, subsequently received Muslims who created a unique civilization. Since then, Muslims have contributed to Europe's culture and civilization. In this respect both Talbi and Ayoub point out that Islam's long presence in Europe and its contribution to Western civilization has not been fully recognized. Theologically, socially and, most importantly, in the psyche of the West, the West is still Judaeo-Christian. Ayoub and Talbi believe that the West has to acknowledge its 'third heritage', that it is Judaeo-Christian-Islamic. Others, Khurshid, for example, suggest that while the Western political system is democratic, nonetheless its cultural and social behaviour remains monolithic. This monolithic understanding of culture, he argues, is at the heart of many misunderstandings today. In this respect, he also points out that the Western powers continually impose their model, politics and culture upon Muslims, thereby destabilizing them. He finds a lack of full appreciation and understanding of Islamic resurgence on the part of

the West and contends that future relations between Islam and the West will depend upon how the West comes to terms with the phenomenon of Islamic resurgence. This will obviously affect Christian-Muslim relations too.

6. Resurgent Islam has put the question of Shari'ah and its application at the top of the agenda, especially in Nigeria, Sudan and Pakistan. In these countries, relations between the two communities have become tense. On this issue the six Muslims suggest that the misunderstanding about Shari'ah emerges as soon as Shari'ah is compared with the Western understanding of law. Nasr and Talbi suggest that because Roman law has been absorbed into the Christian perspective, Christianity cannot understand Shari'ah. Shari'ah for Muslims also includes daily prayer, fasting and other major and minor details and, importantly, the major and minor cannot be separated. Shari'ah demands the implementation of the whole of Islam. They all agree that there is a great need for *Ijtihad* and to 'contextualize' Shari'ah, according to contemporary needs. Referring to Shari'ah, Khurshid argues that there is a vast area which is open for discussion. The Muslims suggest that in dialogue the importance of Shari'ah to Muslims has to be recognized by Christians and, at the same time, Muslims have to realize that today they cannot always implement strictly the earlier interpretations and applications of Shari'ah. They urge care and flexibility in this direction. They are in favour of involving non-Muslims in a debate on Shari'ah and its implementation as far as their religious, social and cultural rights are concerned.

7. Most of them regard dialogue as a part of *Da'wah*. Talbi would like to see the issue of *Da'wah*/mission taken out of the dialogue issue. However, they all agree that *Da'wah* should not become an instrument of proselytism. They understand *Da'wah*, rather, in the sense of information, communication with and understanding of other religions. Whilst they are prepared to accept the same understanding of Christian mission, they are critical of 'mission' as they perceive it as not being 'a religious mission'. Faruqi suggests that the word 'mission' should be dropped and an alternative word, perhaps 'witness' be adopted.

8. Most of them stress the need for a unit like the Pontifical Council for Inter-religious Dialogue in the Vatican in one of the international Muslim organizations. First, they are aware of the difficulties of convincing such an organization of the need to establish a 'secretariat' or even a 'unit' because the priority of Muslim organizations, as we shall see in the Part III, is much more the human and educational concerns

or the plight of Muslims all over the world. They do not see any urgency to establish a dialogue unit. However, if a Muslim organization were to accept and establish a 'secretariat' or 'unit' for dialogue, then the fear – and this is the second point – has been voiced by several of the Muslims, as to who would lead such a 'unit'. What shade of dialogue they would represent is a genuine concern. Would it be a dialogue unit or an office for polemicists?

9. It is apparent that the Muslim participation in dialogue with Christians has been as 'an invited guest'. In other words, they were not the initiators of dialogue. They were invited by the World Council of Churches at the international level, but even at the national level they have responded to the invitation of the Churches. Although the Libyan-sponsored dialogue conference of 1976 was one such event, it paved the way for subsequent bilateral dialogue between the Secretariat of World Islamic Call Society and the Vatican's Inter-religious Dialogue. Askari's short-lived Inter-Religious Foundation and the Islamic Foundation's Interfaith Unit, established by Khurshid Ahmad, came into existence out of the necessity to respond and redefine the Muslim position. However, a consistent and thorough initiative on the part of Muslims is still called for.

III
International Organizations

Introduction

It is important to view the development of the institutions and organizations in the Muslim world against the background of their struggle for independence from the colonial powers and their search for an *Ummah* identity, especially after the fall of the Ottoman *Khilāfah* in 1924. Muslims were conscious of the educational and social backwardness of their community and the decline of the spiritual and moral aspects of Muslims in the world. They discussed their problems at national level and often took the opportunity to have discussions with other Muslims from various parts of the world in Makkah during the *Hajj*. Even small conferences were held with a political agenda. After the fall of *Khilāfah*, the urgency to find an alternative increased.

Two major conferences were held in 1926 in Cairo (13–19 August) and in Makkah (7 June–5 July). Both conferences were formal and attended by Muslim leaders from many parts of the world. The first conference was initiated by a few members of Al-Azhar University, the second by 'Abdul Aziz Ibn Sa'ud. The first conference faced heavy criticism with respect to its validity to organize such a conference in Egypt and for inviting people from abroad. The second conference included in its agenda a proposal to revive *Khilāfah* which, after criticism from Turkey, was eventually dropped from the agenda. However, this conference also established a permanent institution the *Mu'tamar al-'Alam al-Islami* or the Muslim World Congress, with the intention that the Congress should meet annually in Makkah. The second meeting of the Congress was held in 1931 and the structure of the organization finalized. The Congress has political overtones.

The rise of nationalism and socialism in the Arab world in the 1950s and 1960s, especially in Egypt where national identity quite often clashed with religious identity, produced a series of changes in the educational system of schools and universities, including that of the Al-Azhar University. This tendency alerted a number of orthodox *'Ulamā'* who viewed these changes with scepticism. Saudi Arabia, especially wary of Nassir's Arab nationalism, began to search for alternative educational and social institutions. The increasing national wealth brought about by petroleum exports helped to found a number of educational institutions in the 1960s. The Madinah University (established 1962), King Abdul Aziz University, Jeddah (established 1964) and Higher

Institute for Islamic Law, Riyadh (established 1966) were additions to the already established *Shari'ah* College of Makkah (1949) and the *Shari'ah* College of Riyadh (established 1954). Students sponsored from all over the world attended these universities especially the Madinah University, where they trained as Imams and *Da'is* for various parts of the Muslim and non-Muslim world. In order to counter the influence of atheism and socialist ideas on the one hand, and Western influence and Christian missionary activities on the other, *Rabitat al-'Alam al-Islami*, the Muslim World League, was formed in 1962. It soon established a number of offices in Africa, Asia and Europe and later in America.

Nassir's Nationalism influenced many Arab youth. One of his admirers was Mu'ammar al-Qadhdhafi of Libya. In 1969 after the Revolution which brought him to power, he gradually developed his own ideas, which he called the 'Third Way'. His Green Book became the expression of his thought, written on the basis of his experience of the 1969–73 revolution, but rigorously followed up to 1977. Qadhdhafi's belief in Islam, interpreted and understood perhaps in his own way, is expressed in a strong desire to clarify misunderstandings about Islam, especially in the West, and to educate Muslims in general, of whom a large number are wrapped up in various cultural practices and 'superstitions'. With this in mind, Qadhdhafi held the first conference of the Islamic Call Society within months of coming to power (December 1970), and began functioning on the international level with the World Islamic Call Society in 1982. This organization also has a number of offices in Africa, Asia, Europe and America.

Participation of these institutions in dialogue with Christians needs to be seen against these backgrounds and the circumstances of their establishment.

The study materials are based on the replies to my questionnaire received from these three organizations. I have been helped by the publications and articles published either by the respective organizations or the views expressed in general in their interviews published in journals and magazines, and the views expressed in publications other than their own.

11 International Organizations

MU'TAMAR AL-'ALAM AL-ISLAMI
(WORLD MUSLIM CONGRESS)

In 1926 the *Mu'tamar* was established in Makkah. The people behind it were King Abdul Aziz of Saudi Arabia, the Grand Mufti of Palestine, Al-Hajj Aminul Husseini, Rashid Rida of *Al-Manar* and Sheikh Oemar Tjokroaminoto from Indonesia.

The *Mu'tamar* took another five years to take its proper shape and structure. In 1931 it held its second conference in Jerusalem. The choice of venue was perhaps on the initiative of the Grand Mufti of Palestine himself. This indicated that the organizers were aware of the Muslims' sentimental attachment to the Holy places. As well as finalizing the organizational set-up, the Jerusalem conference also provided *Mu'tamar* with an opportunity to hold its first Council meeting. The Council elected the Grand Mufti Al-Hajj M. Aminul Husseini as President and Dr. Mohammad Iqbal, the famous Urdu poet, who led the Indian subcontinent's delegation to the conference, was elected the first Vice-President and Syed Alouba Pasha of Egypt the second. Syed Ziauddin Tabatabai from Iran was elected the General Secretary. This conference also agreed to set up the *Mu'tamar*'s headquarters in Jerusalem, where it remained until 1939 when it was closed forcefully by the British authorities. By the end of the Second World War, the situation in Palestine had changed, and Israel had been created. The leadership revived the organization and held its third conference in Karachi in 1949. The political climate of the time prevented many of the delegates from participating in the assembly, but the delegates agreed to hold a fourth conference in 1951. In 1951, Karachi was chosen as the new international headquarters and in this conference Inamullah Khan of Burma (Maynmar) was chosen as the Secretary General. Since then it has held several conferences, the fifth in Baghdad (1952), the sixth in Mogadishu (1964–5), the seventh in Amman (1967), the eighth in Kibris (Cyprus) (1980), and the ninth in Karachi (1988), where the vacant place of President (the Grand Mufti had died in 1975) was filled by Marouf al Dawalibi, former Prime Minister of Syria and the tenth in Colombo (1992). At this last assembly Abdullah Omar Naseef was chosen as President and Raja Mohammad Zafar-ul-Haq was chosen as the new Secretary General.

The Structure

The *Mu'tamar*'s 25-member Council meets annually in Makkah or Jeddah. The choice of venue is the result of its increasing links with the Secretariats of *Rabitah* and Organization of Islamic Conference, where the *Mu'tamar* has an observer status in its summit conferences.

It disseminates information through regular publications like *The Muslim World*, a weekly bulletin from Karachi published since 1963. The bulletin is a news and views service, an organ of the *Mu'tamar*.

Objectives

In an interview, Inamullah Khan explained the goals of the *Mu'tamar* in the following words:

1. To build bridges of goodwill and understanding among Muslims all over the world and to work for Islamic solidarity.
2. To acquaint the Muslim people with their faith, ideology, cultural heritage, past history and contemporary situation.
3. To exhort the world-wide Muslim community to march forward with the Holy Qur'an as the Book of eternal guidance and the life example of the Prophet Muhammad (peace be upon him) as the beacon light of the caravan.
4. To organize the *Ummah* to make it a well-knit and homogeneous world entity, able to contribute to world peace as well as working for peace among the countries.
5. To establish conditions under which the dignity and worth of the human person is respected, and racism and apartheid wiped out.[1]

Dialogue

Mu'tamar's various areas of work at the political and social levels do not pertain to our field of study. However, the area of dialogue, especially between Christians and Muslims, does. There are no comprehensive publications of *Mu'tamar* in this field, therefore I have to depend upon Inamullah Khan's interview, speeches and replies to the letters that I wrote to him. It was his personal interest that, in his capacity as Secretary General, he started taking a deeper interest in inter-faith activities and perhaps he used his influence to mould the *Mu'tamar* in that direction. He developed this interest in the late 1950s when Garland Hopkins set up a committee, as he remembers, 'called the

Christian–Muslim Continuing Committee (organizers of Bhamdoun Consultation, 1954) in which he was one of the Presidents and their idea was to achieve better understanding between the two largest world communities'[2] (i.e. Christians and Muslims). The theme of better understanding between the two communities recurs in Dr Khan's concern about dialogue. In a keynote speech in Mindanao in 1984, he outlined the necessity of dialogue between the two religions, which could be summed up as:

> That the Christian-Muslim dialogue is an effort to promote common values of two great religions. This includes belief in one Humanity and one great human family. Dialogue provides an opportunity to 'settle all our differences ... through discussions'. Dialogue is about the defence of 'human rights of all citizens of the country – the basic rights assured by all religions. Dialogue is about soul searching and having the courage to admit past mistakes and discuss freely various issues of mutual accomodation.[3]

Mu'tamar first participated in dialogue with Christians in 1969 in Amman. In 1967, the Israeli occupation of part of Jordan and Jerusalem brought not only Muslims, but also Muslims and Christians together. In this unique show of solidarity, the Roman Catholic Church and the Greek Orthodox Church united with Muslims on the issue of Palestine. Although the issue was of an international nature, the dialogue was held in a regional or Middle Eastern context.

Mu'tamar participated in a joint programme of dialogue with the World Council of Churches in 1982. The dialogue was organized in Colombo (30 March–1 April) against the background of the occupation of Afghanistan by the Soviet Union which had created a large influx of refugees into Pakistan, the Palestinian issue was at its height and Muslims were celebrating the beginning of a new century of *Hijrah*. The theme of the dialogue was selected as 'Christian–Muslim Living and Working Together – Ethics and Practices of Humanitarian and Development Programmes'. In this dialogue 30 Muslims and 30 Christians participated, and several issues directly concerning them, especially in the field of co-operation, were pointed out. They said – and this part was also included in the Final Report of the dialogue – 'co-operation deserves to be built on the foundations of removing obstacles and supporting the victims of aggression and persecution'.[4] The Muslims stressed:

an unequivocal condemnation of Israeli aggression against Palestine and the invasion of Afghanistan by the Soviet Union. They urged Christians to develop a sympathetic understanding of Muslims' *Shari'ah*. They also emphasize to remove obstacles of Christian–Muslim co-operation on the basis of principles agreed upon in the Chambesy dialogue in 1976.[5]

Assessing the achievement of *Mu'tamar*'s participation in dialogue, Inamullah Khan argues that from the very beginning, that is, from the Amman dialogue in 1969 onwards, as far as the cause of Palestine is concerned, no 'dissent or misgiving or apathy was shown from the Christian side' and 'the Christian leaders' viewpoint, also in the Colombo dialogue, 'was in line with the Muslim viewpoint'.[6] Secondly, he takes credit for the earlier participation in dialogue with Christians, by the *Mu'tamar*, which he believes inspired other national and international Muslim organizations.

The *Mu'tamar* now maintains dialogue with Christians, but it is engaged in dialogue with other religions too. It has developed an informal dialogue with Buddhist organizations in Sri Lanka and in Japan.

'Keeping in view the concept of better awareness, meaningful understanding and sustainable co-operation, the *Mu'tamar* and especially I, as the Secretary General', says Dr Khan, 'started taking active interest in WCRP' (World Conference on Religion and Peace).[7] He was one of the presidents of WCRP until 1989. He emphasizes that 'Islam means peace', it is 'peace without discrimination'. He envisages a society ' . . . based on the great concept of peace, love, justice, harmony, mercy and equity for all'.[8]

Minorities

One of *Mu'tamar*'s important areas of work is with the Muslim minorities. Muslim minorities comprise one-third of the total Muslim population of the world. 'One very important aspect which our leaders forget', argues Dr Khan, 'is to give the Muslim minorities the sense of their cultural identity . . .'. He finds an absence of this, saying, 'they may be completely lost in the vast sea of the majority community of their countries', and finds the problem of Muslim minorities in the East, in Burma, in Patani, in Philippines and in India, are serious. But equally, he points out that the problem in the Western countries is no better, if not worse. Muslims in Russia, Bulgaria, Europe and in the Americas 'need a special study'.[9] In Europe he finds some sort of cultural supremacy of the majority against the minority, what he calls a 'cultural racism'.[10]

Christians in Muslim countries are in a minority, too. Perhaps, with this important aspect in mind, the organizers of the Colombo dialogue had a working group on minorities. This group identified six major areas of tension between majority and minority: (a) Each religious group should be enabled to live according to the teachings of its faith, [and] the right to worship, and build places of worship schools. (b) They should co-operate with each other for their freedom of worship. (c) It was agreed that a standing committee should be formed to study instances of discrimination and persecution of human rights and to take appropriate action. (d) Places of worship, religious schools and trusts confiscated in the last 50 years should be returned to their original use and owners. (e) To find appropriate ways of maintaining or creating legal safeguards in matters of marriage, divorce and inheritance are for Muslims, and some Christians, confessions to be respected. (f) Multi-religious, multi-cultural and multi-linguistic communities offer new methods of living and working together and need further study.[11]

The Muslim minorities in Western Europe are under two spheres of influence. Salim Abdullah, *Mu'tamar*'s representative in Germany until recently, points out they are the spheres of 'traditional Islam' and 'the Muslim Movements'. 'Traditional Islam', in his view, is 'co-operative and consequently open for the new status quo the Muslim community is faced with within their diaspora – and subsequently also affirms the necessity of dialogue with other religions'. The 'Muslim Movements' which includes both Shi'is and Sunnis, Abdullah points out, are 'rather unfriendly missionaries'. They are in his opinion 'against Western society', because they consider it a 'society of unbelievers'.[12]

In a situation where 'traditional Islam' could provide a hopeful sign in the European context, Abdullah finds that it in itself is under attack from two sides. On the one hand, the European mass media 'pronounce Islam as undifferential and above all dogmatic, antiquated and conservative', and therefore out of touch with its own people and society at large. Furthermore, Islam has been projected as a missionary religion and therefore as 'an enemy of Christianity'. Islam is also 'accused of having conquest in mind as a delayed continuation of the Turkish siege of Vienna'. On the other hand, the 'Muslim Movement' labels 'traditional Islam' as a 'fifth column' of the 'Saudi royal family and hence an enemy of Islam and an accomplice of the U.S.A.'.[13]

Though Abdullah provides the names of the representatives of 'traditionalist Islam' he avoids mentioning 'Muslim Movement'.

RABITAT AL-'ALAM AL-ISLAMI
(THE MUSLIM WORLD LEAGUE)

The idea of pan-Islamism developed soon after the fall of *Khilafah* in Turkey in 1924. Muslims at various levels began their quest for co-operation and common concern. In India, in the mid–1950s, on a modest scale, a group of Muslim youth, mostly students belonging to *Darul-'Ulum Nadwatul Ulama*, the famous religious seminary in Lucknow, determined to propagate and popularize the universal message of Islamic brotherhood, formed a non-official International Cultural Islamic Organization (ICIO) called *Anjuman Rabitah-i-Islami* in Urdu and *Jam'iyat ar-Rabitah al-Islamiah al-Dawliyah* in Arabic. Since this had an international dimension, its membership was open to an international audience. Soon this 'Utopian idea' received responses from 14 Muslim countries. Eventually its membership increased to 40. Its Patron-Chairman was Abul Hassan Ali Nadwi. It published an Arabic and English bulletin. Even in those early days ICIO published a book in Arabic from Beirut, highlighting the case of Ethiopian and Eritrean Muslims.[14]

The ICIO did not survive long. Perhaps it was only a 'coincidence' that the Makkah *Rabitah* came into existence in 1962 and one of its founder members was Abul Hassan Ali Nadwi, and later, one of the permanent members of its Constituent Council. Others who were associated with ICIO became members of *Rabitah* and eventually took charge of branches, in various positions and in several countries.[15]

Objectives

The objectives of the *Rabitah* could be grouped as:

To convey the message of Islam and its teachings all over the world. To dispel any wrong impressions about Islam and Muslims, created by the false propaganda of the enemies of Islam. To help Muslims, particularly the oppressed ones and those in minority, in the preservation and advancement of their religious, educational and cultural rights and activities. To assist the Muslim communities in the promotion of Islamic *Da'wah* and the achievement of unity and solidarity among them.[16]

The *Rabitah* came into existence with these broad objectives, as a result of the resolution of the Islamic Conference held in Makkah in May 1962.

Rabitah talks of *Da'wah* in a broader sense, not only of preaching and propagation but also as a counter-measure to 'conspiracies of the enemies'. Defining the area of the *Rabitah*'s work, former Secretary General, Sheikh Al-Gazzaz said in a *Rabitah* meeting in November 1975:

> The *Rabitah* . . . was established on the basic of Islamic *Da'wah*. Its basic objectives are to preach the teachings of Islam, enlighten the people about the principles and values of our faith, and explain the meaning of Islamic Shari'ah and practice. Moreover, we Muslims have to be aware of the conspiracies of the enemies of Islam who try their level best to mislead the public opinion about the fundamentals of Islam, and to misrepresent the Shari'ah. It is our duty to combat their nefarious activities, and we should have full confidence that they can never put off the light of Islam.[17]

Who are the enemies? The *Rabitah*'s journals and publications provide an indication of three levels of enemies.

1. The threat of Western imperialism in all its forms. It includes Freemasonry, Rotary Clubs, Lion Clubs and similar other organizations and ideologies, which it terms as 'a secret subversive organization, affiliated with Zionism'[18] to be checked in Muslim countries.

2. The heretical movements like Qadianism or Ahmedism and Bahaism. The League urged all Muslims to ban their activities, as these may be thought of by other Muslims as Islamic activities.[19]

3. Perhaps at a lesser degree but with the same enthusiasm, it urges its member organizations to counter the *Bida'* (innovations) within Islam. Graduates of Saudi universities in Madinah or from Ummal Qura found employment with *Darul Ifta'* (office of legal judgement) and work in close association with the *Rabitah* branches in various parts of the world. Through these associations the *Rabitah* had a mission to 'reform' Muslims. Apart from publishing and sponsoring some basic literature on Islam, the *Rabitah* has two major areas of work where it has made some impact among Muslims.

First, according to its objective to 'assist the Muslim communities', the *Rabitah* has been able to finance the building of mosques and to help in maintaining them. For example, the mosque in Rome is funded and built by the support of the *Rabitah*. It has been instrumental in several countries, including Britain, in providing a platform where the representatives of mosques could be brought together. 'The Council of Mosques' in Britain is one such example. Under such 'representative' councils, the *Rabitah* has been able to establish *Fiqh* Councils (Council of Islamic Jurisprudence) to help the local Muslim communities with their day-to-day problems of marriage, divorce and family affairs, and issues of religious edict.[20]

The second area concerns Muslim minorities and refugees. It has funded schools and institutions, but more importantly, it has to some extent kept pressure and momentum on the issues, e.g. Moro in the Philippines, Eritrea in Ethiopia until its independence, and Kashmir. Regarding refugees, the *Rabitah* established in the late 1970s an agency called the 'Islamic International Relief Agency'. This agency has helped Muslim refugees in Bangladesh, Pakistan, Afghanistan, Ethiopia, Sudan, Somalia and many other countries.[21]

To achieve its objectives the *Rabitah* has a secretariat in Makkah. The supreme body of this organization is its 'Constituent Council' which currently has around 60 members from various parts of the world. New members are added from time to time. The Secretariat, headed by the Secretary General, is responsible for implementing the decisions of the Constituent Council. The Council meets every year, usually at the time of *Hajj* (pilgrimage). It is funded solely by the Saudi government. With a budget of 120 million Saudi Riyal, it employs more than 2000 people of 50 nationalities.[22]

Dialogue and Christian Mission

Dialogue has been perceived as one of the methods of *Da'wah* and is a part of *Da'wah*. As to the reasons why the *Rabitah* participates in dialogue with other religions, and especially with Christians, Abdullah Omar Nasseef, Secretary General until recently, emphasizes 'that the dialogue with different religions will go a long way to erase misconceptions about Islam'. He claims, 'Muslims will be beneficiaries in two ways: one, by putting Islam to others as it really is, and the other, by getting a correct picture of other religions.'[23]

The need for a 'correct picture' has arisen because in many Muslim countries, in the past, missionaries were responsible for the education of Muslim children. The *Rabitah* has viewed Christian missionaries as active agents of Westernization, as well as an 'instrument of atheism'.[24] Therefore, they are perceived as a threat to Islam. For example, one of the *Rabitah*'s representatives in Africa, Yahya As-Saeti, stated in 1982, 'international Christian missionary and communist organizations pose the most serious threat to Islamic society. Especially as its modern life does not exclude the possibility of the realization of such a threat.'[25]

The threat of Christian mission has been highlighted in several of the *Rabitah*'s meetings and conferences. Addressing an African Muslim audience in Senegal, former Secretary General Muhammad Ali al-Harakan said, 'It is worthy of note . . . that the Christian missionary organizations are now distributing the Bible, translated into about a thousand local African dialects, in an area stretching from Mauritania to Liberia', referring to the various students who are in European universities for higher education from Africa. 'The aim of such a programme', he stresses, 'is of course not to preserve the African cultural heritage as is claimed but rather to enrich the canonical [sic; i.e. colonial] heritage by adding to it new publications of the Bible in various African languages'.[26] The Western approach of mission has been seen as an encroachment upon human dignity and rights, termed as the 'forcing of an alien religion on an indigenous population'.[27]

The *Rabitah* finds that the Second Vatican Council's statement on other religions (*Nostra Aetate*) is very encouraging. This declaration, it says, 'assured us of their good intention'.[28] Perhaps this was the reason why both sides, the Vatican and the Saudi government, opened lines of communication, and Muhammad Ali al-Harakan, then the Minister of Justice, later appointed as Secretary General of the *Rabitah*, visited the Vatican on 9–10 October 1974. As one Saudi journalist put it: 'this meeting is a sign, which indicates the end of the Crusades, Pope Paul VI will be remembered for that'.[29] To show solidarity with other religions, the *Rabitah*'s Secretary General participated in 'The Pilgrimage to Assisi' in 1986.

The *Rabitah* sees its role in dialogue at various levels. Naseef points to the *Rabitah*'s participation with the various Churches at both national and international levels. 'We personally attended the meetings and invited the leaders of various church bodies to the Kingdom [Saudi Arabia] on behalf of the Muslim World League. In addition', he says, we 'made contacts with the Orthodox Church of Antioch, the Orthodox Church of Greece and also the Middle Eastern churches in Geneva'.[30] This is a growing sign that the *Rabitah* feels much more comfortable dealing with the regional Arab Christian Churches than the Churches in the West.

Now the *Rabitah* is shifting its emphasis to conservation, economics and peace and green issues, without neglecting the areas of work that it has covered so far. From the very fact that people of religions are consulted and perhaps 'the most important exercise and lesson for Muslims in the interfaith equation is to learn how to deal with people of other religions', the *Rabitah* is now 'considering the founding of a department of Inter-Faith Affairs within the Muslim World League. For if the Muslims are not present in this new and increasingly influential platform to contribute to deliberations armed with the certainty of Islam and vast resources of Islamic thought, then others will do so'.[31]

JAM'IYAT AL-DA'WAH AL-ISLAMIYAH AL-'ALAMIYAH (THE WORLD ISLAMIC CALL SOCIETY)

The World Islamic Call Society was established by the Libyan government in 1982. The Revolutionary Command Council of Libya issued a decree to establish a special 'Body of Public Interest' known as 'The Association of the Islamic Convocation' (in 1970 this was the first congress of the Islamic Call Society). In August 1974, the decree regarding the 'Association' was amended and its scope widened. By 1974, the following objectives of the Association had emerged.

Objectives and Structure

The Association aims especially to propagate Islam in all parts of the world with all available resources. The Association's broad objectives could be summarized as:

to introduce the Holy Qur'an and the Prophet's life by all available means. Teaching of Islam, its ethics, worship and day-to-day dealings in a pure and simple way. Prepare *Da'is* of Islam. Publication of books and periodicals and research work on Islam and translate them in all major languages. Organize seminars for students and professionals in order to introduce Islam to them. Develop contacts with various religious bodies. Spread Arabic language and encourage Muslim countries to accept Qur'an as the basis of legislation and consider Arabic as the official language of the country. All available means.[32]

In August 1982, in a meeting in Libya (the Second Congress of the Islamic Call Society), it was proposed to establish 'The World Council of the Islamic Call', now known as the 'World Islamic Call Society'. The Society's aims and objectives are more or less the same as those of the Association. Of those who participated in the Congress, some were invited to be members of the Council. Currently it consists of 36 members from various parts of the world.[33] They meet annually to plan and formulate policies and the Council's Secretariat in Tripoli is responsible for the implementation of the policies agreed in the Council.

The Society disseminates its information today through Islamic *Da'wah*, a trilingual newspaper (Arabic, English and French) and publishes a monthly magazine, *Rissalat al-Jihad*, in three languages, French, Arabic and English (separate issues). It also publishes the Holy Qur'an in Arabic and translations in various languages. It trains a number of *Da'i* to work amongst Muslims and non-Muslims in various parts of the world.

The Society helps to finance various welfare projects in conjunction with UNESCO (United Nations Educational Scientific and Cultural Organization), e.g. protection and rational use of water in rural sub-Saharan areas.[34] It promotes the use of Arabic alphabets in African languages. This project is carried out in collaboration with the Islamic Development Bank, Jeddah. The Society's publications have highlighted the Arab-Islamic world's contribution to the fields of science, culture, arts and technology.

The Society's humanitarian and welfare activities are not the subject of this study. For this a regular report appears in their publication. Here we shall deal specifically with the Society's participation in dialogue.

Dialogue

When Qadhdhafi came to power in 1969 after a *coup d'état*, the whole emphasis of government and its outlook towards society changed. Libya began to set itself as 'an example' for other Arab countries to follow. The philosophy of the Society, alongside the ideas expounded by the *Green Book*, began the task of changing the world. With this new philosophy Qadhdhafi himself entered into dialogue with some European intellectuals in Paris. In November 1973 a symposium arranged by the newspaper *Le Monde* was held. French intellectuals, newspaper editors and politicians were present. The symposium was hailed 'as a return to the intellectual and civilized dialogue between the East and the West'.[35] Although the discussion touched on issues such as 'Islam and Socialism', 'Democracy', 'Unity of the Mediterranean Region', etc., the discussion, however, was focused mainly on Palestinian issues and Zionism. Although this symposium, it seems, did not produce the desired effect, and at times entered into polemics, nevertheless this was a rare encounter of an Arab leader with European intellectual circles. Furthermore, the symposium paved the way for subsequent Christian–Muslim dialogue, first between the Libyan government and the Vatican, and later between the World Islamic Call Society and the Pontifical Council for Interreligious Dialogue.

After the Paris Symposium, the Libyan government was constantly in touch with the Vatican in order to initiate a dialogue between Muslims and Christians. Finally, in 1976, a delegation from Libya, headed by Ahmad Shaheeti, Secretary for Foreign Affairs, visited the Vatican and finalized the arrangements including a joint preparatory committee to convene a Christian–Muslim dialogue in Tripoli from 1 to 5 February 1976. Four major topics for presentation were agreed.

1. The possibility of religion as an ideology in life and religion in modern society.
2. The joint fundamentals between the two religions and points of agreement between them.
3. The principle that social justice stems from faith in God.
4. How to eliminate wrong concepts and distrust which are still dividing the two religions.[36]

Some 500 people from 70 countries attended the dialogue. In his inaugural speech, Qadhdhafi emphasized that due to 'certain circumstances when dialogue came to a standstill' between Christians and Muslims after the colonial period, now it has become 'possible to establish a dialogue to bring about peace and agreement between us'.[37] He also emphasized that 'our meeting, here, is a gathering for frankness, truth and earnest and positive course of action ... It is time that we cannot cancel history nor reinterpret its events according to the conditions of our time, yet we can deduce lessons from it in order to be able to make the history of our period'.[38] The organizers of this dialogue were aware that this was only the first step, 'which must be followed by many other steps as well'. Soon after the dialogue was over Ahmad Shaheeti visited the Vatican in March 1976 and a protocol was agreed in order to implement the Tripoli resolutions by establishing a joint follow-up committee. Gradually, the responsibility of arrangements, participation and planning fell to the World Islamic Call Society. Since 1976 a number of dialogues between Christians, especially with the Pontifical Council for Interreligious Dialogue and the Call Society have been held, sometimes in Rome and sometimes in Malta, where the Society has a branch office.

It is important to note that the Society's participation in dialogue with Christians is motivated by two factors; first, to put up a common front against atheism and Zionism, and, second, to present Islam in a better way. When the preparation for the Tripoli dialogue was under way, Sheikh Mahmud Subhi, of the Society, said in a statement that 'the Libyan Arab Republic wishing to start a new chapter with the Christian world was looking forward to finding possible ways for joint co-operation in opposing the atheistic trends sweeping the world as well as the political trends created by Zionism',[39] and this is reflected in the inclusion of Articles 20 and 21 in the final communiqué of the Tripoli dialogue.[40] These two Articles became the centre of controversy, and the Western press highlighted these aspects; the progress this dialogue made, in building good relations between the two communities, was overshadowed.

The Society began ongoing efforts at dialogue in the mid-1980s. Its dialogue activities have been arranged mainly through its Malta branch, especially since the completion of its multi-purpose Islamic Centre in the Paola region. This branch has arranged a number of Christian–Muslim gatherings at local level. Since July 1987, it has published a monthly newspaper in the local language under the name *Dialogue*, which has been distributed to churches, schools, government institutions and pubic libraries.[41] This initiative has been welcomed by the local Muslim community.

In 1988 the Society organized a symposium of Muslims and Christians on the theme 'Religion and Conflict of Civilizations'. This symposium looked at the emergence of Christian Zionism and its theology, the Arab and Western cultural clash and others.[42] In March 1989, a delegation of the Pontifical Council for Inter-religious Dialogue, headed by Cardinal Arinze, visited the World Islamic Call Society in Tripoli with the aim of renewing contacts and revising dialogue on the guidelines agreed in the 1976 Tripoli dialogue. A reciprocal visit was made by the Society at the invitation of the Pontifical Council on 15 February 1990. The two sides exchanged views and discussed the subject of 'Mission and *Da'wah*' in some detail under the following agenda:

1. The concept of *Da'wah* and mission.
2. The proper methods to be employed in conducting *Da'wah* and mission, and the attitude required.
3. The methods which are to be avoided.
4. The methods actually being employed and the difficulties which arise in today's world.[43]

This meeting was a small, 'rather limited meeting'. At the conclusion of the meeting, the participants had an audience with the Pope. In his address the Pope emphasized that 'Christians and Muslims can work together, bearing witness before modern civilization to the divine presence and loving providence which guides our steps. Together we can proclaim that He who has made us has called us to live in harmony and justice'.[44] This meeting paved the way for another dialogue in Malta and broadened the participants in the meeting.

A two-day meeting (22–23 November 1990) was held in Malta between the Society and Pontifical Council for Inter-religious Dialogue. The papers presented by Christians in the dialogue drew attention to the social and cultural aspects through:

1. making sure that school books are free from any errors or distortions that could insult religion or misinterpret it,
2. adopting unified methods of education which aim to instil in the teacher the love for dialogue and the understanding of others and inculcate in him the spirit of tolerance and love,
3. the search for ways and means to direct public opinion in such a way as to foster the spirit of tolerance and understanding of others.[45]

Papers presented by the Muslim participants emphasized the importance of contemplating the divine texts, which call for tolerance. The papers point out that 'the divine text is one thing and its application is another, for while the text is divine, its application is human'. The papers further asserted that the 'will to adopt dialogue begins with the recognition of the other'.[46]

The Society sponsored, along with others, a three-day 'International Seminar on Migrants and Refugees: Christian and Muslim Perspectives and Practices', held in Valetta (Malta) 22–24 April 1991. This seminar was 'built on past interfaith discussions' and focused 'specifically on establishing practical co-operation on the global humanitarian problem of refugees and migrants'.[47]

The Society, although committed to maintaining better relations between Christians and Muslims, nonetheless remains strongly critical of Christian missionary activities in the Muslim world in particular and in the Third World in general. Its regular newspapers criticize missionary activities and it has translated into Arabic and French and serialized some publications of the Islamic Foundation, Leicester, on missionary activities.[48] Introducing a series, the editor of *Al-Da'wah Al-Islamiyah* remarks:

Muslims are . . . generally exposed to the crusading Christianizing activity. Therefore Islam as a whole is in danger of it. The Muslim [exposed to such pressures anywhere in the world] is worthy of every support and backing, from all Muslims and from all who are able to present material and ideal help and [do] care for encountering Islam's historic enemies.[49]

12 Discussion

The formation of the two international organizations, *Mu'tamar al-'Alam al-Islami* and *Rabitat al-'Alam al-Islami* needs to be seen in the light of the circumstances in which they have been created. The *Mu'tamar*'s priority lies with the political and social issues of Muslims. As mentioned earlier, the *Mu'tamar* came into existence soon after the fall of *Khilāfah*, and tried to fill the vacuum. In its approach to political issues, the *Mu'tamar* took an anti-colonial stand and a pan-Islamic attitude. The anti-colonial stand became more visible when it began to criticize the Balfour Declaration, which supported a homeland for the Jews in Palestine. Its opposition to a Jewish state became vigorous after the creation of Israel. The pan-Islamic idea of the *Mu'tamar* became increasingly irrelevant, mainly because of the growing nation-state and nationalist feelings amongst the Muslims. *Mu'tamar* received a further setback when the concept of nationhood was introduced by the Arab nationalists like Michel Aflaq, which gained ground in Syria and Iraq, or socialists, and the Arab nationalist message preached by Nasser. 'Co-operation' between Muslims and Christians seems to have existed on the ground even against the political trend of the time, which was fragile. However, *Mu'tamar* wanted co-operation between the Christian and Muslim religious leaders which was the best option for *Mu'tamar*. The *Ulamā* were not ready to co-operate.

The *Ulamā*'s priority in their encounter with Christianity needs to be seen in the image of Christianity created by Christian missionaries in the Muslim world, as well as the *Ulamā*'s image of Christianity, seen by them as the colonial arm of the West. They avoided opening any new avenues, such as co-operation or even dialogue with Christians, simply because their priority at the time seems to have been to preserve 'what is left' of Muslim traditions and culture. In such circumstances *Ijtihad* becomes a risky business. *Mu'tamar*'s priority of a political and social agenda gave little or no thought to opening a new relationship with other faiths. It was not until the mid-1950s that Garland Hopkin, the organizer of the Bhamdoun Dialogue (1954), approached Inamullah Khan, then Secretary General of *Mu'tamar*. Khan participated in a number of dialogues with Christians as well as other religions. It was his personal interest in dialogue which in 1982 persuaded *Mu'tamar* to hold a Christian–Muslim dialogue in Colombo. Again, this dialogue was not the main event of the conference; rather it was an appendix to celebrate the new *Hijrah* centenary.

At the regional level, representatives like Salim Abdullah in Germany, who participated in a number of regional Christian–Muslim dialogues, projected *Mu'tamar* as an organization which encourages dialogue. It did not take any serious decision to establish a unit within *Mu'tamar*. The reason perhaps being, as pointed out earlier, that the leadership was not convinced of the seriousness of dialogue initiated by the Churches in the West. The dominant factor remains the *Ulamā* within, and the decision-making body in *Mu'tamar* were wary of the Churches' intentions about dialogue. Furthermore, they could not convince the larger body of their constituency of the need to initiate and participate in dialogue with other faiths.

There are instances, e.g. in the Middle East, where *Mu'tamar* was involved in 'dialogue'. The Israeli occupation of the West Bank and Gaza as well as East Jerusalem in 1967, the attempt to set fire to the *Al-Aqsa* mosque and the changed character of the Christian holy places in Jerusalem brought Christians and Muslims together in Amman in 1969.

Though there have been some dialogue initiatives and participation of some members of *Mu'tamar* at local level, it does not provide a clear picture that dialogue is an essential programme of *Mu'tamar*. *Mu'tamar* is still guided by immediate political concerns. *Mu'tamar*'s interest in dialogue, and dialogue with Christians and other religions, is not an adopted policy of the organization, but remains an initiative of some individuals at regional and national levels.

Rabitah came into existence in an environment where the nationalist and socialist forces were making headway in the Arab world. Nasser's pan-Arabism was threatening a number of Islamic organizations and institutions. The oldest and prestigious centre of Islamic learning in Egypt, Al-Azhar University, was forced to make a number of changes. The ruler's political grip was making its mark on religious and social institutions. In order to counter this trend and to cover the gaps the *Mu'tamar* left, e.g. on education, relief and rehabilitation, and above all *Da'wah* among Muslims and non-Muslims, the *Rabitah* came into existence in 1962. Patronage of the *Rabitah* was provided by the Saudi Royal family. The emergence of *Rabitah* was again in response to the situation in which Muslims found themselves. Priority has been given to teaching Islam and propagating it among the masses. This includes making Muslims aware of the 'dangers' the Muslim community is facing. These dangers are Western imperialism, Zionism and Christian

missionaries. Once Christians are seen as a 'danger', Muslim understanding and knowledge of Christianity is obviously motivated by that
factor. Dialogue with Muslims and other religions, as the Churches in
the West understood it, becomes a suspect tool and as a result largely
irrelevant. The *Da'i* of the *Rabitah*, trained Muslim clerics, are not
trained to understand Christianity as the Christians understand them.
They are not trained for dialogue as such, but are well aware of
Rahmatullah Kairanawi's argument against Karl Pfander or Ibn
Taimiyah's *al-Jawab-al-Sahih*. Their books have become standard works
for understanding other religions, especially Christianity.

Rabitah's leadership, like that of the late Secretary General Al-Harakan
but more prominently during the period of Abdullah Omar Naseef, has
shown great enthusiasm for participating in international inter-religious
platforms, e.g. sending a delegation of the Saudi government to the
Vatican by the former and participation in Assisi (1986) and in World
Conference on Religion and Peace (WCRP) by the latter. Naseef was
one of the main speakers at the WCRP's Fourth General Assembly in
Melbourne, Australia (1989). He showed an interest in opening a special unit for inter-religious dialogue in *Rabitah*'s headquarters. In order to establish a unit successfully, *Rabitah* has to overcome two
important obstacles. First, the *Ulamā*. The *Ulamā*'s experience of Christianity is through encounter with missionaries, and any initiatives from
the Churches for dialogue is bound to be seen as another missionary
strategy aimed at the conversion of Muslims. Without their approval
or even tacit support dialogue initiatives of any kind are bound to fail.
If *Rabitah* manages to convince the *Ulamā* of the need for a unit of
inter-religious dialogue, the other problem *Rabitah* will face is, who
will lead such a unit? It seems that *Rabitah* will be under pressure to
appoint a person who may follow the line of 'dialogue' adopted by
Ahmad Deedat, who was awarded the King Faisal Award for services
to Islam in 1989. In such case, *Rabitah* may have to go back to the
drawing board.

The Call of Islam Society emerged out of the womb of nationalism
and socialism. Both ideologies – nationalism and socialism – have been
adopted by the Arab leaders against Western hegemony. From its very
inception the Society adopted a policy of providing welfare services,
like medical aid and education, especially in Africa. It has also appointed Imams in various mosques in Africa and Asia, especially mosques
built with the help of the Society. Despite all its philanthropic activities, at its heart lies the preaching of Islam, to non-Muslims and Muslims alike. Qadhdhafi made clear this primary objective from its inception.

The preaching of Islam is not set in a traditional sense of *Sufi* tradition or in a *Madrassah* setting. The preaching is adopted through the appointment of Imams in the mosque but also by adopting the methods, which the Society criticizes of Christian missionaries, of philanthropic activities, in Africa and Asia.

The Society's decision to participate in dialogue with Christians seems motivated by Qadhdhafi's emphasis on cultural issues – a dialogue with the West, where he was trying to create a religious front against the capitalist West. The emphasis of the 1973 Paris symposium, where Qadhdhafi highlighted the plight of the Palestinian refugees and the emergence of Zionism and Western domination in Arab lands, has now changed to lesser publicized Christian–Muslim gatherings. Unlike the 1973 Paris symposium or the 1976 Tripoli dialogue, the issues are now specific and not general. Issues are debated in small groups of representatives from the Call of Islam Society and the Pontifical Council for Inter-religious Dialogue (PCID). There is an ongoing discussion between the two. It seems that the Society is content to keep as its partner only the PCID, and has not moved to seek a partnership with other Churches or even the World Council of Churches. However, while this relationship has provided a close working relationship with the PCID, the Society's influence has been limited to one Church.

There were several requests from various Muslim quarters to establish a secretariat or unit for inter-religious dialogue. The requests are specifically directed towards the Organization of Islamic Conference (OIC). Such requests suggest that Muslim intellectuals are increasingly losing confidence in these three international organizations and hoping that the OIC may open a new chapter for them. It is desirable, but looking at the current political climate of the Muslim world it is most unlikely that the OIC will establish a unit in the near future. Perhaps concentration on regional level dialogue, and providing help to the regional bodies, may be the way out.

13 Conclusion

We began this study by pointing out the context in which Muslims and Christians felt the need for dialogue. The challenge of modernity shook confidence in the metaphysical realities in society. Increasingly, 'individualism', 'liberalism' and 'secularization' became the defining force of modern thinking. Technological innovations and discoveries have been hailed as the success of modernity. Religion, increasingly, became apologetic and began to define its own scope and space. The religious discourse, increasingly dictated by the prevailing social and political climate, generated its own reaction. The European colonialists' understanding of religion was overwhelmingly moulded by the understanding of Western Christianity. They saw other religions in the light of Christian understanding and perception. They were perceived as a deficient way of reaching God, and therefore Christianity has a moral obligation to fill that gap. It was in this context, the context of modernity and colonialism, that Muslims entered into a new encounter with Christians.

The dialogue between the two communities, which began with the 'quest for human understanding', seems set to extend well into the next millenium. But better understanding between the two communities will depend upon how they address the crucial issues such as the nature of dialogue, Shari'ah, human rights, religious pluralism, and Islam and the West in general. How the two communities tackle these issues may create either alienation or much-needed reconciliation between the two.

We shall begin with the nature of dialogue. Dialogue between the two communities, as we have suggested, began with exploration, where the emphasis was more on the understanding of the other and the quest for religion's relevance to the contemporary world. The World Council of Churches and the Vatican both initiated dialogue with Muslims as well as other religions in more or less this direction. But, from the very beginning, both the Church bodies faced consistent pressure from within to abandon this exploratory dimension of dialogue and to bring dialogue within the fold of mission.

In order to clarify this dichotomy between 'mission' and 'dialogue', both the Vatican and WCC issued statements and clarifications. However, it seems, this did not satisfy the Church members. The pressure from the Evangelical Churches increasingly influenced the dialogue–mission debate. By 1990, there was a complete reversal in the Churches' position on dialogue. They began defining dialogue increasingly in terms of mission.

The 'Decade of Evangelism' and dialogue have been defined more or less as a part of the mission agenda. This leaves open several questions. How should non-Christians relate to the question of dialogue, especially in the context where the term 'mission' revives legacies of colonial history and memories of polemical encounter? Understanding 'dialogue' within the mission fold is already creating a problem; it has been seen as 'a kind of scaffolding for mission agencies'. The *Nostra Aetate*, undoubtedly, was a great step forward towards building good relations with other religions and especially with Muslims. However, one cannot ignore the fact that the document was prepared against the background of social and political climate of the time. It was obvious at the time that to issue a seemingly pro-Jewish and, by extension, pro-Israeli document would not go down well amongst the Muslims and might restrict the Church's role in the Middle East. The logical move was to issue a statement about Muslims and, as a result, we find the inclusion of 'Muslims' in the *Nostra Aetate*. If we leave aside the political debate and discussion in the Second Vatican Council, a statement is still awaited from the Vatican in relation to Muslims. The consideration and sensitivities observed by the Conciliar Fathers in relation to Jews is not apparent in even the smallest degree in relation to Muslims. However, Muslims cannot wait to have the shortcomings of *Nostra Aetate* rectified by the Third Vatican Council. They would prefer an encyclical, stating unambiguously that the Church disavows all unjustifiable statements of the earlier Popes and declares them annulled.

Muslims have not developed a coherent position about dialogue. The problems seem to lie within the Muslim community. Though Islam provides an acceptable basis of pluralism and a code of conduct with other religions, this aspect of relations has not been explored and has rarely been debated within the Muslim community. The Muslim community has been able to create a number of platforms to discuss social-political issue, but rarely have they discussed the issue of religious pluralism or pluralism in general and created a forum for such discussion. Once Muslims realize the importance of religious pluralism, they are bound to open a thorough-going discussion about the majority–minority situation of Muslims and Christians and with other religions in the world. Dialogue in this context, perhaps, will be less cavalier and may become a dialogue of substance.

The Muslim position on and participation in dialogue, with few exceptions, has been *ad hoc* and reactive. When invited to participate in such dialogue, they have simply responded. Overwhelmingly, Muslim invitees have been unprepared for dialogue, at times even about its nature and necessity. There is an urgent need to address these weaknesses. Muslims need to discuss and look deep into their religious resources to highlight the need and importance of dialogue and its scope. Not simply 'dialogue' in its generic sense, but also its importance in the context of religious and cultural pluralism. Once Muslims open up such debates they are bound to discuss the nature of Shari'ah and *Fiqh*.

Before we move to the issue of Shari'ah, a small note on the Muslims' understanding of other religions may not be out of place. The Muslims' understanding of the other remains guided by their understanding of the self. The fulfilment of revelations to the Prophet Muhammad it seems sealed all opportunities to look even with curiosity at 'the otherness of the other'.

The Lambeth Conference, the Canberra Assembly of the World Council of Churches and the Vatican, either directly or indirectly, referred to the issue of Shari'ah in relation to Christian minorities. The issue of Shari'ah and its implementation has become a kind of battleground between the two religions, rather between the two civilizations. The problem has been caused largely by military commanders and politicians eager to show their people they are the champions of the cause of Islam and are implementing Shari'ah. In this respect, not only non-Muslims have cause to feel threatened by such 'demonstrative' aspects of Shari'ah; many Muslims also are threatened by such acts of gross misrepresentation of Islam and violation of the spirit of Shari'ah.

Unfortunately, a large number of people, Muslims and non-Muslims, psychologically and practically, reduce Shari'ah to a system of jurisprudence which relates to one aspect, the punishment system. This has overshadowed the whole spirit of Shari'ah. The demand for an 'Islamic state' has been linked to the demand for punishment laws. The punishment laws in fact cannot be implemented unless the obligations towards society are met. The overwhelming aspect of Shari'ah, what is known as *Maqasid al-Shari'ah*, seems largely absent from the Shari'ah debate among Muslims and is hardly discussed in its relation to non-Muslims. Furthermore, Shari'ah incorporates aspects of Muslims' daily life like prayer, fasting and *Hajj*. These cannot be equated with 'law' as perceived in secular modern society.

Today, a large body of Muslim thinkers and jurists are trying to formulate a new model of jurisprudence relevant for our times. If 'Islam is suitable for all times and places', this includes quite literally places where non-Muslims are partners in nation-building. Benefits to a nation – financial or otherwise – are shared by all and so are the losses. In such circumstances, therefore, just to transplant historical models of *Fiqh* would be unwise. The vocabulary of *Dhimmī*, *Jizyah*, *Dar al-Islam* and *Dar al-Harb*, etc., narrated by Muslim jurists in the past, is becoming increasingly 'irrelevant'. The concept of citizenship has drastically altered this situation. The challenge of modernity and colonialism has created a situation in the Muslim and non-Muslim mind alike that the Western models of state and economy are universal. Implementation of Shari'ah means relinquishing the power of secular society and, by extension, democracy and civil rights as well. The extremist position on both sides is adamant not to examine the position of others. Protagonists of the secular model dismiss the whole Shari'ah debate as a waste of time to discuss the 'uncivilized barbaric law' and the extreme protagonists of Shari'ah propagate seclusion from Western thought and cultural influences.

As pointed out earlier, the relevance of dialogue was the growing influence of modernity and the changing political circumstances, where socialism was making its mark. Muslims participated in dialogue with Christians in order to create a religious, moral and ethical front. Muslims today, in their search for religious pluralism within a religious framework, look towards the Church, whether the Church will prefer a religious framework to work with or a modern secular framework. This leads to another important area where a role for the Churches is called for, that of human rights.

The assertion of human rights grew gradually during the eighteenth century and became part of the UN Declaration of Human Rights in 1948. This 'universal' human right is, in fact, in its ethos and spirit, the product of the Enlightenment's debate and values and of a secular rationale. This is quite free from religious or divine dimensions. Today, human rights are projected as a world morality and implemented through the will of the UN Security Council. Human rights is an evolving concept, and should incorporate various new aspects, concepts and developments. In order to incorporate new ideas and thoughts, Muslims and Christians, alongside other religions, need to participate positively in this debate. The problem with human rights is not the idea as such, but increasingly its practice. International order, in human rights, it seems has found a moral language to implement its will with a 'holier than thou' approach. The discrimination in its application is obvious, but importantly the implementation of human rights has an 'us' and 'them' divide. Its implementation against 'them' is not simply that they are 'violating' human rights, but also 'they' belong to a group that does not agree with 'us'. Discrimination and injustices are all aimed at groups. The growing demand of Church leaders to evoke the UN's Declaration of Human Rights in favour of Christian minorities is increasingly seen by Muslims as the Church 'siding with' and in 'favour of' Western secular advancement in the Muslim world. The dialogue of salvation in this context will be meaningless unless the Church clearly states how it defines the concept of human rights and where it stands. The advancement of Western technology has been much less compassionate in warfare; the march of secular man or secularism as such, in the moral sense, has been a disaster. How can the power of the secular state be curtailed which inflicts its authority so devastatingly? This needs to be reassessed by both Christians and Muslims. Here again perhaps Muslims would like to know what route the Church is willing to take.

Muslims are anxious, and hopeful, that the Churches will place their intellectual and human resources behind the St Pölten's consultation of 1974. The Churches quite rightly identified that issues are not only of 'right' but also of 'dignity'. The debate was moved further along the same lines as the Churches in 1994, when the Just World Trust of Malaysia held the 'Rethinking Human Rights Conference' in Kuala Lumpur. This conference urged a multi-faith dialogue on the issue of human dignity. Whether the Church will adopt a multi-faith approach to this issue or remain comfortable with the contemporary Eurocentric view of human rights remains to be seen.

Our study shows that the dialogue discourse is a part of the modern Western Christian discourse. The dialogue between the two religions is not simply a dialogue between religions, but a dialogue of two civilizations. The frontiers of human knowledge have been pushed forward so rapidly and assertively that Muslim theologies and jurisprudence need time to catch up. They are waking up to the fact that they seem to have lost a great deal of the initiative in these areas and are rather more concerned about the bruises left by colonialism. A great push in Muslim thought and imagination is only possible with a great heart and through *Ijtihād*. The sensitivity lies between the relevance of historical models of the *Fuqaha'*, which Muslims regard themselves as an heir of, and at the same time venturing into a new world with a critical gaze. They need to specify their stand on various issues, which we have pointed out in this study, in clear and specific terms. The issue of Christian–Muslim dialogue and its role is intrinsically entwined with the relation between two civilizations – Islam and the West – and their co-existence. The greater responsibility in this respect, however, lies with the dominant civilization. How far the West is prepared to understand other civilizations as they define and describe themselves, and co-exist with them, has a wider impact and repercussions.

Another aspect which is relevant to the previous point we have made is the relations between the two religions, including dialogue, which hinges upon an important question. How far is the West going to recognize or ignore Islam's long presence in Europe? Is the contemporary Muslim presence in the West (especially in Europe and in North America) an asset or a liability? Islam has been a major factor in shaping European history and contemporary politics. It has built as well as threatened the political structure of the European nations in the past and is a dominant factor for the West's contemporary policy-makers. The Gulf War, Bosnia and the Middle East are a few examples. The West, in fact, is not only Judaeo-Christian but also Islamic and it is important to recognize this 'third heritage' of Europe. But will the people in the West accept this third heritage? Only time will tell. Christians and Muslims living in the West have a major task ahead. They need to understand that, without denying the contribution and role of Christianity in the West, to associate everything in the West with Christianity is a fallacy. Similarly, to associate Islam with terrorism and fanaticism, and to see Muslims as a 'problem' would also be a serious mistake. For Muslims, the existential and pragmatic side of the dialogue takes precedence over the theological and the theoretical. Christians and Muslims can contribute by focusing on the historical, social, political, economical and ethical agenda and by involving at some level the policy-makers. It is urgent, especially if political analysts are to be believed, that the 'clash of 'civilizations' will dominate future global politics and the 'fault lines' of civilizations are going to be the future 'battle-grounds'. If this is the case, then Western and Islamic civilizations have many fault lines to mend. Indeed, Muslims consider a 'civilizational' dialogue between the West and Islam more meaningful than simply between the two religions, Islam and Christianity, and in this direction one can detect a noticeable change in the World Council of Churches' position on dialogue with Muslims.

There is a need for a thorough analysis of past dialogue between Christians and Muslims. An assessment of what has been gained and lost would be an important step forward for assessing relations between the two communities. Special reference should also be made to areas like education, *Da'wah*, mission, etc., which Muslims and Christians have agreed in their past consultations to implement according to their capability and resources, to ascertain whether these have been implemented or not. If they have not, what were the reasons why? There are other interesting lines of research which can be pursued, which we believe will throw further light on Christian–Muslim dialogue. Since this study is mainly focused on materials published in the English language on the subject, a thorough assessment of materials published in French, German, Arabic, Turkish and Urdu would be valuable. A comparative study could look at the role of Shi'i and Sunni *Ulamā* in Christian–Muslim relations, especially in the Middle East. Furthermore, regional Christian–Muslim dialogue groups, institutions and organizations and their contributions need to be assessed.

Notes

CHAPTER 1

1. Kant's emphasis is that 'the illusion of being able to accomplish anything in the way of justifying ourselves before God through religious acts of worship is *superstitious*, just as the illusion of wishing to accomplish this by striving for what is supposed to be communion with God is religious *fanaticism*' (New York: Harper & Row Publishers, 1960), p. 162.
2. P.F. Knitter, *No Other Name? A Critical Survey of Christian Attitudes Towards the World Religions* (London: SCM Press 1985), p. 77.
3. See for details, Y. Haddad, 'Muslims and Contemporary Colonialism – Some Facts and Figures', *MECC News Report*, August 1974, pp. 6–7.
4. S.M. Zwemer, *The Moslem World* (Young People's Missionary Movement of the United States and Canada, 1908), p. xiii.
5. A.A. Powell, 'Maulana Rahmat Allah Kairanawi and Muslim–Christian Controversy in India in the mid-19th century', *Journal of the Royal Asiatic Society*, No. 1, 1976, p. 43.
6. *Ibid.*, pp. 42–61.
7. *Ibid.*, p. 50.
8. S. Amritsari, *Tafsir Sanai*, Vol. I (Hoamani Kutub Khana, n.d.), p. 137.
9. C.W. Troll, *Sayyid Ahmad Khan – A Reinterpretation of Muslim Theology* (Delhi: Oxford University Press, 1978/79), p. 15.
10. *Ibid.*
11. He wrote only the first volume out of seven, but his student, Syyid Sulaiman Nadvi, completed five more volumes in the framework prepared by Shibli. The seventh volume was prepared by Abul Hassan Ali Nadvi. Shibli states clearly the reasons for writing this biography, see *Sirat un-Nabi*, (Azamgarh: Dar al-Musannefeen, 4th edition, 1932), p. 7.
12. M. Iqbal, *The Reconstruction of Religious Thought in Islam* (Lahore: Sh. Muhammad Ashraf, 1960), p. 9.
13. *Ibid.*, p. 163.
14. See for details I.H. Douglas, in G. Minault and C.W. Troll, (eds.), *Abul Kalam Azad – An Intellectual and Religious Biography* (London: Oxford University Press, 1988), pp. 154–7.
15. S.A.A. Mawdudi, 'Twenty-Nine Years of the Jamaat-e-Islami' (Part I), *The Criterion*, Vol. 5, No. 6 (November-December 1970), pp. 46–7.
16. S.A.A. Mawdudi, *Sick Nations of the Modern Age* (Lahore, 1966), p. 13.
17. S.A.A. Mawdudi, *The Meaning of the Qur'an*, Vol. XIV (Lahore: Islamic Publications Ltd, 1987), pp. 218–28.
18. 'Muslim–Christian Amity', A letter to the Pope, *The Criterion*, Vol. 3, No. 2, pp. 71–7. This translation is an abridged version of the original letter. See the original letter published and edited by A. Hijaz, in *Khutbat-e-Europe* (Lahore: Idarah Tarjuman al-Qur'an, 1981), pp. 23–35.

19. K. Ahmad, 'Dini Adab', in *Tarikh Adbiyat Musalmanan-e-Pakistan wa Hind*, vol. 10 (Lahore, Punjab University, 1971), pp. 263–378.

20. Deliar Noer, *The Modernist Muslim Movement in Indonesia 1900–1942* (Kuala Lumpur: Oxford University Press, 1973), p. 7.

21. *Ibid.*, p. 21.

22. *Ibid.*, p. 22.

23. Noer, *op. cit.*, pp. 127–30.

24. See a detailed study of modernity and Islam after 1945 by B.J. Boland, *Modern Indonesia* (The Hague: Martinus Nijhoff, 1982). For Muslim–Christian relations, see pp. 224–42, and A.V. Denffer, *Indonesia–Government Decrees on Mission and Subsequent Developments* (1987), and R. Ka'abah, *Christian Presence in Indonesia: A View of Christian–Muslim Relations* (1985), both published by the Islamic Foundation, Leicester.

25. Majid Fakhry, *A History of Islamic Philosophy* (London: Longman, 1983), pp. 336–7.

26. K. Cragg, *Counsels in Contemporary Islam*, Islamic Surveys (Edinburgh: Edinburgh University Press, 1965), p. 35.

27. J.M. Gaudeul, *Encounters and Clashes*, Vol. I (Rome: Pontifico Instituto di Studi Arabi-e-Islamici, 1990), p. 266.

28. Quoted in Z. Badawi, *The Reformers of Egypt,* (London: Croom Helm, 1978), p. 99.

29. Published by Manar, Cairo in 1928. See translation of pages 3 and 4 in Gaudeul, *op. cit.*, Vol. II, p. 302.

30. Kamil Hussain's *Qaryah-Zalimah* (The Evil Town), translated by Kenneth Cragg as *City of Wrong*, and Naguib Mahfuz, *Awlad Haratina* (a novel 'The Children of our Quarter') belongs to the same group of writing. See also Hussayn Haykal's *Hayat Muhammad*, translated by Ismail Ragi al-Faruqi (North American Trust Publications, 1976) and Haykal's view on Christianity, mission and Orientalism in his preface to the book.

31. Zahia Ragheb Dajani, *Egypt and the Crisis of Islam* (New York: Peter Lang, 1990), p. 30.

32. Quoted in *ibid.*, p. 162, from Haykal's *Mustaqbal al-Thaqafa fi-Misr*, p. 63.

33. S. Qutb, *Islam the Religion of the Future* (Kuwait: IIFSO, n.d.), p. 55.

34. The Sanusi leaders, named after Muhammad ibn Ali al-Sanusi (1787–1859), were fully aware of the threat posed by European expansion in the Islamic community. Although they were not as fanatically anti-Christian as the late nineteenth-century French 'propagandists' suggested, they were not willing to accept European expansionism without a struggle. After the invasion of Libya, the 'order was left as the only organized opposition to the Italian Libyan nationalism'. J.O. Voll, *Islam: Continuity and Change in the Modern World* (Boulder: Westview Press, 1982), p. 136.

35. See in H.C. Jackson, *Pastors on the Nile, Being Some Account of the Life and Letters of Llewellyn Henry Gwynne* (London: SPCK, 1960), p. 33.

36. W.C. Smith, *Modern Islam in India* (Lahore: Sh. Muhammad Ashraf, 1963), p. 42.

37. E.I.J. Rosenthal, *Islam in the Modern National State* (Cambridge; Cambridge University Press, 1965), p. 5.

38. Continuing Committee on Muslim–Christian Co-operation, *The Proceed-*

ings of the First Muslim–Christian Convocation (Bhamadoun, Lebanon, 22–27 April 1954), p. 98.
39. *Ibid.*, p. 67.

CHAPTER 2

1. See K. Cracknell, *Justice, Courtesy and Love: Theologians and Missionaries Encountering World Religions 1846–1914* (London: Epworth Press, 1995), pp. 183 and 233.
2. N. Lossky, *et al.* (eds.), *Dictionary of the Ecumenical Movement* (Geneva: WCC, 1991), p. 325.
3. J.N. Farquhar, *The Crown of Hinduism* (London: Oxford University Press, 1913), p. 469.
4. H. Kraemer, *The Christian Message in a Non-Christian World* (London: The Edinburgh House Press, 1938), p. 36.
5. C.F. Hallencruntz, *Kraemer Towards Tambaran* (Uppsala: Cleerup, 1966), pp. 301–2.
6. *Ibid.*, p. 161.
7. *Ibid.*, p. 162. (Hallencreutz in subsequent paragraphs points out that Kraemer perhaps overestimated the Islamic renaissance.)
8. *Ibid.*, p. 165.
9. N. Goodall, *The Ecumenical Movement* (Oxford: Oxford University Press, 1966), pp. 22–3.
10. N. Lossky, *et al., op. cit.*, p. 412.
11. *Ibid.*
12. *One World*, No. 122, January 1987, p. 4.
13. WCC Publications, *Christians Meeting Muslims*, WCC Papers on Ten Years of Christian–Muslim dialogue (Geneva: WCC, 1977), p. 12.
14. *Ibid.*, p. 13.
15. *Ibid.*, p. 15.
16. *Ibid.*, p. 17.
17. David Brewster, 'From Conflict to Dialogue – The Development of Christian–Muslim Dialogue since 1956'. Unpublished MS., p. 12.
18. *Ibid.*, p. 13.
19. WCC, *Christians Meeting Muslims, op. cit.*, p. 67.
20. *Ibid.*, p. 68.
21. C.A. Kimball, 'Striving Together in the Way of God: Muslim Participation in Christian–Muslim Dialogue', PhD thesis, Harvard University, 1987, p. 284.
22. S. Brown (ed.), *Meetings in Faith*, (Geneva: WCC, 1989), p. 15.
23. S.J. Samartha, 'Guidelines for Dialogue', *The Ecumenical Review*, Vol. 31 (1979), p. 130.
24. R.B. Sheard, *Interreligious Dialogue in the Catholic Church Since Vatican II – An Historical and Theological Study* (New York: The Edwin Mellen Press, 1987), p. 18.
25. *Ibid.*
26. K. Rahner, 'Christianity and the Non-Christian Religions', in *Theological Investigations*, Vol. 5, Eng. translation (London: Darton, Longman & Todd, 1966), p. 118.

27. *Ibid.*, p. 131.
28. Quoted by Robert Casper, *Cours de Théologie Musulmane*, Vol. I (Rome: Institut Pontifical d'Etudes Arabes, 1987).
29. Giulio Bassetti-Sani, *The Koran in the Light of Christ, Islam in the Plan of History and Salvation* (Chicago: Franciscan Herald Press, 1977), p. 27.
30. Johannes Cardinal Willebrands, 'Christians and Jews: A New Vision', in *Vatican II, By Those Who Were There*, Stacpoole, A. (ed.) (London: Geoffrey Chapman, 1986), p. 224.
31. A. Flannery, (ed.), *Vatican Council II* (New York: Costello Publishing Company, 1988, revised edition), p. 738.
32. Robert A. Graham, 'Non-Christians', *The Documents of Vatican II*, ed. Walter M. Abbott, (London: Geoffrey Chapman, 1967), p. 656.
33. Flannery, *op. cit.*, pp. 739–40.
34. *Ibid.*, p. 740.
35. Flannery, *op. cit.*, p. 350 (*Lumen Gentium*, para. 1).
36. *Ibid.*, p. 367, (para. 16).
37. *Ibid.*
38. Hastings, *A Concise Guide to the Document of the Second Vatican Council*, Vol. I (London: Darton, Longman & Todd, 1968), p. 40.
39. Flannery, *op. cit.*, p. 814.
40. *Ibid.*, p. 813.
41. *Ibid.*, p. 814 (*AG*, para. 2).
42. *Ibid.*, p. 820 (*AG*, para. 6).
43. *Ibid.*, p. 824 (*AG*, para. 10).
44. *Ibid.*, p. 750 (*DV*, para. 3).
45. *Ibid.*, pp. 751–2 (*DV*, para. 4).
46. Flannery, *op. cit.*, p. 910 (*GS*, para. 9).
47. *Ibid.*, p. 911 (*GS*, para. 10).
48. Flannery, *op. cit.*, p. 800 (*DH*, para. 2).
49. *Ibid.*, p. 807 (*DH*, para. 11).
50. H. Vorgrimler (ed.), *Commentary on the Documents of Vatican II*, Vol. IV (London: Burns & Oates/Heider & Horder, 1969), p. 122.
51. M.L. Fitzgerald, '25 Years of Christian–Muslim Dialogue. A Personal Journey', *Proche-Orient Chrétien*, Vol. XL (1990), pp. 265-6.
52. M. Kinnamon (ed.), *Signs of the Spirit*, official report Seventh Assembly (Geneva: WCC, 1991), p. 105.
53. R. Hoffman, 'Yes, Conversion and the Mission of the Church', in D. McGavran (ed.), *The Conciliar-Evangelical Debate: The Crucial Documents 1964–1976* (South Pasadena: William Carey Library, 1977), p. 71.
54. D. McGavran, 'Criticism of the WCC Working Draft on Mission', in *The Crucial . . ., op. cit.*, p. 235.
55. J.D. Douglas (ed.), *Let the Earth Hear His Voice, International Congress on World Evangelization*, Vol. I (Minneapolis: Worlwide Publications, 1975), p. 26.
56. The text of the Frankfurt Declaration appeared in *Christianity Today*, 19 June 1970, p. 1 and also in D. McGavran (ed.), *Conciliar and Evangelical . . ., op. cit.*, pp. 283–93.
57. R. Winter (ed.), *The Evangelical Response to Bangkok* (South Pasadena: William Carey Library, 1973).

58. *Ibid.*, p. 31.
59. G.W. Peters, 'Contemporary Practices of Evangelism', in Douglas, *op. cit.*, p. 186.
60. David Gitari, 'Theologies of Presence, Dialogue and Proclamation', in Douglas, *op. cit.*, Vol. II, p. 1119.
61. Don M. McCurry, (ed.), *The Gospel and Islam: A 1978 compendium* (California: Missions Advanced Research and Communication Center (MARC), 1978), p. 638.
62. D.R. Brewster, 'Dialogue: Relevancy to Evangelism', in McCurry, *op. cit.*, p. 514.
63. *Ibid.*, p. 515.
64. *Ibid.*, p. 519.
65. See an abridged version of these and several other missionary statements including Roman Catholic and Eastern Orthodox and Oriental Church statements. J.A. Scherer and S.B. Bevans (eds.), *New Directions in Mission and Evangelization*, Vol. I, Basic Statements 1974–1991 (New York: Orbis Books, 1992), p. 324.
66. Rossano Pietro's article, 'The Secretariat for Non-Christian Religions from the Beginnings to the Present Day: History, Ideas, Problems', *Bulletin*, Vatican, Vol. XIV/2–3, Nos. 41–2, (1979), p. 90.
67. *Ibid.*, p. 92.
68. M.L. Fitzgerald, 'The Secretariat for Non-Christians is Ten Years Old', *Encounter*, No. 9, (November 1974), p. 2.
69. Rossano, 'The Secretariat'. *op. cit.*, p. 91.
70. Secretariatus Pro non-Christianis, *Guidelines for a Dialogue Between Muslims and Christians* (Rome: Secretariat for Non-Christians, 1969), p. 171.
71. Published by Paulist Press, New York, 1990, p. 132.
72. George Khodr, 'Christianity in a Pluralist World – The Economy of the Holy Spirit' in Samartha, *Living Faiths . . ., op. cit.*, p. 141.
73. *Ibid.*, p. 141.
74. Samartha, *Living Faiths . . ., op. cit.*, p. 153.
75. *Ibid.*, p. 156.
76. *Ibid.*, p. 154.
77. WCC, 'Central Committee of the World Council of Churches Minutes and Reports of the Twenty-Fourth Meeting, Addis Ababa, Ethiopia, January 10th–21st', (1971), pp. 18–22.

CHAPTER 3

1. M. Kretzmann, 'Analysis of the Encounter to Date', *International Review of Missions*, Vol. LV, No. 220 (October 1966), p. 405.
2. H. Saab, 'Communication Between Christianity and Islam', *The Middle East Journal*, Vol. XVIII (Winter 1964), p. 60.
3. Sulayman S. Nyang, 'Responses to Questionnaire' (R.Q.), dated 13 March 1991, p. 2.
4. 'O ye who believe! Take not the Jews and the Christians for your friends and protectors, they are but friends and protectors to each other. And he among you who turns to them [for friendship] is of them. Verily God guideth not a people unjust' (*al-Maidah*, 5:51).

5. Habibul Haq Nadvi, 'R.Q', and Hassan Makki M. Ahmed, *Interview*, 23 August 1990. Makki refers to President Bush's appeal to Christians to pray for success in the Gulf War.
6. Qur'an, *Kafirun*, 109:6. 'R.Q.' quoted by Professor T.B. Irving, n.d.
7. Gai Eaton, *Interview*, 18 April 1991, p. 4.
8. Z. Sardar, 'The Ethical Connection: Christian–Muslim in the Postmodern Age', *Islam and Christian–Muslim Relations*, Vol. 2, No. 1 (June 1991), pp. 59–60.
9. Farid Eschak, *Interview*, 11 December 1991, p. 5.
10. S.S. Nyang, 'R.Q.', *op. cit.*
11. Farid Eschak, *Interview*, *op. cit.*, p. 6.
12. *Ibid.*, p. 5.
13. M.A. Anees, 'Historical Light on the Present Situation of Christian–Muslim Relations', Part II, *Newsletter of the Office of Christian–Muslim Relations*, Hartford Seminary, No. 38 (July 1988), p. 2.
14. S. Bayln, *Saints, Goddesses and Kings – Muslims and Christians in South Indian Society 1700–1900* (Cambridge: Cambridge University Press, 1989), pp. 260–1.
15. See A.L. Tibawi, *English-Speaking Orientalists: A Critique of Their Approach to Islam and Arab Nation* (Geneva: Islamic Centre, 1965).
16. Quoted in M.R. Buheiry, 'Colonial Scholarship and Muslim Revivalism in 1900', *Arab Studies Quarterly*, Vol. 4, Nos. 1–2 (Spring 1982), p. 5.
17. *Ibid.*
18. *Ibid.*
19. A. Flannery (ed.), *Vatican Council II – The Conciliar and Post Conciliar Documents* (New York: Costello Publishing Company, 1988, revised edition), p. 740.
20. Hamidullah, 'R.Q.', dated 5 March 1991. [I wrote to him asking for a copy of the letter, but he could not find a copy. This letter, he wrote to me, 'was not in my private capacity, but in the name of a Muslim Association in Paris. I don't now remember who had signed it. Anyhow, no reply ever came' (letter dated 15 March 1991)].
21. F. Eschak, *Interview, op. cit.*, p. 8.
22. Anees, *op. cit.*, p. 3.
23. Ibrahim Hewitt, 'R.Q.', dated 27 March 1991, p. 1.
24. Zaki Badawi, *Interview*, 18 April 1991, p. 6.
25. O.S. Noibi, *Interview*, p. 6.
26. Gai Eaton, *Interview*, 18 April 1991, p. 11.
27. A.M. Macdonald (ed.), *Chambers Twentieth Century Dictionary* (Edinburgh: W. & R. Chambers Ltd, 1978, revised edition).
28. Badawi, *op. cit.*, pp. 1 and 2.
29. Khalid Alvi, *Interview*, 12 June 1991, p. 1.
30. Mashuq Ally, *Interview*, 15 March 1991, p. 1.
31. Khurram, Murad, *Interview*, 30 September 1991, p. 1.
32. O.S. Noibi, *Interview*, 30 May 1991, p. 3.
33. *Ibid.*
34. S.Z. Abedin, 'The Role of Believers in Promoting Mutual Trust and Community', paper presented in Christian–Muslim Colloquium organized by World Council of Churches (27 September–1 October 1987), p. 62.

35. Badawi, *op. cit.*, pp. 9–12.
36. Murad, *op. cit.*, p. 1.
37. See in R.W. Southern, *Western Views of Islam in the Middle Ages* (Massachusetts: Harvard University Press, 1978), pp. 22–33. Daniel, Norman *Islam and the West* (Oxford: One World Publications, 1993, revised edition). See for a critique of Orientalism, Edward Said, *Orientalism* (New York: Pantheon Books, 1978).
38. A. von Denffer, 'Muhammad – A Prophet or "a great religious leader"', *Impact International*, (11–24 July 1980), p. 2.
39. D.A. Kerr, *The Prophet Muhammad in Christian Theological Perspective* (Birmingham: Centre for the Study of Islam and Christian–Muslim Relations, Selly Oak Colleges, No. 2, September 1982), p. 8.
40. Abedin, *op. cit.*, p. 62.
41. C. Muzaffar, quoted in *Contemporary Issues on Malaysian Religions*, ed. Tunko Abdul-Rahman Putra *et al.* (Selangor: Pelanduk Publications, 1985), pp. 115–16.
42. M. Kinnamon (ed.), *Signs of the Spirit – Official Report Seventh Assembly* (Geneva: World Council of Churches, 1991), pp. 92–3. (The Assembly was held in Canberra, Australia, 7–20 February 1991.)
43. M. Borrmans, *Interview*, dated 23 January 1991, p. 11. He further remarks 'will it include all jurisdictional verses of the Qur'an or also the Jurisdictional ahadith? Shari'ah seems to be a kind of refuge for a lot of people and seems very little time has been given to analyse and discuss. It becomes very important in the light of the power and functions of modern day state.
44. T. Michel, 'The Rights of Non-Muslims in Islam: An Opening Statement', *Journal Institute of Muslim Minority Affairs*, Vol. 6, No. 1 (January 1985), p. 14.
45. *Ibid.*
46. M. Fitzgerald, *Interview*, 22 January 1991, p. 10. In the same interview he also remarks that Muslims 'have not found convincing and consistent explanations [of what] application of Shari'ah means to them'.
47. T. Michel, *Interview*, 22 January 1991, p. 13.
48. S.V. Utere, in *New Nigeria*, 22 January 1986, p. 7.
49. T. Michel, 'Rights of Non-Muslims ...', *op. cit.*, p. 16.
50. *Ibid.*, pp. 15–16.
51. A letter regarding reservations about the Shariat Bill was written to the Prime Minister of Pakistan, Mr Nawaz Sharif, signed by six bishops of the country. A summary of the letter was published in *FOCUS*, supplement No. 2 (1990), pp. 127–32.
52. A.H. Al-Ghazali (d.1111), *Al-Mustafa*, Vol. 1 (1937), pp. 139–40, quoted in M.U. Chapra, *Islam and the Economic Challenge* (Leicester: The Islamic Foundation, and the International Institute of Islamic Thought, 1992), p. 1.
53. Ibn Qayyim al-Jawziyyah (691–750 CE), *A'lam al-Muwaqqi'in*, Vol. 3 (1955), p. 14, quoted in Chapra, *op. cit.*, p. 1.
54. Usman Bugaje, *Interview*, 18 September 1991, p. 1.
55. Hashir Faruqi, *Interview*, 15 May 1991, p. 1.
56. D.O.S. Noibi, *Interview*, 30 March 1991, p. 18.

57. Zaki Badawi, *Interview*, 18 April 1991.
58. Bugaje, *op. cit.*, pp. 2–3.
59. Badawi, *op. cit.*, p. 10.
60. F. Rahman, 'Non-Muslim Minorities in an Islamic State', *Journal Institute of Muslim Minority Affairs*, Vol. 7, No. 1 (January 1986), p. 21.
61. *Ibid.*, p. 20.
62. Badawi, *op. cit.*, p. 19.
63. *Interview* with Zaki Badawi, *op. cit.*, Abdul Wahab Effendi, 22 February 1991, p. 3, Khurram Murad, *op. cit.*, p. 5, Adeleke D. Ajijola, 12 February 1992, p. 5, Usman Bugaje, *op. cit.*, p. 7.
64. Rahman, *op. cit.*, p. 20.
65. M. Hamidullah, 'Relations of Muslims with non-Muslims', *Journal Institute of Muslim Minority Affairs*, Vol. 7, No. 1 (January 1986), p. 7.
66. Noibi, *op. cit.*, p. 22.
67. Rahman, *op. cit.*
68. Murad, *op. cit.*, p. 5.
69. E.g. Rashid al-Ghanoushi, the leader of the Islamic Trend Movement of Tunisia exiled in Britain. His recent speeches and writings highlight this point very strongly.
70. A.W. El-Effendi, *Interview*, p. 2.
71. Bugaje, *op. cit.*, p. 9.
72. See S.M.N. Al-Attas, *Islam and Secularism* (Kuala Lumpur: ABIM, 1978), especially chapter on 'The Biblical Sources of Secularism'.
73. B.A. Lemu, in *New Nigeria* (January 1986), p. 7. Aisha Lemu wrote this letter in her capacity as President, Federation of Muslim Women's Association in Nigeria (FOMWAN).
74. See for Christian demands and their support of Israel and suspicion of Shari'ah *New Nigeria*, (16 January 1986), p. 7.
75. Rahman, *op. cit.*, p. 20.
76. *Ibid.*, p. 22.
77. Rahman, *op. cit.*, see also Anees, *op. cit.*
78. *Al-Mushir*, Vol. XXVII, No. 2 (Summer 1985), pp. 95, 96. See the debate and having a separate electoral to the minorities, debated by Christian Members of the National Assembly, pp. 93–103.
79. Khalid Alvi, *Interview*, 12 June 1991, p. 11.
80. *Ibid.* He points out that the 'present British or European system, which is a party system, where you are a minority or a majority, you have to vote within that party system. Parties have their own policies and these policies are also approved and implemented with the majority. So even if Muslims join these parties ... still they cannot influence basic policy issues which are sometimes against their moral and their ethical value system.'
81. See A. El-Affendi, 'Discovering the South: Sudanese Dilemmas for slam in Africa', *African Affairs*, Vol. 89, No. 356 (1990), pp. 372, 373.
82. *Ibid.*
83. See the Appendix 'Position of Christian Churches with Regard to the Enforcement of the Islamic *Shari'ah* in Sudan', L. Swindler, (ed.), *Muslims in Dialogue* (New York, The Edwin Mellen Press, 1992), pp. 534–5.
84. *FOCUS on Christian-Muslim Relations*, 6/85, p. 7.

85. El-Affendi, *op. cit.*, p. 386.
86. J.R.W. Stott, 'The Biblical Basis of Evangelism', *Trends*, No. 2 (New York: Paulist Press and Wm. B. Eerdmans Publishing Co., 1975), p. 6.
87. Khurram Murad, *Da'wah Among Non-Muslims in the West* (Leicester: The Islamic Foundation, 1986), p. 12.
88. A. Flannery, (ed.), *Vatican Council II* (New York: Costello Publishing Co., 1988, revised edition), p. 739.
89. *Ibid.*, p. 744.
90. A.F. Glasser, 'Vatican II and Mission 1965–1985', *Missiology*, Vol. XIII, No. 4 (October 1985), pp. 490, 491.
91. Quoted in Glasser, *op. cit.*, p. 492.
92. *Ibid.*
93. *Bulletin*, No. 36 (1977), p. 89.
94. *The Attitude of the Church Towards the Followers of Other Religions – Reflections and Orientation on Dialogue and Mission* (Vatican: Secretariatus pro non-Christianis, 1984), p. 18.
95. *Redemptoris Missio*, Encyclical Letter of the Supreme Pontiff John Paul II, Vatican, 1991, pp. 70–1.
96. *Dialogue and Proclamation – Reflections and Orientations on Inter-religious Dialogue and the Proclamation of the Gospel of Jesus Christ* (Vatican, 1991), pp. 201–50. Offprint of the *Bulletin*, No. 77 (1991), p. 226.
97. *Ibid.*, p. 245.
98. *Ecumenical Chronicle: Documents of the Central Committee* (WCC), Canterbury, England, August 1969. *The Ecumenical Review*, Vol. XXI, No. 4 (October 1969), p. 363.
99. S. Brown (ed.), *Meeting in Faith* (Geneva: WCC, 1989), p. 3.
100. *International Review of Mission*, Vol. LXV, No. 258 (April 1976), p. 145.
101. M. Kinnamon, (ed.), *Signs of the Spirit*, Official Report, Seventh Assembly. (Geneva: WCC, 1991), p. 104.
102. 'The Manila Manifesto', *Evangelism Today*, No. 210 (September 1989), p. 7.
103. 'Dialogue could be taken as a form of *Da'wah*' (Sheikh Jamal Manna, *Interview, op. cit.*, p. 2): 'my understanding of *Da'wah* is that you are creating an awareness with another person, it is one aspect of *Da'wah* . . .' (Khurshid Ahmad, *Interview, op. cit.*, p. 2).
104. Hewitt, I. *R.Q*, p. 1.
105. G.N. Saqeb, 'R.Q.', p. 1, dated 28 March 1991.
106. A.R. Doi, 'R.Q.', pp. 1, 2.
107. G. Basri, 'R.Q.', p. 1, 4 April 1991.
108. Abedin, *op. cit.*, p. 43.
109. F. Eschak, *Interview*, p. 9, 11 December 1991.
110. M.M. Ahsan, '*Da'wah* and its Significance for the Future', in Davies and Pasha, *op. cit.*, p. 13.
111. K.R. Hohn, 'R.Q.', 27 June 1991 p. 2.
112. Khurran Murad, *Interview*, 30 September 1991, p. 2.
113. Manna, *op. cit.*, p. 6.
114. Murad, *op. cit.*, p. 3.
115. Harfigah Ball, 'R.Q.', p. 2, dated 2 March 1991.

116. Akhtar, *Interview, op. cit.*, p. 15.
117. Usman Bugaje, *Interview*, 18 September 1991, p. 11.

CHAPTER 4

1. Isma'il R. Al-Faruqi, '*Urubah and Religion* (Amsterdam: Djambatan, 1962), p. ix.
2. Isma'il R. Al-Faruqi, 'The Problem of the Metaphysical Status of Values in the Western and Islamic Tradition', *Studia Islamica,* Vol. XXVIII (1968), p. 30.
3. Isma'il R. Al-Faruqi, 'Common Bases between the Two Religions in Regard to Convictions, and Points of Agreement in the Spheres of Life', *Seminar of the Islamic-Christian Dialogue* (1976). Tripoli: Popular Office of Foreign Relations, Socialist Peoples Libyan Arab Jamhariya, 1981, p. 243.
4. S. Hossein Nasr, 'The Essence of Dr. Faruqi's Life Work', *Islamic Horizon* (August/September, 1986), p. 26.
5. 'Self-Portrait', *Impact International*, Vol. 16, No. 11 (June 1986), p. 6.
6. Isma'il R. Al-Faruqi, *Christian Ethics – A Historical and Systematic Analysis of its Dominant Ideas* (Montreal: McGill University Press, 1967).
7. *Ibid.*, pp. 11–14, where he describes these principles.
8. Isma'il R. Al-Faruqi, 'Meta-Religion: Towards a Critical World Theology', *American Journal of Islamic Social Sciences*, Vol. 3, No. 1 (September 1986), p. 26.
9. *Ibid.*, p. 24.
10. Faruqi, *Christian Ethics, op. cit.*, p. 17.
11. *Ibid.*
12. *Ibid.* See for details of his meta-religion, pp. 21–32 and also his article 'Meta-Religion', *op. cit.*
13. Isma'il R. Al-Faruqi, 'Islam and Christianity: Diatribe or Dialogue', *Journal of Ecumenical Studies*, (Winter 1968) pp. 45–77.
14. Faruqi, 'Islam and Christianity', *op. cit.*, p. 58.
15. *Ibid.*, pp. 58–9.
16. *Ibid.*, p. 59.
17. *Ibid.*, p. 60.
18. *Ibid.*, p. 56.
19. *Ibid.*
20. *Ibid.*, p. 57.
21. *Ibid.*
22. Faruqi, *Christian Ethics, op. cit.*, p. 313. See also *Christian Mission and Islamic Da'wah*, proceedings of The Chambesy Dialogue (Leicester: The Islamic Foundation, 1982), p. 27.
23. Isma'il R. Al-Faruqi, 'Rights of Non-Muslims Under Islam: Social and Cultural Aspects', *Journal of Institute of Muslim Minority Affairs*, Vol. 1, No. 1 (Summer 1979), p. 95.
24. *Ibid.*
25. *Ibid.*, p. 97.
26. *Ibid.*, p. 96.
27. *Ibid.*

28. Faruqi, 'Common Bases...', *op. cit.*, p. 235.
29. *Ibid.*, p. 234.
30. *Ibid.*, pp. 234–5.
31. *Ibid.*, p. 235. [He quotes in his support from the Holy Qur'an (25:2, 80:19, 54:45)].
32. *Ibid.*, p. 235.
33. Isma'il R. Al-Faruqi, 'History of Religions: Its Nature and Significance for Christian Education and the Muslim–Christian Dialogue', *Numen*, Vol. XII (1965), p. 81.
34. *Ibid.*, p. 82.
35. Faruqi, 'Common Bases...', *op. cit.*, p. 240.
36. 'Islam and Christianity...', *JES, op. cit.*, p. 50.
37. Isma'il R. Al-Faruqi, 'Common Bases...', *op. cit.*, p. 242.
38. 'Common Bases...', *op. cit.*, p. 241.
39. 'Islam and Christianity', *op. cit.*, p. 51.
40. *Christian Ethics, op. cit.*, p. 34.
41. 'Common Bases...', *op. cit.*, p. 244. Also *JES, op. cit.*, and *Christian Mission and Islamic Da'wah, op. cit.*, p. 31.
42. 'Islam and Christianity...', *op. cit.*, p. 53.
43. *Ibid.*
44. 'Common Bases...', *op. cit.*, p. 240.
45. *Trialogue of Abrahamic Faiths* (Washington, D.C.: International Institute of Islamic Thought), (see Foreword by Isma'il Faruqi), 1982.
46. *Ibid.*
47. Isma'il R. Al-Faruqi, 'Islam and Other Faiths', *The Challenge of Islam*, ed. Altaf Gauhar (London, Islamic Council of Europe, 1978), p. 175.
48. 'Islam and Christianity...', *op. cit.*, p. 72.
49. 'Islam and Other Faiths', *op. cit.*, p. 18.
50. 'Islam and Christianity...', *op. cit.*
51. *Ibid.*, p. 74.
52. *Ibid.*, p. 77.

CHAPTER 5

1. 'Interview', unpublished interviews with Ataullah Siddiqui, London, 20 April 1991, p. 1.
2. *Ibid.*
3. 'Interview', *ibid.*, p. 1.
4. 'Interview', *ibid.*, p. 1.
5. *Ibid.*, p. 2.
6. *Ibid.*
7. 'Interview', p. 2.
8. *Ibid.*, p. 3.
9. Speaking at 13th International Summer School, Birmingham, Selly Oak Colleges, 17 July 1991, p. 2.
10. Qur'an al-Baqara (2: 256).
11. In the Sciences of the Qur'an the term is known as *'Asbab al-Nuzul* (the context of revelation).

12. Selly Oak, *op. cit.*, p. 3. See for a detailed discussion on the subject, M. Ayoub, 'Religions Freedom and the Law of Apostacy in Islam' *Islamochristiana*, Vol. 20 (1994), pp. 75–91.
13. *Ibid.*
14. *Ibid.*
15. 'Interview', *op. cit.*, p. 9.
16. *Ibid.*, p. 9.
17. *Ibid.*
18. *Ibid.*, p. 6.
19. *Ibid.*
20. Mahmoud Ayoub, 'Roots of Muslim–Christian Conflict', *The Muslim World*, Vol. LXXIX, No. 1 (January 1989), p. 30.
21. See Pope Urban II's statement in, *Fulcher of Chartres, A History of the Expedition of Jerusalem: 1095–1127*, trans. by Frances Rita Ryan, ed. Harold S. Fink (Knoxville, The University of Tennessee Press, 1969), p. 66.
22. Ayoub, 'Roots of Muslims', *op. cit.*, p. 34.
23. *Ibid.*, p. 34.
24. 'Interview', *op. cit.*, p. 7.
25. Ayoub, 'Roots of Muslims', *op. cit.*, p. 34.
26. *Ibid.*, p. 35.
27. *Ibid.*
28. 'Interview', p. 6.
29. *Ibid.*, p. 7.
30. Mahmoud Ayoub, 'Roots of Muslim–Christian Conflict', *op. cit.*, p. 42.
31. *Ibid.*
32. 'Interview', *op. cit.*, p. 7.
33. *Ibid.*
34. *Ibid.*, p. 8.
35. *Ibid.*
36. *Ibid.*, p. 12.
37. *Ibid.*
38. *Ibid.*
39. *Ibid.*
40. *Ibid.*, p. 10.
41. *Ibid.*
42. *Ibid.*
43. *Ibid.*
44. Ayoub, 'Roots of Muslim–Christian Conflict', *op. cit.*, p. 42.
45. *Ibid.*, p. 43.
46. 'Interview', *op. cit.*, p. 11.
47. *Ibid.*
48. *Ibid.*, p. 4.
49. *Ibid.*
50. *Ibid.*, pp. 4–5.
51. *Ibid.*, p. 14.
52. *Ibid.*
53. *Ibid.*, p. 15.
54. *Ibid.*

55. 'Interview', *op. cit.*, p. 13.
56. *Ibid.*, p. 14.
57. *Ibid.*
58. *Ibid.*, p. 13.
59. Mahmoud Ayoub, 'Towards an Islamic Christology: An Image of Jesus in Early Shi'i Muslim Literature', *The Muslim World,* Vol. LXVI, No. 3 (July 1976), p. 166.
60. Mahmoud Ayoub, 'Towards an Islamic Christology II: The Death of Jesus, Reality or Delusion', *The Muslim World,* Vol. LXX, No. 2 (April 1980), p. 94.
61. *Ibid.*
62. *Ibid.*, p. 70.
63. *Ibid.*, p. 116.
64. *Ibid.*
65. *Ibid.*, p. 117.
66. Ayoub, 'Christology II . . .', *op. cit,* p. 118.
67. *Ibid.*, p. 97.
68. *Ibid.*, p. 98.
69. *Ibid.*, p. 99.
70. *Ibid.*, p. 118.
71. Mahmoud Ayoub, 'Jesus the Son of God: A Study of the Terms *Ibn* and *Walad* in the Qur'an and *Tafsir* Tradition' in Y.Z. Haddad, and W. Haddad, (eds.), *Christian–Muslim Encounters* (Gainsville: University Press of Florida, 1995), p. 66.
72. *Ibid.*, p. 70.

CHAPTER 6

1. 'Interview', unpublished interviews with Ataullah Siddiqui, Leeds, January 1991, p. 4.
2. Hasan Askari, *Spiritual Quest – An Inter-Religious Dimension* (Pudsey: Seven Mirrors Publishing House, 1991), p. 124.
3. Askari, *Spiritual Quest . . .*, *op. cit.* p. 123.
4. *Ibid.*, p. 80.
5. *Ibid.*, pp. 81–2.
6. *Ibid.*, p. 83.
7. 'Interview', *op. cit.*, p. 6.
8. *Ibid.*, p. 7.
9. *Ibid.*, pp. 11–12.
10. *Ibid.*, p. 12.
11. *Ibid.*, p. 15.
12. *Ibid.*, pp. 15–16.
13. *Ibid.*, p. 54.
14. Askari, *Spiritual Quest, op. cit.*, p. 126.
15. *Ibid.*
16. 'Interview', *op. cit.*, p. 58.
17. *Ibid.*, p. 59.
18. Askari, *Spiritual Quest, op. cit.*, p. 126.

19. 'Interview', *op. cit.*, pp. 59–60.
20. 'Interview', *op. cit.*, p. 52.
21. 'Interview', *op. cit.*, p. 53.
22. *Ibid.*, p. 53.
23. *Ibid.*
24. *Ibid.*, p. 54.
25. John Hick, and Hasan Askari, (eds.), *The Experience of Religious Diversity* (London: Avebury Publishing Company, 1985), p. 191.
26. *Ibid.*, p. 192.
27. 'Interview', *op. cit.*, p. 7.
28. *Ibid.*, p. 38.
29. *Ibid.*, p. 39.
30. 'Interview', pp. 40–1.
31. *Ibid.*, pp. 41–2.
32. *Ibid.*, p. 36.
33. *Ibid.*, p. 9.
34. *Ibid.*
35. *Ibid.*, p. 23.
36. *Ibid.*, p. 18.
37. Askari, *Spiritual Quest*, *op. cit.*, p. 108.
38. 'Interview', *op. cit.*, pp. 18–19.
39. Hasan Askari, 'Limits to Comparison: New Testament and Qur'an', *Newsletter* (of the Centre for the Study of Islam and Christian-Muslim Relations), No. 5 (May 1981), p. 24.
40. *Ibid.*, pp. 25–6.
41. Hasan Askari, 'Christian Mission to Islam: A Muslim Response', *Journal Institute of Muslim Minority Affairs*, Vol. VII, No. 2 (July 1986), p. 316.
42. *Ibid.*
43. *Ibid.*, p. 317.
44. *Ibid.*

CHAPTER 7

1. S. Parvez Manzoor, 'Khurshid Ahmad: Faith Turned into Vocation', *Inquiry* (December 1984), p. 57. See an article by J.L. Esposito, and J.O. Voll, 'Khurshid Ahmad: Muslim Activist-Economist', *The Muslim World*, Vol. LXXX (January 1990), pp. 24–36.
2. 'Interview', unpublished interviews with Ataullah Siddiqui, Leicester, 22 April 1991, p. 1.
3. See for details M. Rahman, and S.M. Khalid, (eds.), *Jab voh nazim-i-ala the* (Lahore, Idara Matbuaat-e-Talba, 1982), p. 119.
4. 'Interview', *op. cit.*, p. 1.
5. *Ibid.*, p. 2.
6. *Ibid.*
7. *Ibid.*, p. 3.
8. *Ibid.*, pp. 3–4.
9. *Ibid.*, p. 4.
10. *Ibid.*

11. He remembers this term first coined by Syrian scholar, Mustapha al-Siba'i (1915–64).
12. 'Interview', p. 4.
13. *Ibid.*
14. *Ibid.*, p. 5.
15. *Ibid.*
16. Khurshid, Ahmad, 'Islamic Da'wah in Europe – Problems and Prospects', unpublished paper, p. 2.
17. *Christian Mission and Islamic Da'wah* (Leicester: The Islamic Foundation, 1982), p. 42.
18. Khurshid Ahmad, 'Strategy to Face Challenges from other Religions and Non-religious Ideas'. Paper presented in a symposium on 'The Role of Islam in Development', held in Niamy (Niger), 21–25 May 1992, p. 13.
19. *Ibid.*
20. 'Interview', *op. cit.*, p. 8.
21. *Ibid.*, p. 13.
22. *Christian Mission and Islamic Da'wah, op. cit.*, p. 10.
23. 'Interview', p. 16.
24. *Ibid.*
25. *Ibid.*, p. 8.
26. *Ibid.*
27. *Ibid.*, p. 16.
28. Khurshid Ahmad, 'West in Crisis', speech delivered in Leicester (unpublished), 1984.
29. Khurshid Ahmad, 'Islamic Da'wah in Europe', *op. cit.*, p. 30.
30. Khurshid Ahmad, 'Islam and the Muslims in Europe Today', unpublished paper, p. 1.
31. *Ibid.*, pp. 1–2.
32. Khurshid Ahmad, 'The Nature of Islamic Resurgence', in J.L. Esposito, (ed.), *Voices of Resurgent Islam* (New York: Oxford University Press, 1983), p. 222.
33. Khurshid Ahmad, 'Islam and the New World Order', paper presented in ISNA Conference, USA, p. 6.
34. *Ibid.*
35. Ahmad, 'The Nature of Islamic Resurgence', *op. cit.*, p. 228.
36. *Ibid.*
37. Khurshid Ahmad, 'Islam and the West: Confrontation or Cooperation?' *The Muslim World*, Vol. LXXXV, No. 1–2 (Jan–April 1995), p. 81.
38. Ahmad, 'Islamic Da'wah in Europe', *op. cit.*, p. 20.
39. Khurshid Ahmad, 'Muslims in Western Europe', unpublished paper, p. 11.
40. *Ibid.*
41. Khurshid Ahmad, 'Muslims in Western Europe', unpublished paper, p. 11.
42. *Ibid.*, p. 15.
43. *Ibid.*, p. 16.
44. Ahmad, 'Islamic Da'wah in Europe', *op. cit.*, p. 32.
45. *Ibid.*
46. *Ibid.*, p. 41.

47. 'Interview', *op. cit.*, p. 19.
48. *Ibid.*
49. *Ibid.*
50. 'Interview', p. 9.
51. *Ibid.*, p. 17.
52. *Ibid.*
53. *Ibid.*, p. 10.
54. *Ibid.*, p. 11.
55. *Ibid.*
56. Syyid A. Mawdudi, *The Islamic Law and Constitution*, ed. and trans. Khurshid Ahmad (Lahore: Islamic Publications Ltd, 1969), pp. 65ff.

CHAPTER 8

1. Mohammed Talbi, 'Unavoidable Dialogue in an Unavoidable Pluralistic World: A Personal Account', *Encounters: Journal of Inter-Cultural Perspectives*, Vol. 1, No. 1 (March 1995), p. 57.
2. *Ibid.*, p. 56.
3. *Ibid.*
4. Mohammed Talbi, 'Community of Communities', in John Hick and Hasan Askari, *The Experience of Religious Diversity* (London: Avebury Publishing Company, 1985), pp. 71–2.
5. *Ibid.*, p. 67.
6. *Ibid.*, p. 69.
7. *Ibid.*, p. 70.
8. *Ibid.*
9. *Ibid.*, p. 72.
10. See Ibn Ishaq's *Sirat Rasul Allah* (trans. A. Guillaume, *The Life of Muhammad*, Oxford: Oxford University Press, 1980, pp. 231–3).
11. Talbi, *'Community of Communities'*, *op. cit.*, pp. 74–5.
12. *Ibid.*, p. 83.
13. *Ibid.*, p. 84. Qur'an (21:105).
14. *Ibid.*, p. 77.
15. *Ibid.*, p. 78.
16. *Ibid.*, p. 85.
17. *Ibid.*, p. 86.
18. *Ibid.*, p. 73.
19. Mohammed Talbi, 'Islamo-Christian Encounter Today: Some Principles', *MECC Perspective*, No. 4/5, (July–August 1985), p. 10.
20. Mohammed Talbi, 'Islam and Dialogue: Some Reflections on a Current Topic', in R. Rousseau, (ed.), *Christianity and Islam: The Struggling Dialogue* (Scranton: Ridge Row Press, 1985), p. 54.
21. *Ibid.*, p. 57.
22. 'Suppliqué d'un Musulman aux Chrétiens', in *Les Musulmans* (Paris: Beauschene, 1976), p. 125.
23. Talbi, in Rousseau, *op. cit.*, p. 58.
24. *Ibid.*, p. 59.
25. *Ibid.*, p. 61.

26. Talbi, in Rousseau, *op. cit.*, p. 62.
27. Talbi, 'Unavoidable Dialogue . . .', p. 7.
28. Talbi, 'Islamo-Christian Encounter . . .', *op. cit.*, p. 9.
29. *Ibid.*, p. 10.
30. *Ibid.*
31. Talbi, in Rousseau, *op. cit.*, p. 65.
32. *Ibid.*
33. *Ibid.*, p. 68.
34. *Ibid.*, p. 70.
35. Talbi, 'Unavoidable Dialogue . . .', *op. cit.*, p. 65.
36. *Ibid.*, p. 10.
37. *Ibid.*, pp. 65–6.
38. 'Correspondence', dated 13 January 1993.
39. Talbi, 'Unavoidable Dialogue', *op. cit.*, p. 66.
40. *Ibid.*
41. *Ibid.*
42. Muhammed Talbi, 'Islam and Dialogue', in P.S. Griffiths (ed.), *Christianity through Non-Christian Eyes* (New York: Orbis, 1990), p. 88.
43. Muhammed Talbi, 'Islam and the West: Beyond Confrontation, Ambiguities and Complexes', *Encounter*, No. 108 (September–October 1984), p. 17.
44. Talbi, 'Unavoidable Dialogue . . .', *op. cit.*, p. 11. See also a detailed discussion on religious freedom in his article 'Religious Liberty: A Muslim Perspective', *Encounter*, No. 126–7 (June–July 1986), p. 17.
45. Muhammed Talbi, 'Mohammad: "I am a Gift of Mercy"', *International Journal of Religious Freedom*, Vol. 2, No. 4 (Winter 1990), p. 77.
46. Talbi, 'Islam and the West . . .', *op. cit.*, p. 3.
47. *Ibid.*, p. 4.
48. Muhammed Talbi, 'Possibilities and Conditions for a Better Understanding Between Islam and the West', *Journal of Ecumenical Studies*, Vol. 25, No. 2 (Spring 1988), p. 163.
49. *Ibid.*, pp. 163–4.
50. *Ibid.*
51. *Ibid.*, p. 165.
52. *Ibid.*, pp. 165–6.
53. *Ibid.*, pp. 167–8.

CHAPTER 9

1. Hossein S. Nasr, 'The Philosophia Perennis and the Study of Religion', in F. Whaling, *The World's Religious Traditions, Current Perspectives in Religious Studies* (Edinburgh, 1984), pp. 182–3 (all the above quotations in this paragraph are from these two pages).
2. *Ibid.*
3. Hossein S. Nasr, *Knowledge and the Sacred* (New York: Crossroad Publications, 1981), p. 68.
4. Hossein S. Nasr, 'Comments on a Few Theological Issues in Islamic–Christian Dialogue', in Y.Z. Haddad, and W. Haddad, (eds.), *Christian–Muslim Encounters* (Gainsville: University Press of Florida, 1995), p. 457.

5. Hossein S. Nasr, *Ideals and Realities of Islam* (Boston: Beacon Press, 1972), pp. 21–2.
6. Nasr, 'Comments on a Few Theological Issues in Islamic–Christian Dialogue', *op. cit.*, p. 458.
7. Nasr, *Ideals and Realities of Islam*, *op. cit.*, p. 43.
8. *Ibid.*, p. 45.
9. *Ibid.*, p. 46.
10. *Ibid.*, pp. 43–4.
11. *Ibid.*, pp. 68–9.
12. *Ibid.*, pp. 70–1.
13. Nasr, 'Comments on a Few Theological Issues in Islamic–Christian Dialogue', *op. cit.*, p. 464.
14. Hossein S. Nasr, *Islamic Studies* (Beirut: Librairie du Liban, 1967), pp. 26–7.
15. Nasr, *Ideals and Realities . . .*, *op. cit.*, p. 94.
16. *Ibid.*, pp. 94–5.
17. Nasr, *Islamic Studies*, *op. cit.*, p. 30.
18. Nasr, *Ideals and Realities . . .*, *op. cit.*, p. 95.
19. *Ibid.*, p. 96.
20. *Ibid.*, p. 98.
21. 'Interview', unpublished interview with Ataullah Siddiqui, London, 9 December 1992, p. 1.
22. *Ibid.*, p. 2.
23. *Ibid.*
24. *Ibid.*
25. Hossein S. Nasr, 'A Muslim's Reflections on Hans Küng's', *Studies in Comparative Religion*, Vol. 13, Nos. 3 and 4 (Summer–Autumn 1979), p. 156.
26. *Bulletin Secretariatus Pro non-Christianis*, Vol. XIII/1, No. 37 (1978), p. 26.
27. *The Muslim World*, Vol. LXXVII, No. 2 (April 1987), p. 122.
28. *Bulletin*, *op. cit.*, p. 26.
29. 'Interview', *op. cit.*, p. 4.
30. *Ibid.*
31. *Ibid.*, p. 5.
32. *Ibid.*, p. 3.
33. *The Muslim World*, *op. cit.*, p. 129.
34. *Ibid.*
35. *Ibid.*
36. *Bulletin*, *op. cit.*, p. 26.
37. 'Interview', *op. cit.*, p. 14.
38. *Ibid.*, p. 16.
39. *Ibid.*
40. *Ibid.*
41. *Ibid.*, p. 17.
42. Nasr, 'A Muslim's Reflection . . .', *op. cit.*, p. 149.
43. *Ibid.*, p. 151.
44. *Ibid.*, p. 152.
45. Nasr, 'A Muslim's Reflections . . .', *op. cit.*
46. 'There will be no peace among the people of this world without peace

among the world religions', *Christianity and the World Religions* (New York: Doubleday and Co. Inc., 1986), p. 443.
47. *The Muslim World*, Vol. LXXVII, No. 2 (April 1987), p. 96.
48. *Ibid.*, p. 98.
49. *Ibid.*
50. *Ibid.*, pp. 99–100.
51. *Ibid.*, See pp. 101–3.
52. *Ibid.*, pp. 120–1.
53. *Ibid.*, p. 105.

CHAPTER 11

1. *The Journal of Muslim World League* (May 1981), p. 21.
2. Correspondence with Dr Inamullah Khan, dated 10 June 1991.
3. *The Muslim World*, Vol. 22, No. 22 (8 December 1984).
4. 'Final Report of the Colombo Dialogue', (1982), p. 2.
5. *Ibid.*
6. Correspondence, *op. cit.*
7. *Ibid.*
8. *Ibid.*
9. 'The Present Day Condition of the World of Islam – A Special Interview' with Dr Inamullah Khan, *The Muslim World League Journal*, Vol. 17, Nos. 1 and 2 (September/October 1989), p. 24.
10. Correspondence, *op. cit.*
11. Resolution from Working Group B on Refugees and Minorities in the Colombo Dialogue, 1982.
12. M. Salim Abdullah, 'Muslim Minorities in Western Europe', I & II, in *The Muslim World* (Karachi), Vol. 22 (2 and 9 February 1985), p. 6.
13. Abdullah, *op. cit.*
14. Mushirul Haq, 'The Rabitah: A New Trend in Pan-Islamism', *Islam and the Modern Age*, Vol. IX, No. 3(August 1978), pp. 55–6.
15. *Ibid.*, p. 57
16. *Muslim World Gazette*. (Karachi: Muslim World Congress, 1985), 781pp.
17. *The Journal of Muslim World League*, Makkah, Vol. 3, No. 1 (1975), p. 35.
18. *The Journal MWL* (May 1974), pp. 45–62.
19. *The Journal MWL* (February 1982), p. 35.
20. *The Journal MWL* (July–August 1987), p. 31. See also a short report, 'European Mosque Council – Aims and Objectives', *The Journal MWL* (February 1982), p. 11.
21. *The Journal MWL* (July–August 1987), p. 30. See a list of areas which the Constituent Council has discussed in past years in *Rabitat al-'Alam al-Islami fi 25*, MWL's publications (1987), pp. 24–6.
22. *The Journal MWL* (July–August 1987), p. 31.
23. *Ibid.*, p. 30
24. Haq, *op. cit.*, p. 58.
25. *The Journal MWL* (February 1982), p. 36. Also in *Al-Akbar al-Alam Al-Islami*, Makkah, (8 May 1978).

26. *The Journal MWL* (February 1982), p. 35.
27. Correspondence with Hatim H. Qudi, assistant to the Secretary General, MWL (4 Safar 1412 H.).
28. *Ibid.*
29. *Ibid.*
30. *The Journal MWL* (July–August 1987), p. 29.
31. *The Journal MWL* (January–February 1989), p. 17.
32. See Law No. 58, 1972 and 1974, pp. 15–19, n.d.
33. Introductory leaflet of the organization.
34. *Ibid.* (Since 1992, United Nations has imposed sanctions and this co-operation might have been stopped.)
35. See, e.g., 'Islamic Medical Caravans to Africa', report in *Al-Da'wah al-Islamiyah* (September 1991).
36. *The Muslim World*, Vol. 13, No. 22 (20 December 1975).
37. Preparation and Publication Office of Foreign Relations in the Congress General, *Documents and Research of Seminar of the Islamic-Christian Dialogue* (Tripoli, 1981), p. 47.
38. *Ibid.* p. 47. See for Qadhdhafi's religious views, M. Ayoub, *Islam and the Third Universal Theory: The Religious Thought of Mu'ammar al-Qadhdhafi* (London: Kegan Paul International, 1987); also M.K. Deep, 'Islam and Arab Nationalism in Al-Qaddhafi's Ideology', *Journal of South Asian and Middle Eastern Studies*, Vol. 2, No. 2 (Winter 1978), pp. 12–26.
39. *The Muslim World, op. cit.*
40. See the Articles in 'Preparation and Publication . . .', *op. cit.*, p. 144.
41. 'Malta and Islam Between the Past and the Present', *Rissalat al-Jihad*, No. 67 (June 1988), p. 24.
42. See *Rissalat al-Jihad*, No. 7 (June 1989).
43. Press release issued by the World Islamic Call Society, Malta branch.
44. *L'Osservatore Romano*, 16 February 1990.
45. 'Co-Existence Between Religions: Reality and Horizons'. A consultation between the Pontifical Council for Interreligious Dialogue and World Islamic Call Society, n.d., p. 45. See report in Arabic, *Rissalat al-Jihad* (Arabic edition), No. 95 (January 1991), pp. 8–15.
46. 'Co-Existence . . .', *op. cit.*, p. 45.
47. See six-page Seminar Declaration, n.d.
48. For example, Abdul Karim Khan's study paper, *Christian Mission in Bangladesh – A Survey* (Leicester: The Islamic Foundation, 1981), is serialized in *Al-Dawah al-Islamiyah*, first part in August 1988, p. 3, and in subsequent issues.
49. *Ibid.* p. 3.

Bibliography

Abedin, Syed Z., 'The Non-Believers' Identity in Islam', *Islam and Christian–Muslim Relations*, Vol. 3, No. 1 (June 1992), pp. 40–57.

Affendi, Abdelwahab El-, 'Discovering the South: Sudanese Dilemmas for Islam in Africa', *African Affairs*, Vol. 89, No. 356 (1990), pp. 371–89.

Ahmad, Khurshid, *Islam and the West*, Lahore: Islamic Publications Ltd, 1967.

Ahmad, Khurshid, *Fanaticism, Intolerance and Islam*, Lahore: Islamic Publications Ltd, 1967.

Ahmad, Khurshid, 'Family Life in Islam', in *The Family in Islam and Christianity*, Dialogue conference paper, Bradford Metropolitan District Community Relations Council, Bradford, 1974, pp. 3–16.

Ahmad, Khurshid, 'Propagation of Islam: The Basic Principles', *Islam*, Vol. 1, No. 3–4, (1975), pp. 184–91.

Ahmad, Khurshid, 'A Muslim Response', in *World Faiths and the New World Order: A Muslim–Jewish–Christian Search Begins,* edited by J. Gremillion and W. Ryan. Lisbon: The Interreligious Peace Colloquium, 1978, pp. 171–93.

Ahmad, Khurshid, 'Man and the Future of Civilisation', *Encounters: Journal of Inter-Cultural Perspectives*, Vol. 1, No. 1 (March 1995), pp. 39–55.

Ahmad, Khurshid, 'Islam and the West: Confrontation or Cooperation?' *Muslim World*, Vol. LXXXV, No. 1–2 (May–April 1995), pp. 63–81.

Akhtar, Shabbir, *The Final Imperative: An Islamic Theology of Liberation.* London: Bellew Publishing, 1991.

Al-Albait Foundation, *Common Concerns and Values for Family Life*, The 2nd Muslim Christian Consultation. Amman: Al-Albait Foundation, 1986.

Al-Albait Foundation, *Model of Historical Co-existence between Muslims and Christians and its Future Prospects*, Vol. 1. Proceedings of the 4th Muslim–Christian Consultation. Amman: Al-Albait Foundation, 1988.

Al-Albait Foundation, *Religious Education and Modern Society*. Acts of a Muslim–Christian Colloquium organized jointly by the Pontifical Council for Interreligious Dialogue (Vatican City) and the Royal Academy for Islamic Civilization Research, Al-Albait Foundation (Amman), 6–8 December 1989, Rome, Italy. Vatican: Polyglot Press.

Al-Albait Foundation, *Common Humanitarian Ideals for Muslims and Christians*, Vol. 2. The 4th Muslim–Christian Consultation. Amman: Al-Albait Foundation, 1989.

Al-Albait Foundation, *Religious Pluralism*, The 6th Muslim Christian Consultation. Amman: Al-Albait Foundation, 1989.

Ali, Michael Nazir, *Frontiers in Muslim–Christian Encounter*. Oxford: Regnum Books, 1987.

Ali, Michael Nazir, *Mission and Dialogue: Proclaiming the Gospel Afresh in Every Age,* London: SPCK, 1995.

Amaladoss, Michael, *Making All Things New. Dialogue, Pluralism and Evangelization in Asia.* Maryknoll, New York: Orbis Books, 1990.

Amjad Ali, Charles, 'Mission and Evangelism in the Context of Other Faiths', *Al-Mushir*, Vol. XXX, No. 1 (Spring 1988), pp. 1–9.

Amjad Ali, Charles, 'Towards a New Theology of Dialogue', *Al-Mushir*, Vol. 33, No. 2 (Summer 1991), pp. 57–69.

Amjad Ali, Christine, 'The Shariat Bill'. *Al-Mushir*, Vol. 32, No. 4 (Winter 1990), pp. 108–41.

Anderson, Norman, *Islam in the Modern World: A Christian Perspective.* Leicester: Apollos, 1990.

Anees, M.A., 'Historical Light on the Present Situation of Christian–Muslim Relations', *Newsletter of the Office of Christian-Muslim Relations*, Hartford Seminary, No. 38 (July 1988), pp. 1–7.

Ansari, Zafar Ishaq, 'Some Reflections on Islamic Bases for Dialogue with Jews and Christians', *Journal of Ecumenical Studies*, Vol. 14, No. 3 (1977), pp. 433–47.

Arinze, Cardinal Francis, *Church in Dialogue: Walking with Other Believers.* San Francisco: Ignatius Press, 1990.

Arkoun, Mohammed, 'Explorations and Responses: New Perspectives for a Jewish–Christian–Muslim Dialogue'. *Journal of Ecumenical Studies*, Vol. 26, No. 3 (Summer 1989), pp. 523–9.

Askari, Hasan, 'Modernity and Faith', *Islam and the Modern Age*, Vol. I, No. 3 (November 1970), pp. 39–48.

Askari, Hasan, 'The Dialogical Relationship between Christianity and Islam', *Journal of Ecumenical Studies*, Vol. 9, No. 3 (1972), pp. 477–87.

Askari, Hasan, 'Worship and Prayer', in S.J. Samartha, (ed.), *Christian-Muslim Dialogue, Papers from Broumanna, 1972.* Geneva: World Council of Churches, 1973, pp. 120–36.

Askari, Hasan, 'Unity and Alienation in Islam', in S.J. Samartha, (ed.), *Living Faiths and Ultimate Goals: A Continuing Dialogue.* Geneva: World Council of Churches, 1974, pp. 45–55.

Askari, Hasan, *Society and State in Islam: An Introduction.* New Delhi: Islam and the Modern Age Society, 1978.

Askari, Hasan, with John Hick (ed.), *The Experience of Religious Diversity.* London: Avebury Publishing Company, 1985.

Askari, Hasan, *Spiritual Quest: An Inter-Religion Dimension.* Pudsey: Seven Mirrors Publishing House Ltd, 1991.

Askari, Hasan (with Jon Avery), *Toward a Spiritual Humanism: A Muslim–Humanist Dialogue.* Pudsey: Seven Mirrors Publishing House Ltd, 1991.

Attas, S.M.N. Al-, *Islam and Secularism.* Kuala Lumpur: ABIM, 1978.

Ayoub, Mahmoud, 'Towards an Islamic Christology: An Image of Jesus in Early Shi'i Muslim Literature', *The Muslim World*, Vol. LXVI, No. 3 (July 1976), pp. 163–88.

Ayoub, Mahmoud, 'Towards an Islamic Christology II: the Death of Jesus – Reality or Delusion', *The Muslim World*, Vol. LXX, No. 2 (April 1980), pp. 91–121.

Ayoub, Mahmoud, 'Dhimma in the Qur'an and Hadith', *Arab Studies Quarterly*, Vol. 5, No. 2 (1983), pp. 172–82.

Ayoub, Mahmoud, 'Muslim Views of Christianity, Some Modern Examples', *Islamochristiana*, Vol. 10 (1984), pp. 49–70.

Ayoub, Mahmoud, 'The Word of God in Islam', *Greek Orthodox Theological Review*, Vol. 31, No. 1–2 (1986), pp. 69–78.

Ayoub, Mahmoud, 'Uzayr in the Qur'an and Muslim Tradition', *Studies in Islamic and Judaic Traditions*. Paper presented at the Institute for Islamic-Judaic Studies, Centre for Judaic Studies, University of Denver, W.M. Brinner, and S.D. Ricks (eds.) (Atlanta: Scholars Press, 1986), pp. 3–16.

Ayoub, Mahmoud, 'Roots of Muslim–Christian Conflict', *The Muslim World*, Vol. LXXIX, No. 1, (January 1987), pp. 25–45.

Ayoub, Mahmoud, 'Islam and Christianity between Tolerance and Acceptance', *Islam and Christian–Muslim Relations*, Vol. 2, No. 2 (1991), pp. 171–82.

Ayoub, Mahmoud, 'Religious Freedom and the Law of Apostasy in Islam', *Islamochristiana*, Vol. 20 (1994), pp. 75–91.

Basetti-Sani, Giulio, 'For a Dialogue between Christians and Muslims', *Muslim World*, Vol. LVII (1967), pp. 126–37, 186–96.

Basri, Ghazali, *Nigeria and Shari'ah: Aspirations and Apprehensions* (Leicester: The Islamic Foundation, 1994).

Bennett, Clinton, *Victorian Images of Islam*, London: Grey Seal Books, 1992.

Bijlefeld, W.A., 'Recent Theological Evaluation of the Christian–Muslim Encounter', *International Review of Mission*, Vol. LV (1966), pp. 430–41.

Borrmans, M., 'Islam and Christianity: Common Doctrinal Basis and Areas of Convergence', *Encounter*, No. 23 (March 1976), pp. 1–15.

Borrmans, M., 'Recent History of Christian-Muslim Dialogue', *Encounter*, Nos. 61–2 (January–February 1980), pp. 1–23.

Borrmans, M., *Guidelines for Interreligious Dialogue*. New York: Paulist Press, 1990.

Braybrooke, Marcus, *Pilgrimage of Hope – One Hundred Years of Global Interfaith Dialogue*. London: SCM Press, 1992.

Breiner, Bert, 'Christian–Muslim Relations: Some Current Themes', *Islam and Christian–Muslim Relations*, Vol. 2, No. 1 (June 1991), pp. 77–94.

Breiner, Bert, 'Two Papers on Shari'ah', CSIC Papers Europe, Birmingham: Selly Oak Colleges, 1992. pp. 1–18.

Brown, Stuart E. (ed.), *Meeting in Faith: Twenty Years of Christian–Muslim Conversations Sponsored by the World Council of Churches*. Geneva: World Council of Churches Publications, 1989.

Brown, Stuart E., *The Nearest in Affection: Towards a Christian Understanding of Islam*. Geneva: World Council of Churches, 1994.

Carman, John B., 'A New Assessment of the Christian Encounter with Islam', *The Bulletin of the Henry Martyn Institute of Islamic Studies*, Vol. XLVIII (April–June 1960), pp. 38–51, and Vol. XLIX (July–September 1960), pp. 13–32.

Caspar, Robert, 'Islam According to Vatican II', *Encounter*, No. 21 (January 1976), pp. 1–7.

Caspar, Robert, 'The Salvation of Non-Muslims: Muslim View', *Encounter*, No. 31 (January 1977), pp. 1–16.

Cracknell, Kenneth, 'Christianity and Religious Pluralism', *Christian–Jewish Relations*, Vol. 18, No. 2 (June 1985), pp. 40–58.

Cracknell, Kenneth, *Towards a New Relationship: Christians and People of Other Faiths*. London: Epworth Press, 1986.

Cracknell, Kenneth, *Justice, Courtesy and Love: Theologians and Missionaries Encountering World Religions*, London: Epworth Press, 1995.

Cragg, Kenneth, *The Christian and Other Religion*. Oxford: A.R. Mowbray, 1977.

Cragg, Kenneth, *Muhammad and the Christian: A Question of Response*. London: Darton, Longman and Todd Ltd, 1984.

Cragg, Kenneth, *The Pen and the Faith: Eight Modern Writers and the Qur'an*. London: George Allen and Unwin, 1985.

Cragg, Kenneth, *Jesus and the Muslim: An Exploration*. London: George Allen and Unwin, 1985.

Cragg, Kenneth, *Troubled by Truth: Life-Studies in Inter-Faith Concern*, Durham: The Pentland Press Ltd, 1992.

Daniel, Norman, *Islam and the West: The Making of an Image*. Oxford: One World Publications, 1993, revised edition.

D'Costa, Gavin, *Theology and Religious Pluralism: The Challenge of Other Religions*. Oxford: Basil Blackwell, 1986.

Denffer, Ahmad von, *Christians in the Qur'an and the Sunnah*, Leicester: The Islamic Foundation, 1987.

Denffer, Ahmad von, *Some Reflections on Dialogue Between Christians and Muslims*, Leicester: The Islamic Foundation, 1989.

Dobers, Abdullah and Khoury, Eri (eds.), *Religion in Culture, Law and Politics*. Mainz: Hase and Koehler Verlag, 1982.

Dobers, H. *et al.* (eds.), *Development and Solidarity Joint Responsibility of Muslims and Christians*. Mainz: Hase and Koehler, 1985.

Douglas, Elmer H., 'Christian Witness in the World of Islam'. *The South East Asia Journal of Theology*, Vol. 8, No. 4 (April 1967), pp. 6–16.

Douglas, J.D. (ed.), *Let the Earth Hear His Voice, International Congress on World Evangelization*. Two volumes, Official Report of the International Congress on World Evangelization, 16–25 July 1974. Minneapolis: World Wide Publications, 1975.

Esposito, John L., *The Islamic Threat: Myth or Reality?* New York: Oxford University Press, 1992.

Farias, Terence, 'Muslim Image of Christians'. *Encounter*, No. 110 (December 1984), p. 22.

Farquhar, S.N., *The Crown of Hinduism*. Oxford: Oxford University Press, 1913.

Faruqi, I.H. Azad, 'The Qur'anic View of Other Religions', *Islam and the Modern Age*, Vol. XVIII, No. 1 (February 1987), pp. 39–50.

Faruqi, Ismail R. Al-, *Urūbah and Religion*, Amsterdam: Djambatan, 1962.

Faruqi, Ismail R. Al-, 'History of Religions: Its Nature and Significance for Christian Education and the Muslim–Christian Dialogue', *Numen*, Vol. XII (1965), pp. 35–65. Continued to the next issue of *Numen*, pp. 81–6. See also B.E. Meland's response in the same issue of *Numen*, pp. 87–95.

Faruqi, Ismail R. Al-, 'Islam and Christianity – Diatribe or Dialogue', *Journal of Ecumenical Studies*, (Winter 1968), pp. 45–77.

Faruqi, Ismail R. Al-, 'The Essence of Religious Experience in Islam', *Numen*, Vol. XX (1973), pp. 186–201.

Faruqi, Ismail R. Al-, 'Islam and other Faiths', in A. Gauhar (ed.), *The Challenge of Islam*, London: Islamic Council of Europe, 1978, pp. 82–111.

Faruqi, Ismail R. Al-, 'Rights of non-Muslims under Islam: Social and Cultural Aspects', *Journal of Institute of Muslim Minority Affairs*, Vol. I, No. 1 (1979), pp. 90–102.

Faruqi, Ismail R. Al-, 'The Role of Islam in Global Interreligious Dependence', in Warren Lewis (ed.) *Towards a Global Congress of the World's Religions*. Barrytown: N.Y.: Unification Theological Seminary, 1980, pp. 19–38.

Faruqi, Ismail R. Al-, *Trialogue of the Abrahamic Faiths* (edited work). Washington, D.C.: International Institute of Islamic Thought, 1982.

Faruqi, Ismail R. Al–, 'Meta-Religion: Towards a Critical World Theology', *American Journal of Islamic Social Sciences*, Vol. 3, No. 1 (September 1986), pp. 13-57.

Fitzgerald, Michael L., 'Christian-Muslim Dialogue: Foundations and Forms', *Encounter*, No. 52 (February 1979), pp. 1–16.

Fitzgerald, Michael L., 'Muslims and Christians in the Arab World'. *Encounter*, No. 113 (March 1985).

Fitzgerald, Michael L., '25 Years of Christian–Muslim Dialogue: A Personal Journey', *Proche-Orient Chrétien*, Vol. XL (1990), pp. 258–71.

Fitzmaurice, Redmond, 'The Roman Catholic Church and Interreligious Dialogue – Implications for Christian–Muslim Relations', *Islam and Christian–Muslim Relations*, Vol. 3, No. 1 (June 1992), pp. 83–107.

Flannery, Austin (ed.), *Vatican Council II: More Post Conciliar Documents*. Collegeville: The Liturgical Press, 1982.

Flannery, Austin, *Vatican Council II: The Conciliar and Post Conciliar Documents*. New York: Costello Publishing Company, 1988 (revised).

Gaudeul, Jean-Marie, *Encounters and Clashes: Islam and Christianity in History, Vol. I: A Survey*. Rome: Pontifico Instituto di Studi Arabi e Islamici, 1990.

Gaudeul, Jean-Marie, *Encounters and Clashes: Islam and Christianity in History. II: Texts*. Rome: Pontifico Instituto di Studi Arabi e Islamici, 1990.

Genisichen, H.W., 'The Second Vatican Council's Challenge to Protestant Mission', *International Review of Mission*, Vol. LVI, No. 223 (July 1967), pp. 291–309.

Ghrab, Saad, 'Islam and Christianity: From Opposition to Dialogue', *Islamochristiana*, Vol. 13 (1987), pp. 99–111.

Ghrab, Saad, 'Islam and Non-Scriptural Spirituality', *Islamochristiana*, Vol. 14 (1988), pp. 51–70.

Goddard, Hugh P., 'Contemporary Egyptian Muslims View of Christianity', *Renaissance and Modern Studies*, Vol. XXXI (1987), pp. 74–86.

Goddard, Hugh P., *Christians and Muslims: From Double Standards to Mutual Understandings*. Richmond: Curzon Press, 1995.

Goodall, Norman (ed.), *The Uppsala Report 1968 – Official Report of the Fourth Assembly of the World Council of Churches, Upsala, July 4–20, 1968*. Geneva: World Council of Churches, 1968.

Gremillon, J. and W. Ryan, *World Faiths and the New World Order*. Lisbon: Interreligious Peace Colloqium, 1977.

Griffiths, Paul J., *Christianity through Non-Christian Eyes*. Maryknoll, New York: Orbis Books, 1990.

Haddad, Y.H. (ed.) *Muslims of America*. New York: Oxford University Press, 1991.

Haddad, Y.H. and W. Haddad (eds.), *Christian–Muslim Encounters*, Gainesville: University Press of Florida, 1995.

Haines, Byron L. and Frank L. Cooley (eds.), *Christians and Muslims Together: An Exploration by Presbyterians.* Philadelphia: The Geneva Press, 1987.

Hallencreutz, Carl F., *New Approaches to Men of Other Faiths.* Geneva: World Council of Churches, 1970.

Hallencreutz, Carl F., *Dialogue and Community: Ecumenical Issues in Inter-Religious Relationships.* Uppsala: Almquist and Wiksell, 1977.

Hamidullah, M., 'The Friendly Relations of Islam with Christianity and How They Deteriorated', *Journal of the Pakistan Historical Society* (Karachi), Vol. 1, Part 1 (1953), pp. 41–5.

Hamidullah, Muhammad, 'Relations of Muslims with Non-Muslims', *Journal Institute of Muslim Minority Affairs*, Vol. 7, No. 1 (January 1986), pp. 7–12.

Hesselgrave, David J., 'Evangelicals and Interreligious Dialogue', *Mission Trends 5*, Faith Meets Faith Series, ed. Gerald H. Anderson and Thomas F. Stransky. New York: Paulist Press, 1981, pp. 123–7.

Hick, John, *Problems of Religious Pluralism.* London: The Macmillan Press, 1985.

Hick, John and Brian Hebblethwaite, (eds.), *Christianity and Other Religions.* London: William Collins, 1980.

Horton, John and Harriet Crabtree (eds.), *Toleration and Integrity in a Multi-Faith Society.* York: University of York, 1992.

Iqbal, Mohammad, *The Reconstruction of Religious Thought in Islam.* Lahore: Sh. Muhammad Ashraf, 1960.

Islamic Foundation, *Christian Mission and Islamic Da'wah,* Leicester: 1982.

Jackson, H.C., *Pastors on the Nile, Being Some Account of the Life and Letters of Llewellyn Henry Gwynne.* London: SPCK, 1960.

Johnstone, Penelope (introduction and translation), 'Articles from Islamic Journals, An Islamic Perspective on Dialogue'. *Islamochristiana,* Vol. 13 (1987), pp. 131–71.

Joseph, S. *et al., Muslim–Christian Conflicts: Economic, Political and Social Origins.* Boulder, Colorado/Folkestone: Westview Press/Dawson, 1978.

Kandil, Fuad, 'Inter-cultural Learning and Inter-religious Dialogue', *Islam and Christian–Muslim Relations,* Vol. 1, No. 2 (December 1990), pp. 244–51.

Kateregga, B.D. and D.W. Shenk, *Islam and Christianity: A Muslim and Christian Dialogue.* Ibadan: Daystar Press, 1980.

Kerr, David A., 'Christian Witness in Relation to Muslim Neighbours', *Islamochristiana,* Vol. 10 (1984), pp. 1–30.

Kerr, David A., 'The Prophet Muhammad in Christian Theological Perspective', *Encounter,* No. 106 (June 1984), pp. 1–14.

Kerr, David A., 'Mary, Mother of Jesus, in the Islamic Tradition: A Theme for Christian–Muslim Dialogue', *Encounter,* No. 155 (May 1989).

Kimball, Charles A., *Striving Together: A Way Forward in Christian–Muslim Relations.* Maryknoll, New York: Orbis Books, 1991.

Kinnamon, M. (ed.), *Signs of the Spirit, Official Report Seventh Assembly.* Geneva: World Council of Churches, 1991.

Knitter, Paul F., *No Other Name? A Critical Survey of Christian Attitudes Toward the World Religions.* Maryknoll, New York: Orbis Books, 1985.

Kraemer, H., *The Christian Message in a Non-Christian World.* London: The Edinburgh House Press, 1938.

Lopez Gay, J., 'Current Criticism of Dialogue: Its Theology and its Practice', *Encounter*, No. 59 (November 1979), pp. 1–11.

Lossky, N. *et al.* (eds.), *Dictionary of the Ecumenical Movement*. Geneva: World Council of Churches, 1991.

Lubbe, Gerrie, 'Muslims and Christians in South Africa', *Islamochristiana*, Vol. 13 (1987), pp. 113–29.

McCurry, Don M. (ed.), *The Gospel and Islam: A 1978 Compendium*. California: Mission Advanced Research and Communication Centre, 1979.

McGavran, Donald (ed.), *The Conciliar–Evangelical Debate: The Crucial Documents 1964–1976*. California: William Carey Library, 1977.

Magnin, J.G., 'A Venture of Christian Faith in View of Dialogue with Islam', *Encounter*, No. 84 (April 1982), pp. 1–11.

Mangalam, J.J., 'A Dialogue on Religious Dialogue: Its Need, Problems and Facilitating Conditions', *Al-Mushir*, Vol. XIX, Nos. 3–4 (July–December 1977), pp. 117–35.

Mawdudi, Syyid A.A., *Rights of Non-Muslims in Islamic State*. Lahore: Islamic Publications, 1961.

Mawdudi, Syyid A.A., 'Muslim–Christian Amity: A Letter to the Pope', *The Criterion*, Vol. 3, No. 3, (March 1968) pp. 71–7.

Michel, Thomas, 'Christianity and Islam: Reflections on Recent Teachings of the Church', *Encounter*, No. 112 (February 1985), pp. 1–22.

Michel, Thomas, 'Pope John Paul II's Teaching About Islam in his Addresses to Muslims', *Islam and the Modern Age*, Vol. XVIII, No. 1 (February 1987), pp. 67–76.

Mitri, Tarek (ed.) *Religion, Law and Society: A Muslim–Christian Discussion*. Geneva: World Council of Churches, 1995.

Murad, Khurram, *Da'wah Among Non-Muslims in the West. Some Conceptual and Methodological Aspects*. Leicester: The Islamic Foundation, 1986.

Muslim-Christian Research Group, *The Challenge of the Scriptures: The Bible and the Qur'an*. Faith Meets Faith Series. Maryknoll, NY: Orbis Books, 1989.

Nasr, S. Hossein, *Ideals and Realities of Islam*. London: George Allen and Unwin, 1966.

Nasr, S. Hossein, 'Islam and the Encounter of Religions', *Islamic Quarterly*, Vol. 10 (July and December 1966), pp. 47–66.

Nasr, S. Hossein, *Islamic Studies – Essays on Law and Society, the Sciences and Philosophy and Sufism*. Beirut: Librairie du Liban, 1967.

Nasr, S. Hossein, 'The Western World and its Challenges to Islam', *Islamic Quarterly*, Vol. XVII, No. 1 and 2 (January–June 1973), pp. 3–25.

Nasr, S. Hossein, 'A Muslim's Reflections on Hans Küng', *Studies in Comparative Religion*, Vol. 13, No. 3–4, (Summer–Autumn 1979), pp. 149–547.

Nasr, S. Hossein, 'A Muslim Reflection on Religion and Theology', *Journal of Ecumenical Studies*, Vol. 17, No. 1 (Winter 1980), pp. 112–20.

Nasr, S. Hossein, 'The Islamic View of Christianity', *Concilium* (February 1986), pp. 3–12.

Nasr, S. Hossein, 'Response to Hans Küng's Christianity and World Religion', *Muslim World*, Vol. LXXVII, No. 2, (April 1987), pp. 96–105.

Nasr, S. Hossein, *Religion and Religions: The Challenge of Living in a Multi-Religious World*, The Long H. Witherspoon Lectures in Religious Studies, 5 April, 1985. The University of North Carolina at Charlotte, n.d., p. 31.

Neill, Stephen, *Christian Faith and Other Faiths: The Christian Dialogue with Other Religions*. Oxford: Oxford University Press, (2nd edition), 1970.

Newbigin, Leslie, 'The Missionary of the Ecumenical Movement', *Ecumenical Review*, Vol. XIV, No. 2 (January 1962), pp. 207–14.

Nielsen, J. (ed.), *Religion and Citizenship in Europe and the Arab World*. London: Grey Seal, 1992.

Njoya, Ndam, *et al.* (eds.), *Development and Solidarity: Joint Responsibility of Muslims and Christians*, Maiz: v. Hase & Koehler Verlag, 1985.

Nwaiwu, O., *Inter-Religious Dialogue in African Context: Christianity, Islam and African Religion*. Munich: Publications Universitaires Africaines, 1990.

Oloyede, I.O., 'Secularism and Religion: Conflict and Compromise (an Islamic Perspective)', *Islam and the Modern Age*, Vol. XVIII, No. 1 (February 197), pp. 21–38.

Orthodox Centre of the Ecumenical Patriarch, *Peace and Justice*, The 5th Muslim–Christian Consultation, Chambesy: The Orthodox Centre, 1989.

Osman, Fathi *et al.* (eds.), 'Jesus in Jewish–Christian–Muslim Dialogue', *Journal of Ecumenical Studies*, Vol. 14, No. 3 (1977), pp. 448–54.

Panikkar, Raimundo, *The Intra-Religious Dialogue*. New York: Paulist Press, 1977.

Parshall, P., *New Paths in Muslim Evangelism. Evangelical Approaches to Contextualization*. Michigan: Baker Book House, 1980.

Powell, A.A., 'Maulana Rahmat Allah Kairanawi and Muslim–Christian Controversy in India in the mid-19th Century', *Journal of the Royal Asiatic Society*, No. 1 (1976), pp. 42–63.

Preparation & Publication, Office of Foreign Relations in the Congress General of People, *Documents and Researchers of Seminar of the Islamic–Christian Dialogue*, Tripoli: Popular Office of Foreign Relations, 1981.

Putra, Tunku A.R. *et al.* (eds.), *Contemporary Issues on Malaysian Religions*. Kuala Lumpur: Pelanduk Publications, 1985 (2nd edition).

Race, Alan, *Christians and Religious Pluralism: Patterns in the Christian Theology of Religions*. London: SCM Press, 1993 (2nd edition).

Ragashekar, J.P. and H.S. Wilson, (eds.), *Islam in Asia: Perspectives for Christian–Muslim Encounter*. Geneva: Lutheran World Federation, 1992.

Rahman, Fazlur, *Islam and Modernity: Transformation of an Intellectual Tradition*. Chicago: University of Chicago Press, 1982.

Rahman, Fazlur, 'Non-Muslim Minorities in an Islamic State', *Journal Institute of Muslim Minority Affairs*, Vol. 7, No. 1 (January 1986), pp. 13–24.

Register, R.G. Jr, *Dialogue and Interfaith Witness with Muslims*, Kingsport: Moody Books Inc., 1979.

Renard, John, 'Christian–Muslim Dialogue: A Review of Six Post-Vatican II Church-Related Documents', *Journal of Ecumenical Studies*, Vol. 23, No. 1 (Winter 1986), pp. 69–89.

Robinson, Neal, 'Massignon, Vatican II and Islam as an Abrahamic Religion', *Islam and Christian–Muslim Relations*, Vol. 2, No. 2 (December 1991), pp. 182–205.

Robinson, Neal, *Christ in Islam and Christianity*, Basingstoke: Macmillan Press, 1991.

Rodrigo, Michael, 'A Basis for Dialogue in Community: A Christian Point of View', *Dialogue*, Vol. IV, Nos. 1 and 2 (January–August 1977), pp. 17–26.

Rousseau, Richard W. (ed.), *Christianity and Islam: The Struggling Dialogue.* Scranton: Ridge Row Press, 1985.

Samartha, Stanley J. (ed.), *Dialogue Between Men of Living Faiths.* Geneva: World Council of Churches, 1971.

Samartha, Stanley J. (ed.), *Faith in the Midst of Faith: Reflection on Dialogue in Community.* Geneva: World Council of Churches, 1977.

Samartha, Stanley J., 'Guidelines on Dialogue', *The Ecumenical Review*, Vol. 31 (1979), pp. 155–62.

Samartha, Stanley J., *Courage for Dialogue: Ecumenical Issues in Inter-Religious Relationships.* Geneva: World Council of Churches, 1981.

Samartha, Stanley J. and John B. Taylor (eds.), *Christian–Muslim Dialogue.* Papers Presented at the Broumana Consultation, July 1972. Geneva: World Council of Churches, 1973.

Samartha, Stanley J., *Betweet Two Cultures: Ecumenical Ministry in a Pluralist World.* Geneva: World Council of Churches, 1996.

Sardar, Ziauddin, 'The Ethical Connection. Christian-Muslim Relations in the Post Modern Age', *Islam and Christian-Muslim Relations*, Vol. 2, No. 1 (June 1991), pp. 56–76.

Schlorff, S.P., 'The Catholic Program for Dialogue: An Evangelical Evaluation with Special Reference to Contextualization', *Missiology*, Vol. XI, No. 2 (April 1983), pp. 1–29.

Schumann, Olaf, 'Present-day Muslim Writers on Christ', *Al-Mushir*, Vol. XIX, No. 1 (January–March 1977), pp. 31–43.

Sheard, R.B., *Interreligious Dialogue in the Catholic Church Since Vatican II – An Historical and Theological Study.* New York: The Edwin Mellen Press, 1987.

Shepard, W., 'Conversations in Cairo: Some Contemporary Muslim Views of Other Religions', *Encounter*, No. 93–4, (March–April 1983), pp. 1–25.

Siddiqui, A., 'Muslims' Concern in Dialogue: A Study of Christian–Muslim Relations since 1970', University of Birmingham PhD Thesis, 1994.

Siddiqui, A., 'Muslims in Dialogue with Christians: Context and Concerns', *Christian–Muslim Reflections, CSIC Papers*, Birmingham: Selly Oak Colleges, 1995, pp. 1–8.

Siddiqui, A., 'Muslims in Dialogue with Christians: Expositions and Explanations', *CISC Papers*, Birmingham: Selly Oak Colleges, 1996, pp. 1–9.

Slomp, Jan, 'Committed to the Ecumenical Movement: Nairobi and After', *Al-Mushir*, Vol. XIX, No. 1 (January–March 1977), pp. 44–58.

Smith, Wilfred Cantwell, *The Meaning and End of Religion.* New York: The Macmillan Press, 1962.

Smith, Wilfred Cantwell, 'Interpreting Religious Interrelations: An Historian's View of Christian and Muslim', *Studies in Religion*, Vol. VI, No. 5 (1976–7), pp. 515–26.

Southern, R.W., *Western Views of Islam in the Middle Ages.* Cambridge: Harvard University Press, 1962.

Spae, Joseph J., 'Missiology as Local Theology and Interreligious Encounter', *Missiology*, Vol. VIII, No. 4 (October 1979), pp. 479–500.

Speight, Marston R., 'A Conference on Human Rights from the Faith Perspectives of Muslims and Christians', *Islamochristiana*, Vol. 9 (1983), pp. 161–7.

Stacpoole, A. (ed.), *Vatican II by Those Who Were There*. London: Geoffrey Chapman, 1986.

Stott, John R., 'Dialogue, Encounter, Even Confrontation', *Mission Trends 5*, ed. Gerald H. Anderson and Thomas F. Stransky. New York: Paulist Press, 1981, pp. 156–72.

Swidler, Leonard (ed.), *Muslims in Dialogue: The Evolution of a Dialogue*. Lewiston: Edwin Mellen Press, 1992.

Talbi, Mohammed, 'Islam and Dialogue: Some Reflections on a Current Topic', *Encounter*, No. 11–12 (January/February 1975), pp. 1–19.

Talbi, Mohammed, 'A Community of Communities: The Right to be Different and the Paths to Harmony', *Encounter*, No. 77 (August/September 1981), pp. 1–14.

Talbi, Mohammed, 'Abraham's Faith and Islamic Faith', *Encounter*, No. 92 (1983), pp. 1–16.

Talbi, Mohammed, 'Islam and the West: Beyond Confrontation, Ambiguities and Complexes', *Encounter*, No. 108 (September/October 1984), pp. 1–23.

Talbi, Mohammed, 'Islam–Christian Encounter Today: Some Principles', *MECC Perspective*, No. 4–5 (July/August 1985), pp. 7–11.

Talbi, Mohammed, 'Possibilities and Conditions for a Better Understanding Between Islam and the West', *Journal of Ecumenical Studies*, Vol. 25, No. 2 (Spring 1988), pp. 161–93.

Talbi, Mohammed, 'Unavoidable Dialogue in an Unavoidable Pluralistic World: A Personal Account', *Encounters: Journal of Inter-Cultural Perspectives*, Vol. 1, No. 1 (March 1995), pp. 56–69.

Talbi, Mohammed, 'Is Cultural and Religious Co-existence Possible? How Can We Deal with our Points of Agreement and Disagreement? Harmony and the Right to be Different', *Encounters: Journal of Inter-Cultural Perspectives*, Vol. 1, No. 2 (September 1995), pp. 74–84.

Taylor, John B., 'Christian-Muslim Dialogue: Colombo, Sri Lanka, 30 March–1 April 1982', *Islamochristiana*, Vol. 8 (1982), pp. 201–17.

Troll, C.W., 'Islam as a Missionary Religion. Some Observations with Special Reference to South and Southeast Asia', *Encounter*, No. 130 (November–December 1986).

Troll, C.W., 'The Qur'anic View of Other Religions: Ground for Living Together', *Islam and the Modern Age*, Vol. XVIII, No. 1 (February 1987), pp. 5–20, also in *Encounter*, No. 140 (December 1987), pp. 1–16.

Vahiduddin, Syed, 'Islam and Diversity of Religion', *Islam and Christian–Muslim Relations*, Vol. 1, No. 1 (June 1990), pp. 3–11.

Vaporis, N.M. (ed.), *Orthodox Christians and Muslims*. Massachusetts: Holy Cross Orthodox Press, 1986.

Visser't Hooft, W.A., *The Genesis and Formation of the World Council of Churches*. Geneva: World Council of Churches, 1982.

Waardenburg, Jacques, 'World Religions as Seen in the Light of Islam'. In *Islam: Past Influence and Present Challenge*, ed. Alford T. Welch and Pierre Cachia. Edinburgh University Press, 1979, pp. 245–75.

Waardenburg, Jacques, (ed.), *Scholarly Approaches to Religion, Interreligions Perceptions, and Islam*, Bern: Peter Lang, 1995.

Waddy, Charis, *Shaping a New Europe – the Muslim Factor*. London: Grosvenor Books, 1991.

Watt, W. Montgomery, 'Thoughts on Muslim–Christian Dialogue', *Hamdard Islamicus*, Vol. 1, No. 1 (1978), pp. 1–52.

Watt, W. Montgomery, *Islam and Christianity Today: A Contribution to Dialogue*. London: Routledge and Kegan Paul, 1983.

Watt, W. Montgomery, *Muslim–Christian Encounters – Perceptions and Misperceptions*. London: Routledge, 1991.

Werff, Lyle L.V., *Christian Mission to Muslims, 1800–1938*, California: William Carey Library, 1977.

Woodberry, J. Dudley (ed.), *Muslims and Christians on the Emmaus Road*. California: MARC, 1989.

World Conference on Religion and Peace, *Believers in the Future*, Inter-Faith Conference, 2–4 December 1990, Capetown: World Conference on Religion and Peace, 1991.

Zakzouk, Mahmoud, 'Cultural Relations Between the West and the World of Islam: Meeting Points and Possibilities of Co-operation on the Academic Level', *Islam and Christian–Muslim Relations*, Vol. 3, No. 1 (June 1992), pp. 69–82.

Zebiri, Kate, 'Relations Between Muslims and Non-Muslims in the Thought of Western Educated Muslim Intellectuals', *Islam and Christian-Muslim Relations*, Vol. 6, No. 2 (1995), pp. 255–77.

Index

232